Job Surfing:
Media and
Entertainment

Job Surfing: Media and Entertainment

Using the Internet to Find a Job and Get Hired

Jeff Adams and Jim Blau

Random House, Inc.
New York
www.review.com

Princeton Review Publishing, L. L. C.
2315 Broadway
New York, NY 10024
E-mail: comments@review.com

ISBN 0-375-76236-1
Editors: Anton Malko and Russell Kahn
Designer: Scott Harris
Production Editor: Julieanna Lambert
Production Coordinator: Greta Englert

Manufactured in the United States of America.

9 8 7 6 5 4 3 2 1

Acknowledgments

Many thanks to the people that helped make this book possible: Anton Malko, who did three important things—accepted pages right up until the last possible second, took the idea for the *Job Surfing* series and turned it into a reality, and gave me the opportunity to work on this book (thanks to Corey Podolsky for that, too); Jim Blau, who took all the sites I discussed in my sections of the book and then found so many more to give you the most complete directory possible; and Russell Khan, for having the initial idea for the *Job Surfing* series. Thanks also to all the people I work with at The Princeton Review who make this job the best I've had on so many levels (with extra special thanks to my staff in particular who make each day fun and rewarding: Rob Franek, Sarah Kruchko, Anton Malko, Erik Olson, and Amy Kinney). To the people who gave their time to be interviewed for this book—Jonathan Frank, Niku Kashef, Sebastian LaCause, Clint Rebik, Hamilton Tamayo, and Rosadel Varela—your participation was invaluable and I thank you for it. And now for the most important thanks: to my mom, Linda Adams, who finally gets thanked in print for her years of love and nurturing; and to Will Knauss, for all of his support, not only during the writing of this book, but in life as well.

Jeff Adams

Thanks to Julieanna, Anton, and Russ for giving me this opportunity; to Greta for providing the hardware, time, patience, and support; and to our landlord for not locking the door to the roof.

Jim Blau

Contents

Part One
Introduction

Chapter 1

Media, Entertainment, and the Internet: A Feeding Frenzy

Media, entertainment, and the Internet: Together, what a powerful triumvirate they make as we delve into the twenty-first century. If the distinguishing characteristics were hard to define ten years ago between the "real" drama of news, the foodstuff of media, and the "produced" drama that comprises the lifeblood of entertainment, the relatively recent evolution of the Internet into an everyday part of our lives has made it nearly impossible. Newsstands and televisions have long relied on the allure of news as a powerful form of entertainment, translating it into revenue streams in the form of subscriptions and viewer ratings, all while making the lives and inner workings of the entertainment industry news in itself. Now, thanks to the ultimate information-delivery system we call the Internet, part of the entertainment we derive from any drama, real or produced, comes at us as fast as it can be streamed into our PC.

Morning and evening news broadcasts, along with the morning and late editions of newspapers, have been supplanted by real-time stock quotes and ten-minute newswire updates delivered to your desktop or wireless device. Marketplaces that were once composed of dozens of TV channels, radio stations, and print publications have mushroomed to cover thousands of media options, each of which also has at least dipped its toe into the Internet, where countless of entertainment- and media-based sites (created by both corporations and private citizens) deliver information to an insatiable public.

What does it all add up to, this feeding frenzy? An incredible range of exciting career opportunities for you.

The Internet, in the course of opening up countless avenues for professional involvement, has also made the potential to deliver news and/or entertainment open to everyone. Anyone with very little cash can strike out on the Web and provide information or entertainment to anyone with access to a computer.

Entertainment and Media: A Brief History

Merriam-Webster's Collegiate Dictionary defines *entertainment* in a pretty simple way: "something diverting or engaging: as **a:** a public performance **b:** a usually light comic or adventure novel." The same dictionary defines *media* (or, more accurately, *mass media*) as "communication (as newspapers, radio, or television) that is designed to reach the mass of the people."

Entertainment has been around nearly forever—one only has to think about the cave paintings of early man to come up with an early form of entertainment. The word, however, has been around since the fifteenth century, when it was a synonym for maintenance, provision, or even employment (although most of us don't find employment very entertaining, but rather a means by which to earn money to be entertained).

Mass media, on the other hand, came into the cultural lexicon in the 1920s, when they were looked upon as a way to deliver the news of the day via newspapers and later radio. Even now when you think about the word *media*, there's an implication of something newsworthy associated with it. The capabilities of media have evolved along with each successive generation of technology, the Internet being the latest and perhaps most profound. The Internet has revolutionized the delivery of information and entertainment into a form that is instantaneous, continuous, and limitless.

The vast size of this "media machine" demands a flow of information that must continue regardless of its importance, leaving a vacuum that is readily filled by forms of information delivery that were once considered something separate: entertainment. Even that early form of media, the newspaper, had some bits of lighter news (today what we'd call the features section) that wasn't earth-shattering but more of a pleasant diversion from the day's events. Radio brought entertainment to the forefront as families gathered not just for the news, but also for comedy shows, soap operas, and the chance to be spooked as a nation with Orson Welles's historic 1938 version of H.G. Wells's classic *The War of the*

Worlds. That was just the beginning of the blurring of the line between media and entertainment. Today, the line often does not exist at all.

Over the decades, the media tried their best to keep entertainment and news apart, in large part because the journalistic integrity of news organizations depended on a reputation for fairness that resisted the urge to entertain at the expense of accuracy. Today it's virtually impossible. During the 1990s there was a definite trend toward news programs and magazines seeming more entertainment-oriented. But by fall 2001, news was back to taking itself more seriously.

But while news became a bit more serious, voyeurism continued. The late 1990s and early 2000s will be remembered as the era of "reality" television. What started innocently enough with MTV's *The Real World* back in the early 1990s has become a sensation with *Survivor, Big Brother, Road Rules, Fear Factor, Spy TV,* and other shows that set out to show us how normal, everyday people react under extreme circumstances. It no longer has the innocence of *Candid Camera;* it is harsh, oftentimes cruel, and sometimes dangerous.

There's also the media covering the entertainment, which has been around since the 1950s movie magazines, such as *Look*, which of course today are augmented by TV shows like *Entertainment Tonight, Access Hollywood,* and *Extra.* Lest we forget, there's even exploitation news, which masquerades as media but is better classified as entertainment—at least the traditional news media would rather you think that. That started in 1986 when *A Current Affair* premiered in syndication and paved the way for the tabloid papers to hit television.

One thing about entertainment and media: You are surrounded by them every day. There are few things in life that you've practically no choice but to bear witness to every day. You can't help but catch a glimpse of a newspaper or magazine headline, hear a bit of news or maybe a song on the radio, see a moment of television, or catch a peek of someone's computer screen as they're checking out a site on the Internet.

Putting It Together

With the far-reaching power of the entertainment and media juggernauts, it's no wonder so many people want to work in one or the other (and sometimes both), whether in front of the camera or behind it, at the keyboard creating content or managing the controls and servers that send it out over the airwaves or the Net. Performers, writers, directors, camera operators, technicians, choreographers, makeup artists, producers, and even agents, accountants, studio execs, and lawyers keep the wheels of these industries moving.

How many people comprise the entertainment and media industries? CNN, as an example, employs some 4,000 people worldwide to keep the 24/7 news flowing into televisions, radios, and the Internet. Over at NBC there are forty people listed between the series stars and crew that work to churn out the hit show *Friends* every week—and that doesn't include a weekly turnover of guest stars, bit players, and writers, nor does it include the people who work to make you aware of the show via publicity streamed to your senses in every way imaginable. A major-release Hollywood film involves a cast and crew that can reach nearly 1,000. Even something that may seem smaller, such as the Broadway megahit *The Producers,* involves the participation of more than 200 people among the people onstage, backstage, and in the back office. And, unlike a film that's in production for a set number of months and then finishes, a Broadway show can run for years and involve many of the people on its cast and crew working eight times a week.

Popular magazines such as *Vanity Fair* list more than 100 people responsible for getting that magazine onto newsstands each month. Staffs of big-city newspapers, like *The New York Times* or *Chicago Tribune*, easily double that to get their daily print and online editions out. And, even though a torrent of dot-coms went bust and it's still hard to make a buck off Internet advertising, news outlets are fascinated with the concept of instant news and try to keep their Internet site staffs working, waiting for the impact of the Internet to be fully understood and harnessed. As people figure out the criteria that define success online and the kinds of business models that create that success, look for the employment figures for Internet ventures to rise once again.

A typical hit CD recorded by a musical artist has a staff in the hundreds, too, composed of musicians, sound engineers, arrangers, and composers, plus the staff at the record company that gets it produced and distributed. Then, of course, there's the crew of fifty-plus on the video that gets shot for the single. That single thereby ends up on TV, the Net, and the radio, each medium supporting hundreds of additional jobs.

Who gets an entertainment product mentioned on TV and radio and written about in magazines? The publicity machine. The eyes and ears are what matter to the publicity machine; every publicist wants to get something from his or her production into the minds of many as part of the pop culture of the moment.

Talk about a lot of job opportunities. But make no mistake: it's not exactly easy to get a job in some of the professions covered in this book. Roles for actors, singers, and other performers are as highly prized as ever. Crew jobs, too, can be more difficult initially, although with some of the newer technologies, actually breaking into some behind-the-scenes jobs is getting a little easier. A journalist might not feel as compelled to start out working at *Time* or *People* when there are hundreds of media outlets to hone one's skills.

The Internet is poised and ready to provide you with all the information you'll need to make the connections, find out about opportunities, and market yourself, all more efficiently than ever before. Many professionals who embarked on their careers prior to the rise of the Net now marvel at how much information exists online that they could have used, from casting news to union news to how an event might be affected by the weather that day. People entering their thirties did not have this resource when they were getting their first jobs less than ten years ago.

Time is of the essence when it comes to everyone having access to the same information. This book will not only guide you through the careers that make up the media and entertainment industries, showing you where to research and find job information and how to connect with others in the field, but will save you precious hours sourcing and judging the value of countless Internet resources that may or may not be useful to your quest. So read on with your computer fired up and at the ready so you can point and click your way along as you separate the wheat from the chaff.

Media, Entertainment, and the Internet: A Feeding Frenzy ● 7

Chapter 2
Countless Careers to Consider

Yes, there are a lot of career opportunities available—and there are many applicants for every one of them. Most of the creative positions in entertainment and media are coveted positions and not jobs you can just happen into (unless you're "discovered" at your local drugstore, school, or gym). Crew and technical jobs are difficult to obtain, too, but there are many more places to put those crafts to work on local levels than there are for the performers. No matter what career you want in the media and entertainment industries, this book will help you use the Internet by showing you the best sources online to identify and research the job you want, plus the ways to get your foot in the door.

Following is a list of the careers tackled in this book, along with some vital statistics about each one. All labor statistics are taken from the 2000-2001 edition of the U.S. Department of Labor's Bureau of Labor Statistics' *Occupational Outlook Handbook*.

Actors

From A-list movie stars (think Julia Roberts or Brad Pitt) on through TV series stars (along the lines of Kelsey Grammer or Heather Locklear) to TV guest stars to all those people who populate the background of this week's club scene on *Sex and the City,* these are some of the most visible entertainers. But they are just a part of the actor pool. There are also stage actors, who range from major Tony Award-winning stars to the boys and girls in the back row of the chorus who give their all at every performance, whether on Broadway or at the smallest of community theaters. And let's not forget commercial actors, voice actors, and those who work in institutional training videos. There are also the new media actors who star in CD-ROM games and Internet film projects.

In the future, as entertainment grows and the Internet eventually gets harnessed to deliver broadband entertainment, demand for actors should grow along with every advancement—as long as real actors are preferred over digital clones such those featured in the overhyped and underdelivering film *Final Fantasy* in the summer of 2001.

Many actors now have websites, as a way either to stay in touch with fans or to provide employers with an online résumé, a headshot, and even a reel that can be viewed at anytime. It's rare these days for TV shows, films, and theater productions not to have websites of their own. Aspiring actors can capitalize on the Net on its most fundamental level, joining virtual communities to network with colleagues in the industry.

Dancers and Choreographers

Dancers perform in TV shows and movies in musical numbers, in stage plays, in concerts and other stage presentations, and for dance companies. It's the choreographers who direct the dancers in the movements to perform. Many dancers take on the role of dance captain, assistant choreographer, or choreographer as they gain experience. There are approximately 29,000 working dancers and choreographers earning a median yearly salary of $21,430. Except for some possible employment in productions that get shown on the Internet, it is not likely that the dance employment rate will be very affected by the Net revolution.

Dancers and choreographers have not yet hit their strides with personal representation on websites, though it is becoming more common for individuals to post their résumé and headshot, much like the actors do. Dancers also get Net visibility through their shows or companies, often showcased as featured dancers in photography. Eventually, as streaming video quality improves, companies will start offering video clips of performances as well.

Singers and Musicians

These artists are not just the people you hear on the radio belting out the latest hit or those on the opera stage hitting a high C note. They are those whose musical talents, vocal and instrumental, on traditional as well as digitally re-created instruments, find their way to our ears in infinite ways as we walk through life. Some 273,000 people choose to make this their profession in musical careers, including singers, musicians, composers, conductors, and arrangers. These talented people earn an average of $30,020 per year.

Musicians and singers have fully realized how the Net can connect them to more opportunities to perform their work and refine their craft. A personal website with biographical information, photographs, and audio clips *can* lead to being discovered—or at least to developing a fan base that can come see you at gigs. Musicians can now make and market their own CDs over the Net, but there's no guarantee that anyone will buy them rather than pirate and trade them—the other edge of the sword for a working musician. While exposure for musicians has never been easier, just how to make a profit outside of traditional approaches to the careers is a question being answered right now, by the activities of people like you. Did you pay for that CD you're listening to right now?

DJs and Announcers

Disc jockeys are rather specialized members of the announcers' profession. They keep the music going on the radio, interview special guests, and interact with the listeners. Announcers can be anyone else you hear on the radio or TV—doing commercials, announcing the program coming up next, and recording all other voiceover work. Disc jockeys, in another form, bring entertainment to parties, weddings, and other events. More than 50,000 people call disc jockeying a career; the average salary barely breaks $20,000. With Internet radio one of the few areas of the Internet still seemingly viable for growth, voice talent should continue to be solid employment for those lucky enough to get it.

Radio DJs and announcers don't have much individual visibility on the Net outside of sites that are usually tied into radio shows. DJs whose forte is spinning at clubs, events, and parties have many Web communities and organizations to help them do their jobs.

Writers and Editors

Newspaper and Magazine Reporters/Editors

These are the people who report on everything from local news to the weather, from Hollywood gossip to the atrocities on the front lines of a military action. For midsize and larger publications, reporters gather the news and write the articles while the editors make the assignments and plan out what goes into print. In many organizations, however, writer, reporter, and editor job titles can be fairly interchangeable. More than 350,000 people produce these publications, ranging in positions from a staff reporter on a beat to the editor of *The Wall Street Journal* to a technical writer who reports on the latest medical breakthroughs so that laypeople can understand these advances. These professions also include writers working for Internet publications, though in many cases staffers on the Internet also work on a print publication as well. Median earnings for writers and editors come in under $40,000.

As the Internet continues to be used as an information resource by consumers, the number of writers needed to keep up the information flow is likely to increase. Before that happens, however, the business side of the media empire must figure out how to make money while delivering information.

Meanwhile, writers don't often have sites that promote their writing, although they do have sites that act as résumés with descriptions and clips of stories they've written. Journalists also maintain active communities through online clubs and trade organizations.

Television and Radio News Reporters/Writers

Depending on the type of TV or radio station you work for, you could specialize in a specific type of reporting—legal, city government, investigative—or you could do a wide variety of general assignments. There are also positions where you can write copy for those on the air to read. Typically, the larger the station, the more specialized the job. The median yearly pay for these positions is in the $23,000-to-$26,000 range, depending on the type of job, size of the station, and responsibilities. If you get an on-air job, the median salary goes up to $33,000 for TV-news reporters and $32,000 for radio-news reporters. Sportscasters on TV jump up to a median of $52,000, while their radio counterparts average out at $57,000. Weathercasters in both media earn an average of $55,000.

The Internet won't fully impact most of these jobs until there's an Internet-based video news service. That requires on-air talent. As soon as broadband video is easily accessible from homes and a critical mass of people have DSL or cable-modem connections, a new avenue of opportunity will open. Right now these jobs are all in over-the-air TV and radio stations and cable TV networks.

Much like their print counterparts, these writers and reporters don't put much about themselves on the Internet outside of résumé information. They do maintain communities because the networking is critical to maintaining contacts for both stories and potential future jobs.

Screenwriters for Television and Film

These are the people responsible for writing the scripts we see onscreen—whether the small screen in our living room or the big screen at the theater. Numerous writers are often involved in episodic television shows, each writing and polishing different episodes or plot lines. Films' requirements vary depending on the project between a single writer and an army of writers, some of whom may go uncredited (but not unpaid) for their work. Accurate salary and staffing figures are hard to come by for this category of writers. On television shows, staff writers, on the low end of the scale, make $20,000 to $40,000 per year. Meanwhile, some feature-film writers can earn paychecks into the seven-figure range for their work—and some are paid closer to the television rate.

Screenwriters who are actively working don't have much presence online, except through sites for their shows and through the Writers Guild of America. Those who wish to become screenwriters, though, do make use of the Internet to stay in contact with one another and get helpful advice from their peers and mentors. As the average user can support greater bandwidth and scripted entertainment becomes part of the Net—as it's already doing at places like Warner Bros. Online, where there are cartoon shorts based on Looney Tunes characters—more work for screenwriters is inevitable.

Directors

Behind every performance is a director. From music videos to sitcoms, documentary short films to blockbuster films, stage performances, rock concerts, and even video games, directors pull all the component pieces together into an entertainment work that, done right, is a critical and commercial success. The median salary for directors falls at just $26,000—and that's a combination of all directors. With the salary that low you can be sure that there are far more directors earning below the average rather than the multimillion-dollar salaries that Spielberg-type directors make.

Directors, especially those striving to make a name for themselves, often have homepages to showcase their work. They're also members of online clubs and chats to help draw people toward their work. For them, the Net is about making a name for yourself so you can make the next, hopefully bigger, project. Just like musicians who put their songs online, directors are finding ways to make short films—or offer short clips of longer work—that utilize the available technology of Internet video to further their careers. Like some of the other video/film-based careers, when Internet video matures, look for more directors getting hired to fill the programming need.

Crew

There are very few salary estimates available for crew positions because of the wildly broad pay scales involved and the freelance nature of jobs that are contracted on an as-needed basis.

Cinematographers and Camera Operators

Cinematography is the art of creating film images for television and the big screen. It is the cinematographer's responsibility to plan and coordinate the film shoot. In many cases, the cinematographer doesn't actually operate the camera, but some do. You may think it's just someone saying, "Point the camera there," but keep in mind that there's a huge difference between a home movie of a fishing trip and, say, *A River Runs Through It* (the 1992 Academy Award winner for best cinematography). Cinematographers work with camera operators and assistant camera operators to get the shots they want. Work in these fields will remain steady and pick up a bit as more entertainment productions need to be filmed.

This is another field where personal homepages help showcase an individual's work. Online communities also exist through the guilds and professional publications available to the cinematographer.

Composers, Arrangers, and Conductors

Composers write the songs they hope the whole world will sing (and pay royalties to the composer in order to do so). This includes everything from a commercial jingle to a film score, a Top 40 hit for the latest boy band, and any other piece of music that you hear. Arrangers, meanwhile, take the composition and adapt it to a particular musical style. To put it simply, an arranger takes Madonna's latest hit and transforms it into elevator music, or a totally different-sounding song for a man to sing. Arrangers can also translate a composition so it can be played on just a piano or by a full symphony. Conductors often lead orchestras and vocal ensembles to perform the arranged music.

The Internet remains an underutilized resource for composers and arrangers that is poised to grow as the Net continues to be a gathering place for the industry.

Sound Engineers, Recordists, and Boom Operators

If there's sound involved, these people are, too. Sound designers make sure microphones are placed correctly and that everyone and everything is heard—and what shouldn't be heard (such as a police siren going down the street) isn't. The engineers supervise the actual recording, recordists are in charge of setup and individual recorders, and the boom operators hold those long poles with mikes on the end to capture dialogue (some boom microphones can even show up in finished programs—watch closely and sometimes you'll see them).

This is another underrepresented group on the Web, sans a few personal homepages. Even though Internet-delivered audio is good, a truly good sound engineer isn't going to let his or her creation become corrupted by compressing it into an MP3 (many complain that MP3s sound hollow because of the file compressions that makes these clips so easily shareable). So, while résumés do get posted online, often they don't include audio clips of the work. A rising demand by consumers for the same sound quality from their PC that they get from their home stereos will increase the work for these professionals.

Directors of Photography, Gaffers, and Lighting Designers

These folks are responsible for making sure the production is lit properly. The director of photography supervises the lighting in cooperation with the gaffers, the lighting technicians carrying out the work. For stage and live entertainment, the supervisory role typically falls to the lighting designer, who works with a crew to hang and coordinate the lights.

These jobs are often found on the Internet in the form of personal homepages designed primarily by freelance workers. For them, the Web is a calling card when productions come to their local areas. Work opportunities found solely through the Internet, however, are few at this point. And there's not much of a virtual community right now for lighting pros, either.

Costume Designers

Somebody's got to dress all those people. While it may sound as easy as keeping up with current trends and shopping at retail stores to put the cast of *Law & Order* into costume, it isn't. Imagine coming up with costumes for the alien of the week on *Star Trek* or dressing hundreds of actors in exacting garb, circa 1912—everything from sailor uniforms to proper attire for the rich and the poor— for *Titanic*.

While there are lots of resources for costume designers to find, trade, and buy costumes, representation on the Web is sparse, outside of information about them found on sites about individual productions.

Art Directors, Scenic Designers, Painters, Carpenters, Electricians, Set Decorators, Illustrators, and Model Makers

The art director is responsible for the look of a production, supervising the staff to create sets and executing the vision of the director. You'll find scenic designers, painters, carpenters, electricians, and set decorators on almost every production, no matter how small, from stage to screen. Illustrators are involved if matte paintings are needed, anything from a starscape outside a starship viewport to a cityscape outside an apartment window. Model makers get into the act, too; if there's a miniature city to blow up or rock with an earthquake, the model maker will get it built.

There are lots of resources for these careers on the Internet, from associations and guilds to professional magazines. Individual practitioners of these crafts, though, aren't very front and center on the Net. Work for these people will rise as more Net productions and short films are undertaken.

Special Effects Crews

If something needs to be blown up, look otherworldly, get flooded, or do anything else out of the ordinary, the special effects crew takes over. Today, special effects encompass almost every aspect of the film, even actors in some cases. *Star Wars* films are a perfect example. Much of *Star Wars Episode II: Attack of the Clones* was shot before a blue screen so all the sets and stunts, and even virtual characters, can be added in by effects crews later. As this trend continues, more effects people will be needed to handle the workload.

There are a handful of effects creators with online résumés that show off some of their creations, but a Net presence for this profession is still in the offing. There are plenty of resources out there, though, for those who want to break into the field, from how to do it to where to get work.

Animators

Where the world of animation used to be the realm of cell-animation artists, there's a new wave that encompasses working in front of the computer to create animated work. While the 1995 Disney movie *Toy Story* was the first fully digital-animated feature film, the bar for animation was raised to a new level with the summer 2001 release of *Final Fantasy: The Spirits Within*, which showed the most lifelike digital humans ever. But the work for animators can be shaky as the movie studios grapple with the expense of making animated fare. Twentieth Century Fox, for example, folded its animation unit after box-office duds like *Titan A.E.* But rest assured, there will always be work out there for talented people in this field.

Because animation can be delivered over the Internet with better quality than live-action, full-motion video, animators have work in many facets of the Internet. There are personal sites where they post their latest creations or works in progress; there are also thriving communities of animators online in virtual clubs and chat rooms. There are also jobs creating original animations, as Warner Bros. Online is doing with original Looney Tunes shorts. And with so many places to post their finished work, such as Apple's iMovie site, people can easily explore this line of work on the Net.

Makeup Artists

Here again, there's a vast variety of work to be done: touching up anchor-people's makeup for the evening news, applying makeup for sitcom actors, creating makeup so a stage actor looks as though he's received a black eye, or constructing elaborate makeup for an alien creature in a feature film. There are many subtleties in applying even basic makeup that require expertise in the field. An actor who is playing a modern-day Wall Street broker, for example, will need a different style of makeup depending on the lighting, scenic design, and artistic vision of the production.

There are many makeup artists online. It's easy to make an online résumé and portfolio with photographs of your makeup work. There are also online resources such as *Make-Up Artist Magazine* (www.makeupmag.com) to serve the online community. The Net effect for employment in this area, however, is still being realized as these artists create online communities for networking and job opportunities.

Casting Directors

Who is right for the part? That is a rather daunting question with so many actors vying for a finite number of parts. The casting director coordinates the process of filling roles, from the principal players through all the extras needed. Casting directors are involved in most aspects of stage and screen work to help the directors find the right people to make the characters come to life.

Casting directors, as well as directors and producers who need to cast projects, have established a presence online so actors can find them. There are many resources for casting directors on the Net, especially sites that help actors get noticed. The Casting Site (www.thecastingsite.com), for example, is a place where actors can read casting notices and submit their résumés; meanwhile, casting directors can surf through the actors who use the site to see if anyone is right for projects they're casting. And other sites like Casting Site are popping up, such as the résumé/headshot posting service that Playbill.com runs for actors, in an effort to get actors more visibility and casting directors an easier job of finding talent.

Casting directors are always in demand. Because of the volume of entertainment produced for the Net—everything from TV shows and CD-ROMs to short films—there'll be more demand for talented people to cast the roles. Become a trusted casting director, quickly bringing directors exactly the right actors, and you'll be working nonstop.

Assistants

This is where many of the above crew get their start. Nearly all of these people listed have an assistant of one sort or another who is one part gopher, one part slave, and one part pupil. The wage is low or even nonexistent, but the experience is crucial—and so is the networking. Impress the right person and that's all you need to jump-start your career. An assistant sees everything happening on the set, in the newsroom, or in the recording studio—from top to bottom.

Assistants are generally the heart and soul of getting the work done, keeping the set quiet, running errands, and solving problems. Open positions for assistants are all over the Net—every guild talks about assistantships, which are sometimes presented as internships, as the way to begin. What you don't find a lot of is production assistants talking about their jobs on the Net. After a twelve- to fifteen- hour workday, you can't really blame them for not wanting to spend that free time on the Net. Once you've proven yourself as a great assistant, the work comes easier because you'll get recommended as someone who gets the job done and done right.

Office Staff

So, maybe actually producing the entertainment isn't for you. There are still plenty of positions involving the art of the deal and getting the finished product in front of the public.

Agents and Managers

They don't have the best reputation in the business, but for anyone involved in film, television (in some cases even top news reporters at the networks have agents), stage, and music, there are agents and/or managers involved in making the deal. It's up to these people to make sure their client gets the best deal and takes the best jobs to maintain their exposure and keep their "star" on the rise. Employment statistics are hard to come by for these professions. While some agents and managers work for agencies, others are self-employed and look after only one client (Britney Spears's mom, for example, is her manager).

Agents and managers, much like casting directors, are beginning to use the Net to look for talent. Finding the next big talent is what these people are all about, so all but the largest and most prestigious agencies have some online representation. Look for more work for agents and managers as more productions kick off, no matter what the medium.

Lawyers

Here is another crucial player in the deal-making process. Contracts are a must in this business for everyone, from an ensemble/extra player to the highest paid stars to the director and crew. Usually all parties have a lawyer to make sure their part of the deal is to their specifications, with no loopholes or anything else the signee may regret later. You've probably heard stories of singers and songwriters from the 1950s and 1960s who lost a lot of money because they signed away rights to their songs for just a few hundred dollars. Having an attorney look over your deals can protect you against that. Being the attorney means you bring in lots of money and get to rub elbows with the famous folk—and in some cases even become famous yourself (Johnnie Cochran and Alan Dershowitz, for example, have become household names). There are, of course, numerous lawyers out there, but there is no specific breakdown of how many are in the entertainment specialty.

Accountants

No need to hang out your shingle as a solo CP A; you can specialize in entertainment accounting. There are several opportunities to choose from here: You can work with a production company to help manage its participation in projects; you can work with magazines, newspapers, television stations, and radio stations to ensure their cash flow; you could work with a producer, whose job it is to raise the money and account for how it is used in productions; or you can work on a personal level with the cast and crew of the productions, who can have many streams of money coming in from the array of work they do—or in some cases don't do. Helping people and businesses through lean financial times is just as important as managing the prosperous, successful ventures.

Entertainment accountants are not easily findable on the Net because they are usually one part of an accounting firm or production studio. The work in this field, however, will increase as firms keep looking for a way to make money by entertaining and spreading information on the Web.

Public Relations Teams and Publicists

Every aspect of entertainment and media has its PR machine. It is the job of PR to make sure the public is very aware of their client's business. Magazines have PR firms to beat the drum about each issue's top stories. Movies, television, music, and live performances rely on someone getting the word out so people tune in or drop their hard-earned cash on a ticket, CD, or DVD. Even the talent gets involved, with many performers having their own public relations firm or individual publicist to ensure the right spin for their projects and image. It's certainly not an easy job, with often millions of dollars riding on a campaign for the "latest thing." You could be riding high one moment, preparing to unleash a major singer's motion picture debut, then be in damage-control mode the next as that singer has a very public emotional breakdown. Here's a crowded profession, with more than 120,000 people holding down PR and publicist jobs. Average wages are good here, at almost $50,000 per year.

These people are very happy being behind the scenes and prefer to create the story rather than being the story. You'll find most PR firms on the Web; however, you'll locate only the individual PR practitioner and publicist through personal sites, and in those cases only when they've chosen to talk about their careers. There will be an ever-increasing market for these professions. One of the things the Internet has proven that it can do well is market and promote entertainment, and that will keep these people busy for a long time.

Marketing Coordinators

This is another part of the machine that gets the word out. While the PR people and publicists spin the stories, the marketing folks are getting the word out via every outlet possible—creating websites, posters, television and radio commercials, sweepstakes, advance screenings or listening parties, and gala events keyed to the debut of the new thing. Make no mistake: While it's often TV, movies, and music that have the most overt use of marketing, magazines do, too. Think for a moment about the marketing hoopla that surrounds each year's *Sports Illustrated* swimsuit issue or *Playboy*'s Playmate of the Year or *People*'s Sexiest Man Alive. How big is this marketing machine? More than 480,000 hold marketing jobs. They're paid well for their time, too, earning an average salary of $57,300 per year.

These people fit into the same category as the PR folks, part of the out-of-sight, out-of-mind crew, making the machine turn. And they, too, will ride high on the employment scale as the Net continues to market entertainment really well.

Publishers

At the top of the print-media empire, these are the "producers" of magazines and newspapers. They oversee the entire operation, working to hold together the triangle of editorial, advertising, and production to keep a smooth-running organization while making sure they are serving the needs of the audience.

Publishers who work on the print editions of publications tend to also work on the Internet side of the business. Their visibility on the Internet is primarily through these online editions. There are, of course, publishers for Internet-only publications. However, many Net-only publications are dying out, since most consumers are not yet willing to pay for Internet magazines.

Studio Heads

It's the top job in Hollywood: running your own studio. But there are many subordinate positions to consider here, too, that can groom you for this spot— jobs like vice president of worldwide production or vice president of programming. There are a lot of avenues that can lead to becoming someone like Walt Disney CEO Michael Eisner, about the only studio chief you can routinely find on television (as host of *The Wonderful World of Disney*). And Eisner certainly didn't start out at the top; he spent years in other positions, such as president of Paramount Pictures and senior vice president of prime-time programming at ABC. If this is what you want to be, start learning it all. It'll take twenty or thirty or forty years before you reach this position. And, except for the few studio heads who are household names (like Eisner), you won't find much on the Net concerning people in this position outside of biographies that are posted on studio sites.

There you have it. Any of these jobs sound like something you want to take up? Read on and find out how you can get started in these professions by using the Net.

Part Two
Past, Present, and Future

Chapter 3

Entertainment and Media: The Past

Getting jobs in the entertainment and media fields in the pre-Internet era of the 1980s and early 1990s was a matter of being in the right place at the right time and knowing the right people. Of course, you had to have the skill and/or talent to stand out in your field. That was true even before the 1980s, especially in entertainment, which is quite possibly the most subjective field in which to get employed. The news media, especially for the written word, are generally a little easier. What makes solid reporting is more quantifiable than what makes a good film, song, or play.

Think about it for a moment. You read a great, investigative article in *The New York Times;* you know by the number of angles covered, people interviewed, and conclusions drawn that a good, solid reporter wrote the piece. If you pass that article around you'll probably get the same reaction—it's an airtight story because the rules of good journalism were followed.

Now, go to a movie with a group of friends and discuss it afterward. How many people feel exactly the same way? There is no tried-and-true method to formulate a good piece of entertainment; some will love it and some will hate it. Even productions that are universally panned by critics can find some audience that thinks it's the best thing ever.

And while journalistic styles can differ, a seasoned editor will be able to spot a good writer during the job interview process. It's harder for a director to spot the right talent and guarantee that the talent will translate to the project. If you doubt that, remember that even the most successful stars and directors make movies that simply turn out, well, bad.

Don't Call Us, We'll Call You

That's the most common entertainment business cliché there is. And like any good cliché, it's also a way of life. Prior to the Internet age, you had to live in one of the bigger cities to have any hope of getting discovered and moving up the ranks to where you could reach the level of "star" in your field. Prior to the cable television/ independent film boom of the late 1990s, if you didn't live in New York or Los Angeles or another large city, you really weren't considered "in" the business.

If breaking into film was your thing, you could narrow down the places to live to one—Hollywood—because the bulk of the production work was centered there. It could take years to climb your way up, more so in the pre-Internet era than it did even during the studio system of the 1940s and 1950s, because back then the movies were actively scouting talent. As movies became more money-driven and agents became the dealmakers, getting discovered in a drugstore became less likely.

To break into the field as an actor in the days before the Net, it wasn't a "right place/right time" thing as much as it was about hitting the streets for audition after audition. For filmmakers, getting started often involved graduating from film school with a solid final project, and then getting an internship or apprenticeship through one of the unions or guilds. Competition was fierce all the way around and the information you needed to get a job was held in a few industry publications like *Variety* and *The Hollywood Reporter*.

Then there's television. In the 1980s, cable was an upstart industry, in some circles regarded even lower on the pecking order than local television. The home audience in the 1980s had access to fewer than twenty channels—a far cry from today's digital satellite systems that offer up to 300 channels. That changed as Ted Turner launched a media empire in Atlanta with TBS Superstation, which went national via satellite in 1976, albeit to an audience of only 24,000 on four cable systems. CNN was next, launching in 1980 with 1.7 million subscribers. At nearly the same time, 1979 to be exact, the Entertainment and Sports Programming Network was born in Bristol, Connecticut. Today it's known simply as ESPN, and similar to what Ted Turner did for sitcom reruns and twenty-four-hour news, sports television has never been the same. For that matter, television wasn't the same. As a result of the 300-channel universe, the pool of possible work opportunities has evolved exponentially with each traditional media outlet supported by at least one online component.

Building the Cable Empire

Here's a quick rundown of some critical launches in the multichannel universe:

@ 1976: WTCG (eventually to be called TBS Superstation) launches to 24,000 subscribers

@ 1979: Entertainment and Sports Programming Network (ESPN) launches

@ 1980: Cable News Network (CNN) debuts to 1.7 million subscribers

@ 1994: DirecTV and United States Satellite Broadcasting (USSB) launch digital broadcast satellite to homes, making a 300-channel universe possible

Those who graduated from the local college or university television program in years past, at least in small and midsize markets, often filled television jobs in those cities. This new talent provided TV stations with good employees who were eager to learn, especially behind the scenes on the technical jobs. From those starting positions, the path was to work your way up to other, higher-profile jobs. For example, a cameraman starts out covering local traffic accidents, and if he's good, he moves on to larger TV stations or into camera work on entertainment shows or films.

Cable television expanded the places to go after paying your dues. Where the pinnacle of television prior to the cable boom was to work your way up to one of the big three networks (yes, there was a time before Fox, UPN, and the WB), now there was the new business of cable. As the channel numbers grew, original programming began to claim more airtime from the reruns. All the new talk shows, craft shows, game shows, cooking shows, and even new dramas and sitcoms needed was for production crews to realize them all. It was a win for everyone looking for work in front of or behind the camera.

There was also the rise of home video. Sony's Betamax videocassette recorder hit the consumer market in 1975. Initially intended as a way for people to record television shows so that they could watch them at a more convenient time, the technology was eventually embraced by Hollywood as a new market to distribute theatrical movies. By the early 1980s you could purchase your favorite films for your home library. Also in the 1980s, Betamax and the rival format, VHS, duked it out, and VHS won the home-video-format war, primarily because you could record more on a single cassette (six hours on VHS compared to two and a half on Beta).

By the 1990s, video was an outlet for films that never made it to theaters. Yes, that meant a lot of B movies (and, in many cases, Z movies), but it opened up an array of new employment for actors, directors, producers, and the entire moviemaking crew. The late 1990s gave rise to DVD and a new market to collect films on disc (DVD, it should be noted, succeeded as a video-disc format after CED discs and LaserDiscs failed in the marketplace during the 1980s and early 1990s).

Music Reinvents Itself

Music transformed itself in the 1980s, too. The introduction of the CD in 1983 revolutionized music by making it more portable and compact—it went from the twelve-inch, easy-to-damage vinyl album to the five-inch, fairly indestructible compact disc. MTV was also born and suddenly music was riding a new wave of popularity with acts that not only could sing, but looked good on TV as well—or at least you hoped the artists had both qualities going for them.

Radio genres started expanding. Even in the smaller cities, there became more options of music to listen to. As cable TV expanded its reach, music expanded, too, with delivery services like Digital Cable Radio (today named Music Choice). Digital Cable Radio pumped narrowly themed genres into people's homes via their cable service. Suddenly you could get twenty or more genres of music at the touch of a button—everything from top hits to oldies to gospel to salsa and everything in between.

People trying to make it in music certainly didn't stop in the 1980s and 1990s. Garage bands were nothing new and aspiring musicians were out in force, performing wherever they could to get noticed. There were more venues for musicians as well with the rise of college radio and music conferences that began to actively look for new talent. The South by Southwest Music and Media Conference and Festival (www.sxsw.com), formed in Austin, Texas, in 1987, is a perfect example. The conference was created with the idea of getting bands heard by producers and has worked so well that *Sound and Vision* magazine said of the two-week event held in 2001, "SXSW reigns as the music industry's single most important gathering of artists, talent scouts, journalists . . . a music conference that still puts music first."

For disc jockeys as well it was a time of growth. DJs tend to start out much like local television workers, getting their feet wet at small stations and climbing to larger and larger stations. An excellent example of this is Mark and Brian, currently morning radio show hosts in Los Angeles. Back in the 1980s they were doing morning radio for a station in Birmingham, Alabama. In the 1990s the duo hopped to Los Angeles and KLOS-FM. Now they host a morning show heard not only in L.A., but on twenty other stations across the country. They even had a short-lived series on NBC in 1991 called *The Adventures of Mark and Brian,* which tried to capture their radio high jinks for a different audience. More recently they had a cameo in the summer 2001 Disney film *The Princess Diaries.*

On the Boards

The biggest thing to happen to the United States theater scene during this time was the British invasion—specifically the arrival of megamusicals like *Cats, The Phantom of the Opera,* and *Les Miserables.* Huge casts, huge crews, and huge audience response marked a paradigm shift on Broadway and eventually across the country as those shows went out on tour. Behind the scenes, computers were fueling advances in special effects and stage wizardry, but the Net effect was yet to be tapped into by the research and job seeker.

Regional theaters—both professional and community—struggled to maintain funding, but remained active breeding grounds for actors and tech crews to get the necessary skills to work in larger venues. It's often the regional professional theaters that provide the necessary training and time commitments to gain entrance to the appropriate union.

Besides traditional theater settings, theme park revues grew as entertainment widened its net to snare more of the almighty dollar. Additions to existing parks (or the opening of parks) like Disney's EPCOT Center, Universal Studios in Florida, and several new Six Flags parks brought work to actors and tech crew at each park in the form of numerous stage shows. Many a current Broadway actor got his or her start working these shows back in the 1980s and 1990s. After all, once you've done six or twelve shows per day at a theme park, doing eight a week might seem like nothing at all.

For employment, however, while there was more work for stage actors and crew, other than the size and technology behind some of the shows, not much else changed.

Stop the Presses

Not much happened to the print media during the 1980s and 1990s in terms of how words got written. Where things took off was with desktop publishing, which make designing a publication far more efficient. Gone were the days of waxing sheets of copy and laying them out on boards. The rise of computers for layout and design opened a new route of employment in the print world.

The media busted out of a late-1980s recession that saw jobs harder to come by, especially in the print media; the 1990s brought a story of growth. Even before the Internet, the trend toward publishing a magazine for seemingly every interest on the planet began. Suddenly, if you were interested in a topic, there seemed to be a publication (or several) to which you subscribe, with titles for woodworking, model building, sewing, doll collecting . . . you name it. Newspapers, meanwhile, saw the birth of *USA Today* and had to grapple with the rise of CNN as a fierce competitor for the news audience.

For journalists and other people who put magazines and newspapers together, the 1990s brought the same growth that other factions of the economy saw. Jobs became more plentiful. Plus, with so many niche publications, it was even easy to write about a subject that interested you. Demand for production, art, advertising sales, and distribution jobs grew right along with them.

Jobs in print journalism were obtained in the old-school way: Get an internship while in college and that would translate directly to a job, or at least be a good résumé item to help get the first job. For broadcast majors, the same was true of working at television or radio stations. From there you'd climb up the ladder from the reporter who had to cover any story until you eventually became specialized and moved to a bigger station. The concept of freelancing also hit its stride in this period. People liked the idea of writing at home, and while there were certainly writers who had always done it, journalists were finding it easier to work this way with the ease of e-mailing stories to editors. For the publications, it was a more cost-efficient way of having a network of reporters; for the writers, it was a way to work for many different outlets simultaneously.

The Back Office

There are tons of people behind the scenes who make the creative work look easy. They are the accountants, public relations and marketing people, lawyers, publishers, publicists, agents, mailroom personnel, receptionists, and so on. Without them, the chances of the creative work actually getting seen by the public are diminished.

Mailroom personnel, assistants, and receptionists get their jobs through traditional channels—temp agencies, seeing an ad in the help wanted section, or getting a tip that a position has opened up. Competition for those jobs can be fierce, though, because a foot in the door of an entertainment company is often a way to move past the entry-level job and into a "creative" job.

The entry-level jobs people want today are slightly different on the media side. It's rare that a job as a receptionist at a newspaper, magazine, or local TV station leads to a position as a reporter. The entry jobs at these places are more on the order of assistants—positions like junior writer, photographer, camera operator, and so on—and these jobs are just as competitive as any other.

For positions such as accountants, publicists, and lawyers, entry-level people start like most others in those professions. The key is to get hired by entertainment or media-centric companies as an entrée to the business.

Internet and the Consumer

But what effect did the Internet have on consumers? In the workplace, people started using e-mail as a way to stay connected even in the late 1980s and early 1990s. Online services started popping up in the early 1990s as well and were a far cry from the slick interface and "You've Got Mail" friendliness of AOL.

Everyone Online

According to a 2001 U.S. Census Bureau report, one-half of all U.S. households (54 million) have at least one computer. Many homes are wired for the Internet as well, with 42 percent reporting Web access (up from only 18 percent in 1997). One-third of all U.S. adults use e-mail. In addition, according to a Gartner Dataquest report, nearly 25 percent of wired households use a broadband (DSL, cable modem, T1, or T3) connection.

CompuServe was the first to offer e-mail in 1979 and moved into real-time chat in 1980, long before most people even thought of going online. America Online (or simply AOL) debuted in 1985 as an easy-to-use alternative to accessing the Internet. Today, AOL owns CompuServe. Prodigy, meanwhile, started in 1990 as a partnership between IBM and Sears.

What about the actual World Wide Web? It came into consumer use in 1994 when the Netscape (at the time called Mosaic Netscape) browser came to market. The search engine Yahoo! was born the same year (Trivia note: Did you know that Yahoo! is really an acronym for Yet Another Hierarchical Officious Oracle?). With all this innovation, the way we access information, buy goods, and conduct our lives has changed dramatically.

Chapter 4

Entertainment and Media: The Present

The Internet revolution didn't change only the way we shop for books, CDs, and other merchandise from the comfort of our home. It changed the way we research and get jobs. It also changed the very ways the fields covered in this book operate. Entertainment marketing is far different now than it was a decade ago. So is the way we get our news and information from the media. In a short time, the Internet has moved from a way to get e-mail and chat with people across the room or across the world to a media form all its own, with news, information, and entertainment available on more "channels" than ever imagined possible prior to its existence.

The Net became an amazing marketing machine in the process. All you have to say to prove the point is *The Blair Witch Project*. This simple, small, cheap, independent horror film was master-marketed by its distributor, Artisan Entertainment, to gross $140 million at the box office and become the tenth highest grossing film of 1999. The *Blair Witch* site (www.blairwitch.com) let people check out the "background" of the film's characters before the release—and had a lot of people wondering if *Blair Witch* was fiction or documentary. Industry analysts say that without the site, *Blair Witch* would've just been another horror flick that would've been lucky to gross $50 million. In fact, the sequel made less than $30 million, showing that lightning doesn't strike twice. The sequel, which had a website as well, somehow just didn't create the same sizzle.

Blair Witch shows the power of the Internet in today's marketplace. The big question is, how can you harness that power to get a job in the entertainment and media field? Whether you want to flex your marketing muscle and create the next *Blair Witch* phenomenon, get a part in a play or a movie, get a job at a news organization, or work behind the scenes in any of these fields, the Net is chock-full of information to help you. Once you're involved in the field of your choice, there are countless online communities waiting to support your quest on every level, from intern to executive producer.

In the introduction you read details of jobs this book covers. Now it's time to dig in and find out what the Internet can do to get you ready to find a job in those professions.

Television/Film/Stage

Actors/Dancers

For both aspiring and established actors, the Web makes it easier to keep up-to-date with audition notices, production start-up, and industry news than ever before. Prior to the Net you had to buy the daily trades such as *Variety, Hollywood Reporter,* and *Back Stage* to be up on the news. Now, all those trades are online, with some of them, such as *Variety*, offering updates throughout the day in addition to all the news from the daily print edition. Usually there is a subscription charge to some areas of these sites, but with access to critical industry information—especially the constantly updated list of what's in production at any given time—it can be money well spent.

One of the best sites is BackStage.com. This online resource from the publishers of *Back Stage* and *Back Stage West* has a job board listing jobs that are available for actors and crew. BackStage.com is one of many sites that allows you to post your résumé and headshot online. Once you post that information, not only do you have a link you can send out to people trying to cast you, it also becomes part of a searchable database so you can be found by casting directors.

The tough part for actors and dancers is the hunt; the jobs you're looking for aren't on typical job boards, such as Monster.com. You may find the occasional teaching job or theme park listing on those boards. Generally for these professions, however, it's about keeping up with the trades and specialized websites as well as getting information from your network of contacts.

Your Union, Your Friend

Most professional performers in the United States belong to at least one union among this group: Actors' Equity (www.actorsequity.org), the union for stage actors, dancers, and stage managers; Screen Actors Guild (www.sag.org), the union most film and television series actors belong to; or the American Federation of Television and Radio Artists (www.aftra.org), representing actors and other professional performers, along with broadcasters in television, radio, sound recordings, nonbroadcast/industrial programming, and new technologies such as interactive programming and CD-ROMs.

If you're serious about an acting career, these unions and their sites have a lot of information for you. Each union has its own strict rules about what it takes to become a member—usually a certain number of hours worked on approved projects that the union oversees. Actors' Equity, for example, doesn't recognize work in community theater for credit toward Equity membership. You have to get work at an Equity-participating theater and work for nearly a year to get your membership. It's not the easiest thing, but once you're in the union, your employment potential goes up considerably because some productions hire only Equity members.

The union websites have a great deal of information about breaking into the business. During the time you're working toward your union membership, you'll be gaining valuable contacts to get your foot in the door.

Advantages of Online Résumés and Headshots

"An actor who has a headshot and résumé online shows me that he or she is managing their career and taking the initiative to use all the available resources," says Clint Rebik, artistic director of Redwood Curtain, a small professional theater company in Eureka, California (www.redwoodcurtain.com). "If you want me to have an initial look at you and you're in Ohio and I'm in California, a website with those two things can open further communication."

Rebik says his company is receiving an increased number of queries because of the website it maintains. "We've gotten some actors and directors interested in us because of our location or the shows we've done. Communicating with these people electronically is great because I can shoot off a response immediately—or forward it to my colleagues so they can review the person's materials." Rebik typifies the kind of people who like the freedom the Internet gives them to look at information and respond at any time of the day or night. "It's all such a great convenience."

Sebastian LaCause, who created the title role in the 2000 Broadway revival of *The Rocky Horror Show*, started to use the Internet to market himself, not only to his fans but in an effort to showcase himself for future employment as well.

He stresses the importance of a good headshot, whether you're using it on- or offline. "The headshot is your calling card. Go out and meet photographers, look at their portfolios, find a [photography] style you like, and make sure you've got good chemistry with the photographer," LaCause says. "If you're tense around the photographer, they're not going to be able to bring out your personality." Today you can start your photographer search online, but do take the time to meet them to ensure you're getting exactly what was offered online—it's way too easy to fudge on the Internet.

LaCause's website (www.sebastianlacause.com) debuted in November 2000 to hype his appearance in *Rocky Horror.* Since then, however, he has used it to become involved in new projects. His first time testing it out involved sending the URL to a photographer who was considering him for a magazine cover. His site, featuring many different styles of photos, showed his range to the potential employer.

"The Internet is one tool out of many that you can use to find work," says LaCause, who plans to add a section to his site that features his work in short films. "I want to write, edit, and produce short films as a way to show what else I can do."

There are a number of ways to set up your own site. You can go through a service, such as BackStage.com or Playbill.com, to post a basic résumé and headshot. You can get free hosting through companies like Geocities or America Online (though, be advised, that Geocities and other "free" providers often require you to put advertisements on your site, and that can give your site a cluttered look). You can also pay the nominal fees to get your own website domain and hosting. For the first two years it is possible to get the domain and hosting for less than $250; you just have to shop around for the right package. Then with some simple HTML education, which you'll find on page 173, you can have your site up in just a few short days.

All About Networking

LaCause had a fairly typical start in the business. He went to New York City because he knew he wanted to perform. He enrolled at New York University as a dance major, and during this time he started going on auditions. By nineteen, he'd left NYU and joined a European touring company of *West Side Story*. He's since worked as a dancer in eight films, including *Sister Act II, Scream 2, Showgirls,* and *Boogie Nights,* and has done live performances with Madonna, Prince, and Tina Turner. And he's moved onto Broadway with the current revival of *Chicago*, the December 1999 *Minnelli on Minnelli* concerts (featuring Liza Minnelli's return to Broadway), and his role of Rocky.

After the *West Side Story* tour, the jobs were gotten in part because of the contacts he'd made in the business. "Networking is a great tool but it's not easy. I don't know anyone who loves networking," says LaCause. For LaCause, networking includes going to plays (and not always Broadway productions), after-parties, and any other professional or social opportunities to meet people. "Networking is not asking people for jobs. It's about meeting people and establishing relationships. It's also about asking for people's advice and hearing their story about getting into the business."

Networking for actors is no different than networking in any other profession. The more contacts you have within the business, the better the chance you'll find out about available work. You never know when someone you've become friends with becomes the person who helps you land an audition. Conversations happen all the time. Maybe the woman you've run into at the last three parties you attended told a producer friend about you because you've got the look for a lead role. It could happen, and the mere chance of it is the reason you should be putting yourself out there to meet as many people as you can. As painful as it is making the initial introduction, you'll find most people are quite willing to talk about their experiences in the business. Remember, you've got nothing to lose and everything to gain by mastering the networking game.

A question you might be asking yourself is this: With all the chat on the Internet, can I do my networking in a chat room? Maybe some of it you can, but it should not be your only form of networking. It's too limiting. Actors and dancers do hang out online from time to time, just like the rest of the wired community, but given how anonymous Internet chat rooms are, you can rarely be sure of the identity of the person you're talking to. It is best to go out and find the right people to talk to and then, possibly, strike up an online relationship with them as well.

However, if you want to give cybernetworking a try, there are places to do so, such as Yahoo! Clubs, which offer dozens of forums created by performers for performers. Some of them are generic while others are specific to a geographic location or a specific segment of industry.

One part of networking that the Net excels at is getting the word out. Whenever you're appearing in a play, a commercial, or a bit part on TV, immediately let the people on your networking list know. Have a contact list and send a short note to everyone on it with the details. A little reminder that you're appearing in something could lead to a networking contact watching or encouraging others in their networking circle to watch. Just remember not to be a pest about it, and take people off your e-mail list if they ask you to do so.

"I love getting the occasional e-mail from people I've worked with, or have a desire to work with, telling me what they're doing," says Rebik. "If I'm free, I might go and take other people with me, and who knows what that might lead to."

Audition, Audition, Audition

The key to any job for an actor or dancer is the audition. It's your chance to shine in front of the people who have the power to give you a job. It's not always a one-shot thing, either. LaCause, for example, auditioned four times before he was offered the part of Rocky.

For newcomers, LaCause says you should audition for everything possible. "Auditions are practice all in themselves. It starts the moment you walk into the room and how you deal with everyone in that room. Getting a part is not always about who gave the best reading. People want to work with talent, but they also want to work with people who seem good to work with."

Redwood Curtain's Rebik agrees. "There are plenty of good actors out there who do the work and do it well. But I want someone who is a treat to work with. It's such a collaborative process that it's critical to have a good attitude."

Just as with any other job, your employer is likely going to check up on your work history. Therefore, you'd also be advised not to fudge on your online (or offline, for that matter) résumé. It is tempting to fudge on the Internet with it being such an anonymous tool. No matter how tempted you might be to lie on your résumé or retouch your headshot, don't do it. That will only come back to haunt you in the end. You won't get a job based solely on your Net presentation. You'll be seen by a director or someone and your lying will eventually be discovered, and the word in the networking circles about you will not be positive.

On the Net, the best places to find audition information is through unions and trade papers. You should also keep on top of what's happening with local film commissions in your area. These websites typically have information about the film projects shooting in the area. It's a great way to keep up with your local activity, especially if you live outside a film/TV capital, like New York or L.A. You can find the commission(s) in your area—some cities have film commissions in addition to a state commission—by typing in "[state name] Film Commission" in your favorite search engine. Make sure to get yourself listed on the commission's site if it offers a directory of local resources.

Among the best film commission sites out there are the state of Louisiana (www.lafilm.org), New York City (www.ci.nyc.ny.us/html/filmcom/home.html), and Miami (www.filmiami.org). These sites give you an idea of what to expect as you surf other commissions.

The good thing for actors and dancers is that these tips work for jobs in stage, screen, commercials, and industrial features. The important thing is for you to get out there and go for the glory.

Take the Job

So you went for an audition, and you really thought you nailed that role that has a few pages of dialogue. But when you actually get the call from the director, you end up with a small part, with just a couple of lines that has you on stage for about six minutes. Remember, everybody's got to start somewhere. Whether your six minutes is on Broadway or in a sitcom, infomercial, industrial video, or locally produced cable access show that airs at 2 A.M. every other Wednesday, take the job.

Take that job unless you've definitely got something better lined up. Taking even the smallest part gets you experience and gets you seen. Experience is invaluable. It will make you better able to predict what might happen on your next job. Plus, you'll get networking time with your fellow actors, the director, and the crew. That in itself could lead to the next job.

Can I Find It on a Generic Job-Listings Site?

Not usually. Sometimes you'll find listings on Monster.com or other job boards. These are usually audition notices for theme parks and the occasional teaching position. You are better served using the sources mentioned above to find the auditions for the work you want.

Directors: Television/Film/Video

If there's one thing the computer revolution has done for the filmmaking profession, it's given everybody the ability to become a director. These days, for a couple thousand dollars, you can outfit yourself with a digital camcorder, a computer, and editing software to begin producing movies that you shoot with your friends. The editing software gives you the potential to make a film with the same production quality of what you see on TV and on the big screen. In fact, some Hollywood films are put together with computers and software very similar to what you can get for yourself. You will pay, however—and sometimes pay a lot—to get the right software and equipment to do a truly broadcast-quality film.

Depending on the type of filmmaking you're into, it is possible you don't need the camcorder. There's a lot of animation happening out there using tools like Macromedia Flash and Shockwave software to make animated short films that can rival what you see on Saturday morning television.

Taking either route and posting the finished product to your website, or to a website that caters to short films, can get you exposure to people who might give you a job. If nothing else, it's a great way to build an online portfolio.

The homegrown short film is a fast-growing phenomenon on the Web, and services have cropped up to host your work. Type "short films" into your favorite search engine and you'll find dozens of sites ready to accept your film into their library. Sites like Apple Computer's iMovie Gallery (www.apple.com/imovie/gallery/), Atom Films (www.atomfilms.com), and DFilm: Digital Film Festival (www.dfilm.com) give you the chance to see what other filmmakers have done as well as to submit your own work. And many of these virtual screening rooms also let you connect with the filmmakers to talk about the craft. There are sites developed by production companies looking to make Net cinema and other works using an ensemble of performers, writers, and directors, such as Barewitness.com.

Hamilton Tamayo is an aspiring feature film director who took a short animated film into cyberspace in early 2001. For Tamayo, the attraction of the Web is the exposure it brings. His first short film, which he wrote and directed with animation by Sandy Wu, was posted on his personal website (members.bellatlantic.net/~vze27dra/). He sent twenty to thirty e-mails to his friends and colleagues; the result was more than 1,000 hits to the site over a couple of months. He's gotten some good responses, including indications that some within the film industry have seen the short. "Never underestimate the power of word of mouth," says Tamayo.

Tamayo and Wu are working on a longer film with more sophisticated animation that he plans to post to a site like iMovie or Atom Films. Tamayo says the first film was really just an experiment to see what was possible. The new film is designed to push the boundaries—not only to see what he and Wu can do together, but to create something that pushes the standards of Net animation.

The overriding goal, however, remains the same: getting exposure for the work that might lead to a paying job in the field. "I don't expect MGM to call me. But just to have people see your name or say 'Wow, that movie was great,' that is enough for now," Tamayo says. "The intention is not to get paid. It's about building a portfolio of work and possibly getting freelance assignments based on the work. This is a good testing ground to see what's possible. And it's a chance to build some notoriety that could be used as an entrée somewhere."

Tamayo's example of that notoriety is the story of the creators of TV's *South Park*. Before Matt Stone and Trey Parker's characters were a part of the pop culture lexicon, Stan, Cartman, and the clan were merely part of a video Christmas present that some executives at Fox wanted to send out (someone at the company had seen a short Stone and Parker had done called *Jesus vs. Frosty*). The video Christmas card Stone and Parker created, called *The Spirit of Christmas,* was a runaway hit among the people that received it, in turn copied it and passed it along. Comedy Central, in short order, then asked the duo to create a show around the characters, and *South Park* was born. It debuted in 1997 and has since aired more than sixty half-hour episodes and spawned a hit feature film.

Making your own short films is not a bad way to go to become a director. Steven Spielberg was making Super 8 movies as a kid; today, with the digital technology, you don't have to worry about running out of film or waiting to get it developed.

Put It Out There

Just like aspiring writers enter writing contests, filmmakers can participate in a number of short film festivals. Again, your gateway to the festivals is by visiting your favorite search engine and typing "short film festivals." Festivals range in scale from those run by big players in the entertainment community and large regional festivals to fringe events run by people who hope to see their projects win recognition. Festivals worth investigating on the Web include

@ **Alternative Film Festival (alt.sho.com)**
In its second year, the 2001 festival awarded the winner cash and the chance to develop new work for Showtime, which sponsors the festival. Beyond the prizes, however, was the chance for all entrants to have their work seen by thousands of Net visitors as well as the judging committee. Among the competition's judges are actor Michael Rappaport (*Cop Land*) and Chris Young, director of talent and development at Comedy Central.

@ **Los Angeles International Short Film Festival (www.lashortsfest.com)**
The Academy of Motion Picture Arts and Sciences sanctions this competition. That means the films selected for this competition can be nominated for Academy Awards—not a bad way to break into the business if you can get a film accepted here.

@ **The New York Exposition of Short Film and Video (www.nyexpo.org)**
This event, which celebrated its thirty-fifth anniversary in 2001, bills itself as the "longest-running annual festival of independent short film and video." Filmmakers this festival gave early exposure to include Spike Lee, Danny DeVito, Martha Coolidge, Martin Brest, and George Lucas.

@ **Sundance Film Festival (www.sundance.org)**
This famous festival is mainly known for its feature films, but it also has a short film competition that is just as prestigious.

There are hundreds of smaller, regional, genre-specific, and fringe film festivals you can pitch your work to, such as

@ **Women in the Director's Chair (www.widc.org)**
This organization has a mission to raise the visibility of women filmmakers and support the production of alternative media that "defies demeaning stereotypes perpetuated by mainstream media." They have a yearly film festival and conference.

@ **The Visual Communications Los Angeles Asian Pacific Film and Video Festival (vconline.org/filmfest2001/index.html)**
This annual festival celebrates the best in Asian Pacific American and Asian international cinema.

@ **Backyard National Children's Film Festival (www.childrensfilmfest.org)**
This one is all about kids with a mission to provide an opportunity for young people to create and appreciate stories told through film.

You've got nothing to lose by getting your work in front of an audience. So whether the festival is online or in a theater, make your production and set it free for the world to appreciate.

Be an Intern

Want to learn from the best in the business? Get an internship. You'll not only get to work on a project—or an array of projects—you'll also make contacts to use for the rest of your career. The key about internships is this: You've got to make the effort to snag them while you're still in college, because the opportunities aren't available if you're out of school.

Finding an internship using the Web is easy. You can use The Princeton Review (www.review.com) as a resource with its searchable internship database in the career section. You can target companies or organizations you want to work for and check their websites for internship information, which you'll usually find under the Employment or About Us sections. What you won't be able to do very effectively is find these opportunities using a search engine, such as Yahoo!, because the listings are simply part of each company's website.

Something else to keep in mind: You may not be a director during these internships, but you will get exposed to filmmaking and filmmakers—and that's what counts.

Among the more interesting internship programs available are the following:

@ **Paramount Pictures (www.paramount.com)**
The studio offers an array of internships throughout the company, which would make for excellent networking opportunities while you're seeing how the studio operates.

@ **Disney (disney.go.com/disneycareers/)**
These opportunities encompass Disney Studios, the theme parks, ABC Television, and ESPN. The internships are structured to give ten to twelve weeks of training and mentoring to students in the field they've chosen. Check out the website to see what opportunities are currently available, as they differ from season to season.

@ **HBO (www.hbo.com)**
There are internships available here year-round for work in HBO's various departments, including film development and production, TV development and production, and casting.

As you can see, there are a number of opportunities with a number of large companies—companies that would look great on your résumé. And you know what? Everybody wants a piece of these. While you should certainly apply for the positions that these companies and others like them offer, you should also look at what's offered by smaller operations and those near your own locale if you're not located in New York or Los Angeles, where the aforementioned opportunities are based.

Consider cutting your teeth working at a local production company. Most medium- and large-sized cities have more than one film and/or video production company that may, among other things, shoot local television commercials and help with corporate communications. You can find listings for these in your favorite search engine by typing "film production company," "video production company," or "production services." Depending on the search engine you use, you may get back just a listing or you might get back something split up into a geographic breakdown. You also can insert the name of your city into the search, such as "Boise video production company."

What's the advantage of searching online for this opportunity instead of just opening up your phone book and seeing what companies are in town? Looking online gives you an instant perspective on what the company is like, the work it does, and what its public face is. Just in case you were wondering, a search for "Boise video production company" yields two results: one company that provides video services ranging from educational, sales, and promotional material to consumer needs like wedding and home inventories, and a specialized company that deals with legal videotaping of depositions. The companies you find on the Net may not be taking on interns, but you lose nothing by contacting them. Definitely check the company's website for contact and employment information before you make a phone call or send an e-mail. The fact that you've done a little research on the Net shows you took the initiative instead of cold-calling them without a clue as to the work they do.

You should check out the local television stations to see what their interning needs are as well. Check a station's website to see if it has opportunities listed.

If it doesn't, it would be good to make a phone call or send an e-mail. Maybe you'll plant the idea that the station needs an intern and you'd be perfect.

While local television and production companies may not be making the next Hollywood masterpiece, they offer you experience in the field (and that's better than spending your summer working at the local video store). And who knows? Your first project at the local production house could have something that sparks the interest of a local TV station, something you do there could lead to a reel catching the eye of the management of a cable network, and what you do there might get seen by a Hollywood producer. You never know who may see what, and when it might be your time to move forward. The Net is certainly the right place to start the process of your forward momentum.

Training Programs

@ **The Assistant Directors Training Program (www.dgptp.org)**
Got two years to devote toward your career? The Director's Guild of America and the Alliance of Motion Picture and Television Producers jointly sponsor the Assistant Directors Training Program. In the program you work under the supervision of the unit production manager and other assistant directors. As a trainee you provide managerial, administrative, communication, and facilitation support to all of the actors, crew, and production personnel working on a project.

On-the-Job Training

The Assistant Directors Training Program puts participants in the middle of the action. Trainees perform critical functions like checking to make sure actors and crew arrive on time, setting the background action, and helping to solve problems that disrupt shooting.

Rosadel Varela completed her two-year stint in the program in the spring of 2001. She worked on episodes of *Sex and the City* and *Law & Order* as well as the feature films *Shaft* and *Riding in Cars with Boys*. While in the program, Varela was sent out by the program coordinators on the various jobs and was provided a fixed salary and benefits.

"The program was exactly what I expected it to be," says Varela, who spent five years working at MTV before she applied to the program. "The hours are still a shock, though. You don't believe that you'd start at 9 A.M., work until 5 A.M., and then start over again at 9 A.M. until you actually do it."

While you can't apply directly for the program at the DGA's website, you can learn about the program specifics, as well as application requirements and what your day-to-day life will be like during the two years.

@ **ABC/DGA Television Directing Fellowship Program (www.abcnewtalent.disney.com/html/guildmain.htm)**
ABC joined with the Director's Guild with the goal of increasing the diversity among directors in the television field. Program participants are mentored by DGA directors and rotate among a number of participating directors so that trainees see varying directorial styles. The website explains the program, the requirements for applicants, and what the work environment is like. There is currently no online application.

Networking

Besides posting his films, aspiring director Tamayo uses the Internet for networking. He frequents chats on Yahoo! and other sites that host communication among up-and-coming filmmakers and those interested in the film profession in general. Tamayo, through one of his close friends, has met and worked with cinematographer David West. Tamayo's friend initially found West, who has done music videos and TV-movie work, through networking on the Internet. As a result of the networking, Tamayo worked as a grip on a short student film West shot called *No. 2.*

"Before the Internet, you had to live in California and go to the right places to meet these people," says Tamayo. "Now you can find these people online. My friend was just doing a search and came upon West's e-mail address and dropped him a line. From there a relationship was formed."

Tamayo says it's good to stay in contact with the friends you make in school. They can be a critical networking source, especially if any of them take a job in the entertainment field. As they make new contacts, your own circle grows and the potential for your name to get mentioned increases.

You can even learn from directors you don't even meet directly. One of the sites Tamayo likes a lot is that of *Clerks* and *Dogma* director Kevin Smith (www.viewaskew.com). The site features news about what Smith is doing, from directing new films to rewriting films and pitching new projects. There's also commentary by Smith about Hollywood and what it takes to work in the business.

Can I Find It on a Generic Job-Listings Site?

No. You've got to find your directing jobs through the sources listed above.

Directors: Theater/Live Performance

Yes, there is a sizable difference between directing a live performance and directing film or television. Certainly the tricks of the trade can be very different. You can't, for example, have *Matrix*-like slow-motion action sequences on a stage. It just doesn't work.

But there are successful directors who do both well. Take, for example, Sam Mendes. He went from creating the enormously successful London and Broadway revival of *Cabaret* to directing Nicole Kidman in the London and Broadway runs of *The Blue Room* to directing the hit 1999 film *American Beauty*. Along the way he won the 2000 Academy Award, Director's Guild Award, Golden Globe, and numerous other directing awards for *American Beauty,* and was nominated for a 1988 Tony Award for his *Cabaret* direction. On top of that, he's also the artistic director of the Donmar Warehouse, a theater in London (which happens to be where his productions of *Cabaret* and *The Blue Room* got started).

So while it is possible to do both, when you're just starting out in the business it gets back to how to get that first job as a director. Once again, the Net is a powerful ally.

For starters, it will help you find theater companies in your area. Just use your search engine and type in your city along with the word "theatre" or "theater."

Most search engines are smart enough to look for this word both ways, although companies tend refer to themselves with "theatre."

Most community theaters are constantly looking for volunteers, and this can be the chance for you to shine. Understand you will not be assigned a directorship immediately. But you can start out as an assistant to a director or a stage manager and work your way up. Make it known that you'd like to learn the craft, and put yourself in the position to learn everything.

Look for online advice, too. The Web allows you the chance to be a fly on the wall and soak up the wisdom of experienced directors as they communicate in online forums. There are communities of theater directors online that you can access via your search engine of choice, using search phrases like "theater director community." You'll find a community extremely beneficial because you can talk out your job situation with others and, no doubt, find someone who's been in the same situation you are.

The tricky thing for theater directors, like film and TV directors, is that it's rare to find a help wanted listing for a job. You've got to ingratiate yourself to a theater company or producer; start off on smaller projects, usually as an assistant; and then move into bigger projects as your work gets known. Of course, if you're in a college theater-directing program, you'll get some critical experience before you're out of school, and that will help when you graduate.

There are also internships out there for those who want to get in-the-trenches training. Most of these are available for those still in school, but if you do a search for "theater internships" you'll come across many theater companies offering programs for postgrads as well. Many professional and community theaters offer programs as a way to augment their staff. With many local theaters being cash-strapped, internships are a good way for them to train future directors while getting cheap labor. If you don't see an internship at a theater that interests you, check the website for a phone number or e-mail address as well as a contact name so you can approach the theater yourself and see if there are opportunities.

Can I Find It on a Generic Job-Listings Site?

No. Like motion picture directors, theater and live performance directors find work through personal connections.

Crew Jobs: Film/TV/Theater

This is a huge category. In the introduction to this book you saw a partial list of crew positions, but there are many, many more available. How many crew jobs are there? *Planet of the Apes*, released during the summer of 2001, had hundreds of people listed as crew, everything from makeup to best boys to transportation to the marine crew to the casting team to the special effects team to the animal wranglers to the set builders.

Start Early

As soon as you know that you want to snag a job on the crew of an entertainment production, do everything you can to practice your field. In college, that means getting involved with the campus theater, television station, or film department. Even if you're choosing not to major in those fields, take a class and get involved in the productions. Nothing replaces on-the-job experience. Beyond school, there are plenty of opportunities to explore to improve your résumé.

Hit the Internet and do a key-word search to find the position you desire. Want to be a makeup artist? Type that into your favorite search engine and you'll find sites run by makeup artists to show off their work, a connection to the artists' union (www.iatse.lm.com/chair.html), and an industry magazine called *Make-Up Artist* (www.makeupmag.com).

What if you want to be a gaffer? (A gaffer, by the way, is a chief lighting technician.) Plenty of that online, too, from people's individual sites where they showcase their work to the union connection with the A division of the International Alliance of Theatrical Stage Employees and Moving Picture Technicians, Artists and Allied Crafts of the United States and Canada, known simply as the IATSE (www.iatse.lm.com/cfilm.html). Then there's the whole world of animation—both computerized and traditional cell animation. The IATSE covers both of those types of animators (www.iatse.lm.com/animate.html). A ton of resources for animators can be found at Animation World Network (www.awn.com). Casting directors are out there, too; you can find out about the profession at the Casting Society of America (www.castingsociety.com), which includes a robust FAQ section that includes the critical "How do I become a casting director?" And special effects enthusiasts should check out the Visual

Effects Society (www.visual-effects-society.org). Once you start surfing, look for the internship or job opportunities and make contact.

If theater's your thing, you'll find a similar amount of information. Want to be a stage manager? You can hook up to Actors' Equity (www.actorsequity.org), the union to which you'd belong; the Stage Manager's Association (www.stagemanagers.org); and individuals who maintain their own sites. What if stage combat is more your thing? There are ample sites for you, too, such as the Society of American Fight Directors (www.safd.org) or the Academy of Theatrical Combat (www.catalog.com/academy), as well as sites hosted by individual professionals and enthusiasts.

Communities are forming around other crew jobs as well. Creative Planet (www.creativeplanet.com) has a myriad of sites connected to it that act as an online resource for people involved with digital filmmaking, cinematography, film design, directors, film and video editors, postproduction, visual effects, digital cinema, digital television, sound design and engineering, and videography. Each of the sites has a wealth of industry news, chat boards, and job listings.

According to Creative Planet's Niku Kashef, niche sites like Creative Planet are fast becoming a great way to look for work. "Job postings on these boards range from director's assistants to production assistants to vice presidents," says Kashef. "Based on the feedback we've gotten, those using the boards are both experienced people looking for the next highest job on the ladder to younger people looking to break in."

Kashef says that when you've made the decision to job-hunt, make sure you do it daily so you can be among the first to get your résumé in for a job that sounds good. To that end, you should have your résumé and cover letter ready to go, but take time to personalize that cover letter for the job and company you're responding to. In addition, don't search one job board; keep expanding where you're looking, since not all companies use the same boards.

Connections on the Web exist for any of the crew you'd find on a movie set. Sites such as the Internet Movie Database (www.imdb.com), which lists crew for hundreds of movie and television shows, are great resources. Similarly, theater websites such as Playbill.com, which lists all currently running shows, or the

Internet Theatre Database (www.theatredb.com), which lists a broader array of data about current and closed shows, offer online connections, so you can learn about the positions that are available.

How Hard Is It?

Breaking into crew jobs can be extremely difficult, "but people do it all the time," says Rosadel Varela, who worked as an assistant director on films and television after starting out as an intern at MTV. Varela explains that very often teams are built early in people's careers. If you do a little research, you'll find that Steven Spielberg, for example, has worked with cinematographer Janusz Kaminski half a dozen times—from 1993's *Schindler's List* on through to his 2002 film *Minority Report* and 2003's *Memoirs of a Geisha*. Kaminski also has a team he likes to work with who have shown up in the credits of those same movies. The same is true for Michael Khan, who has edited nearly twenty Spielberg movies, beginning with 1979's comedy *1941*. People like to work with others whom they trust—and you'll have to work to become one of those trusted ones.

Varela is a big proponent of internships as a vehicle to get into the business while still in school. It's a great way to start networking for those important contacts, building experience and earning the trust of your fellow crewmates. She started at MTV as an intern during her senior year of college and immediately went to work on *House of Style*. Because she proved herself during the internship, she continued at MTV after graduation, and during her five years there she worked on thirty different shows—everything from game shows to award shows—as an associate producer or segment producer. From there she went into the Assistant Directors Training Program.

Whatever It Takes

"Do whatever it takes to start; work for free, start at the bottom, or be entrepreneurial and make your own movie. Basically get any job you can. And it's truly easier said than done. But people who really want it will make it happen."

—Rosadel Varela

For crew jobs, production houses are among the best places to start out. Most cities have production houses of one sort or another. If you're in a big city, you'll find more specialized houses that break down into trades like lighting and gaffer services, sound design, special effects makeup, editing, set construction, and so on. You can find these through your search engine, looking for words like those listed above. If you want to search with a local angle, add in your city or state along with those words to refine the results.

In the production centers like New York and Los Angeles—or anywhere there's location shooting going on, for that matter—the film or TV show has a production office set up. Keep an eye on the website for the local film commission, which is the organization that does outreach to bring film work to your area. If a production's coming up, the film commission knows about it and has the contact information for the production's office. Depending on how the film commission operates, it may be able to provide information about internships and other openings within productions as well. A great example is the New York City Mayor's Office of Film, Theatre, and Broadcasting (www.ci.nyc.ny.us/html/filmcom/home.html). The website offers the weekly Tech List, a valuable resource about what's happening all over New York, including shoots, open positions for crew and internships, and contact information for production offices.

Once you've identified the company (or companies) you want to approach, the next step is to get your foot in the door. Consider working as a gofer, receptionist, or general office worker if there are no internships available. The company may not need you for the job you really want. The point of the entry-level gofer-type job for you is to start to meet people and watch what goes on.

"If you get a job at an editing house, and you know there's editing going on after you're done working, ask if you can stay to watch," says Varela. "Let them know you're interested and take any opportunity you can to watch. You'll also get to meet people as they come into the office, and that could be the person who gives you work later."

The job you're most likely to get starting out on a film or television set is that of production assistant (in fact, one of the routes to becoming an assistant director in the DGA is to log 600 days as a production assistant). But again, Varela says it helps to know someone to get into a PA position. She offers this example: "I know personally—or through other contacts—over 100 people I can call to be a PA on a shoot. I've got no time for a random person I don't know. If I bring someone onto a shoot, I'm responsible. It's my reputation on the line, too."

However, getting PAs from a production company associated with a shoot does happen. Varela remembers that during the winter 2000–2001 shoot of the Tom Cruise movie *Vanilla Sky,* a call went out for a hundred PAs to work in the middle of the night in a very cold Times Square to keep onlookers under control, traffic moving, and so on. The unit production manager put out word that the PAs were needed and the network went into action to fill all the slots.

"If you're an intern or [entry-level] worker at a production house, you've got to be a good talker, because everyone else wants the PA job, too," she says. It comes down to people remembering your name and identifying you as a responsible worker.

Your Own Piece of the Web

As you have read, many individuals in these jobs have personal websites. It helps you to get your name and credits out there once you've got a résumé. Your site can also become a portfolio. Have you worked on a student film project? See if you can get permission to place clips or photos that showcase your work on your site. It's critical to get permission—you don't own those copyrights, so just to be totally upright, you should get permission from the copyright owner before you place material on your site.

Check out the other Net surfers who use the Web to further their careers in the tech fields. You'll get ideas on what looks good and what doesn't for your own site. And get yourself on search engines so that filmmakers can find you (this involves making sure your site is coded with key words, and then going to the search engines and using its own "add a site" feature). This is crucial if you're still pre-union and available to work on student films and other nonunion work. It can't be overstated that experience and contacts are what counts!

You can also use a résumé-hosting service. Creative Planet has such a service on its Planet Point (www.planetpoint.com) site. The service allows users to post video, audio, and still photos online. "This is a tremendous resource for artists and creative people," says Kashef. "It allows anyone to access an artist's work at anytime. Sometimes when a production is gearing up and a director wants to see a reel of your work, it is easier to have them immediately access your work on the Web rather than having to send a reel to them through the mail."

Training Programs and Internships

There are a number of training programs that can help you get everything you need to get going in the business. All of the programs are out there on the Net waiting for you to find them. A good technique on a search engine is to type the name of your field—"special effects," for instance—followed by "training."

Here's a look at two of the internships and training programs that you can find on the Net for crew jobs:

@ **Film & TV Connection (www.tvconnection.com)**
This is a mentoring program that offers to place qualified applicants with mentors who teach them about their chosen career path while working in the field. Among the supporters of this program are George Lucas and Jeff Goldblum.

@ **ABC/Touchstone Television Production Associates Program (www.abcnewtalent.disney.com/html/touchmain.htm)**
This twelve- to eighteen-month program places applicants within four divisions of ABC/Touchstone: production, production finance, postproduction, and studio crafts management. The positions are entry-level and are paid.

Check out the websites of the studios, TV networks/stations, and even TV shows you'd like to work for and see if there's anything available like ABC's program. Internships generally have cutoff dates about four to six months before the program starts, so if you're planning for a summer internship, you need to find and apply to it before January. Some companies also offer winter internships, normally with application deadlines in June or July. Could you get an internship at MTV? You'll never know until you apply for it.

Most importantly, don't discount any experience you might get outside New York and Los Angeles. Is it glamorous to work in a production house in Austin,

Texas? It may not seem that way, but getting experience working in editing there will start you on the right road. Remember Varela's advice: "Do whatever it takes to start."

Can I Find It on a Generic Job-Listings Site?

Sometimes. You might find listings for videographers, lighting designers, stage managers, and some of the other crafts listed. These are usually low-paying, nonunion jobs.

Writers: Screenplays/Teleplays/Plays

Without a script it is very hard to get a production off the ground. Yes, we've all heard of films that started shooting without a completed script, but that's certainly not the preferred method. And, yes, rewrites can take place during shooting. But no project gets moving until there's some nature of a script to attract the rest of the team to the project.

Something to keep in mind about scripts: Whereas you can send your résumé and headshot, portfolio materials, etc., to anyone unsolicited with the hope that they'll be looked at, it doesn't work that way with a script. Many agents, studios, producers, directors, and so on will not read any script they randomly receive in the mail. This is because of copyright concerns. There is always the chance that if someone reads your material and then writes or produces anything even slightly resembling it, they could be sued for copyright infringement and/or plagiarism. So if you're thinking about sending a script to someone out of the blue—don't. It's a waste of your time and paper. Contact them first to make sure they are willing to receive it.

TV and Film Scripts

Here is another relationship-based business, given that, if you live outside New York and Los Angeles, it may be hard for you to break into the field (see above concerning the situation regarding unsolicited manuscripts). However, the Internet has given birth to a couple of great resources that can help you get your script seen.

Storybay (www.storybay.com) was created as a way for unrepresented writers (i.e., those without an agent) to have their work seen in Hollywood. Storybay works because of its relationships. Among those on its advisory board (known as the Storybay DreamTeam) are Norm Golightly, a producing partner in Nicolas Cage's Saturn Films; Brad Silberling, writer and director of *Casper* and *City of Angels*; and Jane Sindell, former head of the Creative Artist Agency's Literary Department.

When you send a screenplay, teleplay, or treatment to Storybay, its team of readers pores over it and gives you back "coverage," which is an analysis of the work similar to a one- or two-page book report. Studio heads, producers, and directors make most of their initial decisions about a script based on its coverage. Good coverage means your script gets read more in depth; bad coverage means it ends up in the trash can. After the coverage is done, Storybay, with your permission, starts to send the script around on your behalf. There are more than 500 executives signed up to receive Storybay scripts, so if the script is good, you've got a shot at meetings with studios and producers and ending up with representation from an agent. Not to mention the real possibility of selling the script and seeing it produced.

Storybay, however, does cost money (initial fees start at $275 for screenplays), but since there's a fee, that's your insurance that every script you submit gets read and you'll be getting coverage back. In addition to the coverage, you can pay extra and get "notes" done. Notes offer you feedback about the work with tips about what you might want to rewrite. Finally, if the script sells because of Storybay, you pay them a percentage of the money you receive—just like you would to an agent.

In addition to its screenplay service, Storybay has a similar one for novelists. The company also offers a number of resources for the writer, including access to its chat board where writers (and Storybay staff) offer guidance and support to one another.

Go for the Gold

Screenplay competitions are another way to get your work read by industry people. Here's a look at a couple of competitions you might want to consider (of course, search for "screenwriting competitions" and you'll find plenty more).

@ **Project Greenlight (www.projectgreenlight.com)**

This competition was formed as a joint venture among Live Planet (an "integrated media" company owned by Matt Damon and Ben Affleck), HBO, Miramax Films, and Samuel Adams Beer. The prize was a $1 million production budget to direct the winning screenplay, as well as a guaranteed theatrical release from Miramax. During filmmaking, HBO chronicled the behind-the-scenes making of the film for a documentary it will air about Project Greenlight. If everything stays on track, the winning film, *Stolen Summer* by Pete Jones, will be in theaters in the spring of 2002.

The contest was structured in such a way that many screenplays were read. Initially a pool of 7,000 screenplays for the 2000–2001 competition was narrowed to 250 (scripts were read by contestants and anyone who registered as a Project Greenlight reviewer). The 250 scripts were winnowed down to thirty through process that asked the screenwriters to shoot a video about themselves and the project to see how they would direct the feature should they win. Damon, Affleck, their producing partner Chris Moore, and executives at Miramax reviewed those tapes. Miramax and Live Planet executives then read the top thirty scripts. Those in the top ten were awarded a digital video filmmaking package and asked to shoot a three-minute scene from their scripts. Those ten finalists were brought to Los Angeles for an event to screen the videos. The top ten became a top three list, and then an ultimate winner was chosen.

This process ran from September 25, 2000 (when a call for scripts went out), to March 1, 2001, when the winning script was announced. It's quite the excellent deal when you consider the winner gets to write and direct a film to be distributed by Miramax. Opportunities don't get much better than this.

@ **Screenwriting Showcase Awards (www.screenwritingawards.com)**

Founded in 1996, this competition is judged by professional screenwriters (among the 2001 judges was George Armitage, director of *Grosse Pointe Blank*). The winner gets cash, a professional read of the screenplay (complete with notes), and an array of writing resources, such as screenwriting software. Winners are listed in the contest's database, from which industry people can get in contact with entrants about their scripts.

Other Programs to Consider

@ **ABC Entertainment and Walt Disney Studios Writing Fellowship Program**
(www.abcnewtalent.disney.com/html/writmain.htm)
Under this program, which began in 1990, up to eight writers work full-time for a year at either ABC or Disney to develop their craft in either television or film writing. Those chosen get round-trip airfare to L.A. and one month's accommodations before they have to start paying rent out of their salary. ABC is in negotiations with the Writers Guild to develop a writing fellowship for daytime television writers.

@ **Sundance Institute Writers Fellowship Program**
(www.sundance.org/jsps/site.jsp?resource=pag_
ex_programs_featurefilm_labs)
This fellowship includes breakouts for feature film writers, Native American writers, and screenwriters living abroad. Fellows take part in retreats where they interact with working writers, and they work on their projects with the support of creative advisors. This program is hard to get into because you must be recommended by a school or industry professional to be considered. Besides the fellowship, there is also the Sundance Screenwriters Lab, a five-day workshop that allows participants to, again, work with the support of established screenwriters. There is an open call to select participants for the Screenwriters Lab. Check the website for dates for upcoming labs and fellowships.

And a Program of a Different Kind

@ **Screenplay Systems (www.screenplay.com)**
This software company makes acclaimed programs, such as Movie Magic Screenwriter, to help you plan your screenplays. Among its proponents are Ben Affleck and Matt Damon (Movie Magic is the official software of Project Greenlight), Francis Ford Coppola, and Guy Ritchie. While the software formats the script as you write with all the headers, page numbers, etc., that are considered standard format, it also allows for online collaboration and exporting the script to Adobe PDF for posting on the Internet. The program can also read—yes, literally read out loud—your screenplay using a variety of voices so you can hear what it really sounds like as it's spoken.

Playwrights

In some ways it is easier to get a play produced than a screenplay. Consider that there are hundreds of theaters across the country looking for plays to put on. Consider also that it would be possible for you to rent a theater, get some actors together, and have your play performed for much less than it would cost to produce a movie.

Of course, no one said you were out to become a producer, so to place your work at a theater, you've got a few routes to take. You can, of course, use the Internet to find theaters around the country. Most community and professional companies have websites, and you'll be able to target them with your script. Make sure your script has gone through the copyright process before you send it out. Need to find out how to copyright? Visit the United States Copyright office (lcweb.loc.gov/copyright/) for everything you need to do to protect your work.

You can focus your efforts even further by looking for theaters that use some— or all—of their season to present world-premiere works. Simply search the Net for "world premiere theater" or "new works theater" and visit each website to see if there's information on submitting plays.

There are also competitions to submit your work, giving it the opportunity to be read and maybe produced. Here are a couple of competitions for you to consider (and don't forget to look for new opportunities using your search engine and key words like "drama contest," "play contest," "playwright competition," and combinations of those words):

@ **Actor's Theatre in Santa Cruz, California (www.sccat.org)**
The theater has two competitions: one for a ten-minute play and one for a full-length play. Entrants must live in California, Oregon, or Washington, so this one is limited in scope. But it is a good example of what to look for in a small playwriting contest. The winners here get a bit of cash and a staged reading (or in some cases a full production if resources of the theater can support it). The ten-minute plays are fully presented during a ten-minute-theater festival.

Other Programs to Consider

@ **Sundance Institute Theatre Program (www.sundance.org/theatre/theatre.html)**
Primarily known for film, Sundance also features the Theatre Lab. It's a three-week workshop that gives playwrights, directors, choreographers, and others involved in the theater an environment to hone plays and musicals outside the pressure of actual production. All of this happens with the support of others in the field providing insight and advice. Up to eight projects per year are selected for the Theatre Lab. Check the site for information on entry schedules.

@ **Playwrights Horizons (www.playwrightshorizons.org)**
This New York–based theater focuses on new works by American writers. Some notable works it has launched include Wendy Wasserstein's *The Heidi Chronicles* and Alfred Uhry's *Driving Miss Daisy,* as well as the musicals *Sunday in the Park with George* and *Once on This Island.* Playwrights Horizons accepts unsolicited manuscripts, and commissions four to six new works per year. As its website says, "The best way to become a candidate for a commission is to start submitting your work."

@ **New Dramatists (www.newdramatists.org)**
New Dramatists is another New York–based group dedicated to fostering new writers. Two programs of note here: The first, an internship program, puts you in the New Dramatists office and provides the chance to watch the inner workings of nonprofit, professional theater—including working with the playwrights; second, there are several fellowships and awards that are available, some only to members of New Dramatists, but others that are open to the general public as well. Check the website for a current list of fellowship and award offerings, as they change often.

The Unions

As a writer, there are a couple of unions you will become involved with as you gain more experience in the field. The unions also want to help you become a writer, so the sites contain resources to help you craft your projects and even get them to the right people for review.

@ The Writers Guild of America (www.wga.org)
This is the guild for film and television writers. This site is a must-visit for all aspiring screenwriters because it features a mentoring program and a list of agents who will look at work (including notations about which agents will look at work by new writers).

Another critical feature here is the ability to register your script, and you don't have to be a WGA member to do it. Why should you register? WGA registration proves a date of completion, which is important should your script (or the ideas within it) ever become challenged in court or a WGA action. Note that this registration does *not* replace going through the copyright process.

@ The Dramatists Guild of America (www.dramaguild.com)
The guild covers playwrights, composers, and lyricists. The great thing this site provides for aspiring writers is a list of agents to whom you can pitch your completed works. The list is sorted by member name; for example, you can see who represents Edward Albee, Marvin Hamlisch, and other famous playwrights and composers. While not as robust as the WGA site, the Dramatists Guild site provides a way for you to make connections within the industry.

Is There More?

If it looks like there are fewer opportunities here than in other crafts this book covers, rest assured that's not really the case. There are plenty of opportunities for writers; the difference is that it's harder to find them on the Net. While you may have the perfect script in you, it's harder to get that work in front of people than with the acting and directing positions we've talked about so far. There are always audition notices for actors, and directors can shoot their work and put it on the Web to start inspiring word-of-mouth buzz. It's far more difficult for a writer, especially when it comes to placing unsolicited manuscripts.

Follow the tips given and keep searching the Internet for competitions (especially for opportunities like Project Greenlight). Consider partnering with independent directors, whom you can find via the Net. You could both pool your contacts and shoot a film based on your script using cast and crew you know through your networking. Then you can place the finished film on the Net or in a film festival for all the world to see.

Teaming up with others leads to the critical point made throughout this book: You must network. Find a support group of writers, such as the discussion board provided through Storybay. The more people with whom you form relationships, the better your chances that you're going to end up knowing someone who can help you, even indirectly, land your script with someone who has the power to get it made.

Can I Find It on a Generic Job-Listings Site?

In a word, no.

Producers

Oscar Hammerstein defined a producer as "an idealist, a realist, a practical dreamer, a sophisticated gambler, and a stage-struck child." The Producers Guild of America (www.producersguild.org), by comparison, defines the all-encompassing role of producer like this: "A producer initiates, coordinates, supervises, and controls, either on his own authority (entrepreneur producer) or subject to the authority of an employer (employee producer), all aspects of the motion-picture and/or television production process, creative, financial, technological, and administrative, throughout all phases from inception to completion, including coordination, supervision, and control of all other talents and crafts, subject to the provisions of their collective bargaining agreements and personal service contracts."

That's one huge job description. As you can see, being a producer is more than just putting up the money. The definition from the PGA holds true for theatrical producers as well. As a producer, you're the person—or perhaps one of a group of producers—everyone works for on a production.

I Want to Be a Producer

Matthew Broderick makes becoming a producer seem so easy on stage in *The Producers*, the 2001 Broadway smash that won a record-breaking twelve Tony Awards. Broderick's character, Leo Bloom, goes from singing "I Want to Be a Producer" to inadvertently ending up with a hit show with his producing partner,

Max Bialystock, played by Nathan Lane. And, yes, it could be that easy for you, too, if you find the right property, get it funded, and hire the right people to realize the dream.

Odds are, though, like the other professions covered in this book, you're going to start out at the bottom of the producer chain, as an assistant to a producer or another entry-level position. The good news is the Net is full of opportunities to latch onto this key role in the entertainment business.

Start Small

While you certainly can strike out on your own, set up a production company, find scripts that interest you, hire cast and crew, and distribute or stage the finished product, that's going to be tough if you've got no experience. You can lay out the best plan in the world, but with no proof you can pull it off, it's not likely that backers or workers will take a chance on you.

There are, however, plenty of jobs to cut your teeth on. Most of the internships and training opportunities mentioned in the director and crew sections of this book can prepare you to be a producer. In fact, Rosadel Varela, who took part in the DGA Assistant Directors Training Program, plans to use her training to make herself into a producer. Her route makes sense. As a producer you are, essentially, the captain of the ship, and as captain, it behooves you to know how every job works. That's not to say you need to know how to do the job of cameraman, lighting designer, or makeup artist, but if you have a good understanding of those jobs, you'll be a more effective producer.

No matter where you are in the country, opportunities to become a producer exist. Use the Net to search out local film and video production companies and TV stations as well as theater companies. Even if there's no available entry-level producer jobs, simply working within the environment and getting to know people there is a step in the right direction.

Finding the Job—And Yes, You Can Find It on a Generic Job-Listings Site

Yes, it's true; producer jobs can occasionally be found on job boards like Monster.com. It's not often, and they're usually for industrial video and occasionally for TV stations, but they are out there.

To find a wealth of jobs, however, you need to look at more industry-specific websites, or on the websites of the companies you've targeted as places you want to work. Among the places to look for television jobs are the National Association of Broadcasters (www.nab.org), which maintains a large job board; *Broadcasting and Cable* magazine (www.broadcastingcable.com), an industry publication covering local, network, and cable industries and including job classifieds; and the Hollywood trades, such as *The Hollywood Reporter* (www.hollywoodreporter.com) and *Variety* (www.variety.com) that have job boards that occasionally have producer jobs available.

It's far harder to land an out-of-the-box producing job with a theatrical company. By nature, theater companies are often run on small budgets and produce their own work without an individual's name attached to it. Of course, the bigger the company, the better the odds that a show will have a single producer or producer team. You should approach theater groups you're interested in working with—and for that you can do all your research on the Net, as more and more theater groups go online every day.

For theatrical internships, there are positions offered at Richard Frankel Productions (www.rfpny.com), which has produced *Stomp*, the megahit show *The Producers*, the 2000 revival of *The Rocky Horror Show,* and other touring productions. You'll find more using a search engine and typing in "theatrical internship."

Case Studies in Film/TV/Theater

Check out these movies to see what it's like to work in some of the professions profiled here. Some of the examples are parodies, while others are grittier portrayals. The links given are from the Internet Movie Database site, where you can find out everything about the film, including additional websites.

Television/Film Production

@ *Welcome to Hollywood* (us.imdb.com/Details?0169376). This "mockumentary" charts the course of a young actor in Hollywood in 1998. And while it is "mock," it's also a pretty good look at how things work for actors.

@ *Soapdish* (us.imdb.com/Details?0102951). Go behind the scenes of a network soap opera in this 1991 comedy with Whoopi Goldberg.

@ *The Big Picture* (us.imdb.com/Details?0096926). Kevin Bacon stars in this 1989 movie about a film student who gets a shot at the big time after producing an award-winning short film.

@ *The Player* (us.imdb.com/Details?0105151). A comedy/drama/thriller from 1992 about a studio executive who's being threatened by a writer he turned down.

Theater

@ *Waiting for Guffman* (us.imdb.com/Details?0118111). This 1996 film is total parody, but it's hysterically fun and shows the importance of working with people you get along with.

@ *Fame* (us.imdb.com/Details?0080716). This is the definitive 1980 film about the New York School of Performing Arts and its students, who want nothing less than fame.

@ *All That Jazz* (us.imdb.com/Details?0078754). This nine-time Oscar-nominated 1979 semiautobiographical film follows a Broadway/film director (patterned after Bob Fosse) as he prepares his latest projects despite failing health.

@ *Moon Over Broadway* (us.imdb.com/Details?0125412). This 1997 documentary studies the Broadway mounting of *Moon Over Buffalo*, which starred Carol Burnett and Phillip Bosco.

Producers

@ *The Producers* (us.imdb.com/Details?0063462). This 1968 Mel Brooks film that became the 2001 Tony Award–winning musical on Broadway is a hilarious parody of the producing business. See one or see them both; you won't regret it.

Directors

@ *Making of Steven Spielberg's Jaws* (us.imdb.com/Details?0251821). This documentary, which is available on the twenty-fifth-anniversary-edition *Jaws* DVD, chronicles the behind-the-scenes action of Spielberg's first hit film.

@ *Hearts of Darkness: A Filmmaker's Apocalypse* (us.imdb.com/Details?0102015). This documentary, released in 1992, focuses on the making of Francis Ford Coppola's *Apocalypse Now*. The film mixes footage shot during the 1979 filming along with interviews done ten years later. With *Apocalypse's* legacy as one of the most difficult film shoots ever, this documentary is a must-see for insight into what can happen on a film set.

Music

The Internet radically changed the way music is made, how the audience enjoys it, and how artists and executives seek to make money from it. It boils down to two digital formats: MP3s and recordable CDs (CD-Rs). The MP3 craze—supercharged during 2000 because of the legal battle waged between Napster, a software program that enabled people to share music files over the Internet, and the music industry—revolutionized the way people store their music library, discover new tunes, and, much to the dismay of the record labels and artists, trade songs without paying for them. Combine MP3 with CD-R and you've got the ability to store a few hundred MP3s on a single disc as well as make perfect digital copies of CDs in your—or your friend's—library. Hence a new music paradigm was born for both the music professional and the listener.

The birth of CD-R and sophisticated computer music creation and editing software made it possible for anyone with musical ambition and some computer savvy to make a music demo with quality that is a far cry from that of the noisy tapes made in a basement on a simple tape recorder. MP3 technology also benefits the up-and-coming musician because the files are an ideal way to share songs, either clips or the whole tune, with your fans—or potential fans—on the Net.

Of course, there's more to the music business than just singers and musicians. There's the team that engineers the professionally made recordings, the producers, the songwriters (who are not always performers in their own right), the DJs who get the songs played, and the back-office staff running the companies and promoting the talent. And in the age of video music, the entire troupe of professionals who support the visual element of a musician's identity are not far behind (the music-video jobs consist of identical jobs to the TV and film careers in the previous section).

Singers and Musicians

"The Internet is a tool for you to help yourself," says Seattle-based cabaret singer and recording artist Jonathan Frank (www.jonathanfrank.com). "It would take a lot more work to be where I am today without it."

Frank launched his site in 1998 with his debut CD, *Sleeping in the Arms of Love*. Initially conceived to promote the CD, the site now serves as a critical marketing tool. "The site is a great way for people to get to know me," he says. "From general searches for 'cabaret' and the fact that I'm linked off so many sites, it's amazing the snowball effect it can have as more people find you."

In addition to using the Internet to sell his CDs and promote his upcoming club appearances, Frank researches songs he wants to perform in his act. The American Society of Composers, Artists, and Publishers (www.ascap.com) and Broadcast Music Inc. (www.bmi.com) are the primary licensing organizations in the music industry and offer comprehensive information about who holds the rights to songs artists may wish to perform. Both sites have search engines to help performers secure rights and pay royalties (to learn more about ASCAP and BMI, read the Songwriters section later in this chapter). Frank says those two websites make the process of researching songs much easier than in the pre-Internet days.

When he gets ready to take his show on the road, Frank uses the Net research venues. Once he's found a club that fits his musical style, it's back to some old-style techniques of making contact, including sending a press kit, making some phone calls, or possibly sending an e-mail. "The website is a great follow-up tool after the initial contact" by phone, e-mail, or snail mail, Frank says. His press kits and other promotional materials all have his Web address on them, so potential employers can check his site as part of their decision process to book him for a gig.

Old-fashioned networking is still very much alive in the music business, just as it is in the other entertainment-based careers. Meeting people in person at industry events and parties is always a valuable tool. For Frank, there are cabaret conventions; for others there are conferences like South by Southwest (www.sxsw.com) and *Billboard* magazine-sponsored events (www.billboard.com). You can easily find conferences for any genre of music you participate in by using your search engine and general key words like "music industry conferences," or get more specific with phrases like "orchestra conferences," "cabaret conferences," "heavy metal conferences," and so on.

Making Connections

The Internet is full of opportunities to make connections, with community groups like Yahoo! Clubs as well as genre-specific music sites on the Web. You can look for communities and chat by typing in either "musician community" or "musician chat" (or substitute "singer" for musician) into a search engine. You'll find hundreds of sites devoted to every kind of music imaginable from all over the world. Between live chat and message boards, you should be able to begin talking to musicians and/or singers immediately.

As you search for chat, you'll find loads of other sites out there, too, including fan sites, trade organizations, and file-sharing sites where people trade tunes (although in the era of the Napster trouble, these are becoming fewer—at least the free services are). With so many of these sites offering chat, make sure you're arriving at a one that will take care of your needs. It's great to hook up with music fans, but if what you need is to get tips from fellow musicians, you'll want to be on the right site. The best way to do that is to read the introductory message on the chat board. Also, if it's a discussion board or any type of nonlive chat, check the dates on the most recent entries as well to make sure you're visiting an active discussion board and not one that's been long since abandoned.

MusicPlayer.com is a particularly good source for networking and information. The site has resources broken down by instrument type as well as information about computers, gigs, and more. There are active discussion boards to connect you with others in the business, as well as a classifieds section that includes job listings.

Keep in mind that sometimes the Web can network you in ways you don't expect because you never know whom you might meet online. Jonathan Frank's participation in this book is a perfect example. Frank bought some Broadway show memorabilia from an author of this book over eBay (www.ebay.com). As the two completed the transaction and discussed Broadway via e-mail, Frank let on that he was a cabaret singer with his own website. The website stimulated a series of e-mail exchanges, and in the end his story fit the bill for a profile in this book, since his presence online fuels his career.

Burn, Baby, Burn

Distributing your own music is possible online through MP3 or selling discs from your website. And while MP3 has a stigma attached to it as an illegal music form because of the Napster brouhaha, it remains a great means to send songs over the Internet because of the compact file size. A five-minute song takes only five megabytes to store as an MP3 instead of fifty megabyte as a WAV sound file, which is the file standard for uncompressed music files. Just remember that once you put your MP3 on your site, it can easily be passed around. You must make the choice of how much music you offer and if you're offering whole songs or just clips. Many artists, Frank included, offer a mix of short clips with one or two full songs available for download.

If you want to secure your music even further, consider using streaming audio like Real Networks (www.realnetworks.com). This technology allows a site visitor hear your music, but not download it because it is broadcast over the Internet instead of being saved to a hard drive. You'll pay more (upwards of $200 for the conversion software as opposed to less than $50 to make MP3s) to stream audio, but it does give you a higher level of security.

Near-professional quality CDs are possible straight off your computer, too, if you've got the right equipment and software. You can also record professionally now for around $10,000—that's five to ten times cheaper than the cost from five years ago. Like most technologies, CD recording has gotten cheaper over time. But it's the rise in computer technology that fueled the price decrease, as the recording, mastering, and CD-production process is more efficient now.

"Being able to do your own CDs is a double-edged sword. On the one hand it's wonderful because it acts like a business card, and in many clubs you won't even get talked to without a CD. It shows that you're serious. But because everyone's doing it, there is a lot of crap out there and it can be hard for club owners, press people, and even music lovers to winnow through it. You must have something that sets you apart. It can't just be a CD with vocals backed by a piano and a quickly done cover produced in Photoshop."

—Jonathan Frank

Getting Work

Lining up work as a singer or musician is a lot like getting work as an actor or dancer—your audition and presentation carry most of the weight. As Frank said, having a site is a good tool, but it is only one of many. While you're out there playing your music every day, your audio calling cards are always accessible from anywhere off your website.

Self-promotion on the Web is critical. This is especially true if you book gigs for parties, weddings, and other events. Today people use the Internet like a telephone book. Need a singer for a party in Houston? Type in "Houston party singer" or "Houston party band" in a search engine and you'll find the singers and bands that have taken the Web route to get gigs. A site that talks about your song style while featuring some audio clips and some photos can be your recipe for important contacts and future work.

There are many other paths a musician or singer can take, from working in an orchestra, bar band, or choral setting to working on film scores, doing live performances, and headlining major arenas. Here are some sites to look at, broken up by genre, to help you research and find ideas for getting work—or just getting heard:

@ **GarageBand.com (www.garageband.com)**
This site is geared to help sell your music and get heard in the genres of alternative, electronic, rock, rap/hip-hop, metal, pop, dance, punk rock, funk/soul/R&B, hard rock, blues, jazz, pop/rock, and folk/country. You can upload tracks, get reviews from users, and even sell your CDs through the site, as well as promote your live appearances. Among the luminaries serving on this site's advisory board are Beatles producer Sir George Martin, U2 and Dave Matthews Band producer Steve Lillywhite, musician Brian Eno, and alternative country singer Steve Earle.

@ **American Symphony Orchestra League (www.symphony.org)**
American Symphony Orchestra League offers an array of resources to support classical orchestras and musicians around the country. This site features a job board and a résumé-hosting service; however, you have to pay to join the site to get access to those tools.

@ **American Guild of Musical Artists (www.musicalartists.org)**
This is a union for those who work in choral, dance, and operatic music. You can use this site to research how this union can serve you, such as its health benefits, contract information, and protection from unfair work conditions, and browse the audition notices posted there.

@ **The American Federation of Musicians of the United States and Canada (www.afm.org)**
This organization is open to all professional musicians, and its mission is to make sure musicians are treated and paid fairly. Most of the site's resources, such as access to news and audition information, require membership. Other benefits include health insurance, shopping discounts, and an online list of booking agents as well as education opportunities.

@ **American Society of Music Arrangers and Composers (www.asmac.org)**
This is a service, education, and fraternal organization for professional arrangers and composers working primarily for films, television, recordings, and theater. ASMAC hosts master classes, workshops, and luncheons that are usually open to both members and nonmembers. The member spotlight section lets you see

how others got started in the business. There's also a scholarship program for those still in school.

@ **The Center for the Promotion of Contemporary Composers (www.under.org/cpcc/)**
This group's goal is to pull together the resources necessary for composers, such as grants, scholarships, and faculty positions. It also is a way for composers to get connected through its membership directory, which features e-mail and website addresses. Composers can submit works into the site's score catalog to allow others access to their work, which can lead to it being performed.

@ **EntertainmentCareers.net (www.entertainmentcareers.net)**
In addition to its musician and singer job listings, the site offers listings for sound engineers, production managers, and recordists.

@ **The Recording Industry Association of America (www.riaa.org)**
As its industry's watchdog, this site can tell you tons about the art of recording. The overseer of copyright issues, RIAA has been one of the plaintiffs against Napster and its file-sharing business model. RIAA's mission is to protect artists and the record companies from anything that would disrupt the economics of the music industry. As your career grows, this organization becomes more important to you.

Can I Find It on a Generic Job-Listings Site?

Regular job boards are not really the place to find these jobs, although it is possible to occasionally come across listings that would be of interest, such as open audition calls at theme parks.

Songwriters

Songwriters use many of the same resources as singers and musicians, especially in regard to the unions and publications. Those who write the songs, however, do have some special needs because they also are very much like screenwriters or playwrights. Songwriters need their own communities to foster their creative juices and to try out material. There are also songwriter competitions that can help get your material heard.

Just as with musicians and singers, the key for songwriters is to get their works played. They may do that on their own if they're singer/songwriters, or they may look for musicians to pitch songs to. If you plan on going the singer/ songwriter route, the material in the Singers and Musicians section of this book can help you get gigs and market yourself to potential fans. If you're looking for singers, musicians, and bands to perform your songs, the Net can help with that as well. All you have to do is search using key words like "singers," "bands," or "musicians" and you'll find many professionals and aspiring professionals who might be open to your songs. You can also hone your search results by adding in the key words that describe your music genre, such as "blues," "rock," "punk," or "bluegrass." As an up-and-coming songwriter, you'll have the most success placing songs with unknown bands. When you find a performer's website that appeals to you, drop him or her an e-mail and let on that you think there might be a collaboration possibility.

Register Your Material

You must take the necessary steps to protect your work by registering songs with ASCAP (www.ascap.com) or BMI (www.bmi.com) for rights management. To register your compositions, you'll have to become a member with one of the organizations. Both have slightly different membership benefits, so you should read the sites' information to determine which suits your needs. The reason to register your music is clear: You're entitled to a payment each time it's performed, and rather than having to keep track of each performance yourself, ASCAP and BMI will do it for you.

These organizations handle performance rights for your songs, so if it's heard on the radio, performed in a concert setting, or blasted over a Muzak system in an elevator, you'll get paid for it. Once you become a member to either group, registering your composition is as simple as filling out a form with information about your song and filing it with the organization. Presently, BMI allows for song registration online; ASCAP does not, so you have to call or e-mail to get the registration forms.

You should also investigate a music publisher, who would handle your "mechanical" or "synchronization" rights (granting permission for your song to be recorded or to print copies of your song on sheet music). You can learn about music publishers at the National Music Publishers' Association (www.nmpa.org). This site is an excellent source of copyright information with up-to-date details about copyright legislation, court cases, and how they affect songwriters. This site is the best gateway to explore the music copyright issues instead of going to the U.S. Copyright Office website (lcweb.loc.gov/copyright/), which can be a bit overwhelming because the specifics for music and sound recordings are spread throughout the site.

Make Sure You Get Paid for Your Work

Protect your compositions at all costs. Register your works with BMI or ASCAP to ensure yourself royalty payments. Also, find a music publisher to represent your songs so that you also get paid anytime they're recorded.

Community Resources for You

While some of the musician resources serve songwriters well, there are some specific organizations that support songwriters. Point your Web browser toward these sites.

@ **Songwriters Guild of America (www.songwriters.org)**
This guild offers a contract designed to protect its members in dealings with publishers. Anyone can join the union as an unpublished or published writer; the fee scale varies depending on your royalty payments. The guild also stages events, both online and offline, for members to interact with each other. Check out the site for details of upcoming events.

@ **SongLink International (www.songlink.com)**
SongLink lists artists who are looking for songs. The site's recent success includes placing the song "Genie in a Bottle" with Christina Aguilera, who ran a "songs wanted" ad on the site that was spotted by a member who happened to be a songwriter. You pay a fee to subscribe to the monthly e-mails detailing who is looking for songs.

@ **American Songwriter (www.americansongwriter.com)**
This magazine, which reports on the craft and business of songwriting, celebrates its eighteenth anniversary in 2002. When you visit the site, make sure to get details about the latest lyric contest, which runs six times per year. There's also a Collaborator's Corner to help songwriters find partners.

@ **Muse's Muse (www.musesmuse.com)**
This site focuses on songwriting tips and tools, with lots of information for newcomers to the business. The site acts as a portal to other songwriting news on the Web in addition to offering articles and advice by its own columnists. The site is run by a performer/songwriter, so the information is solid.

There are songwriting contests to check out that can be useful to get your songs in front of industry heavyweights you might otherwise be unable to reach.

@ **The Great American Song Contest (www.greatamericansong.com)**
This contest runs multiple categories: pop, rock/alternative, contemporary acoustic/folk, contemporary Christian/gospel, the "special music category" (defined as children's, Christmas, novelty, or instrumental), and lyrics only. The contest is judged by successful songwriters, publishers, and producers in the industry, such as Michael Laskow, producer for Eric Clapton and Neil Young; Michael Anderson, a contemporary Christian songwriter and recording artist; and Pamela Phillips-Oland, who has written lyrics for Bryan Adams and Reba McEntire.

@ **USA Songwriting Competition (www.songwriting.net)**
Competition here takes place in fifteen categories, including pop, rock, and R&B. The site has details about the current competition, in addition to the opportunity to hear winning songs from years past.

Disc Jockeys and Radio Hosts

As much as MTV would like you to believe it, video did not kill the radio star. Maybe it came close, but the Net is preserving and even enhancing the radio star's health. Disc jockeys—or, more simply, DJs—are alive and well on the airwaves across the country. In addition to the thousands of AM and FM radio stations, there are also satellite-delivered radio stations, cable radio stations, and Internet radio stations competing for millions of ears. DJs also have the fields of club and party work they can pursue with a tremendous boost from the power of the Internet.

Whether you're going into talk radio, club work, or music radio, you'll need a good voice and some technical training. Club work requires a fine sense of what your audience expects to hear as well as the technical skills to mix all the music together for a continuous party. Talk-radio hosts need to be current on topics of the day as well as have strong opinions. A little journalistic experience doesn't hurt either, but if you've got an opinion people want to hear, you could go far on the merits of nothing more than your irresistible personality.

Finding Work and Knowing Your Industry: Radio DJs and Talk-Radio Hosts

If radio is what you want, you can certainly help make a name for yourself on the Internet in much the same way musicians do. And with the easy access to streaming audio over the Net, you could even host your own radio show and stream it off your website. That becomes your résumé as you enter the world of radio broadcasting, where you can show potential employers that you have started your own show with your own resources. Streaming audio, however, can cost a lot because of the software required. You can learn more at Real Networks (www.realnetworks.com), one of the premiere streaming-audio providers. One important note: Streaming your own voice over the Net is a perfectly fine thing to do; if you're doing a music show, however, make sure you've got the rights to the music. Streaming songs your friends have written and performed in their own band is fine; streaming the latest hit from Destiny's Child, or even a cover of that done by your friend's band, is illegal without permission. Keep it legal to keep your reputation intact.

Beyond starting your own show, the Net can connect you to radio stations around the country and the world. Simply type "radio station" into a search engine—with or without a city/state name—and the results are lengthy. You can also run searches by radio genres to narrow down your choices. Check out the stations' sites that interest you. From a station's website you'll be able to see the jobs available, link up to the corporate owner of the station and see if there are jobs available at sister stations, and see the names of other contacts you may wish to make at both the station and the corporate level. Send in your résumé and CD (or tape)—see Part Three for lessons on how to build these—and see what happens. Remember, though: You're probably going to start in a small market, but you've got to start somewhere.

Check out these sites to learn more about the industry and find work.

@ **Federal Communications Commission Audio Services Division (www.fcc.gov/mmb/asd/)**
There are tons of rules regulating radio transmissions—covering topics like what you can and can't say, licensing processes, public service programming, and rules governing how stations must be identified—and this site spells it all out.

@ **Radio and Records Online (www.rronline.com)**
This is the radio industry resource for both music and talk formats. Besides up-to-the-minute news, this site maintains a job board with regional and national positions posted. Besides DJ opportunities, you'll find other radio station positions as well, such as broadcast engineer, promotion director, and program director. There are active discussion boards about industry topics, so you can chat with professionals from around the country.

@ **Billboard Online (www.billboard.com)**
This site is also mentioned back in the music section because it is that industry's major trade publication. However, there are resources here for those interested in radio, including classifieds and news about the industry in general.

@ **Talkers Magazine Online (www.talkers.com)**
If talk radio is your thing, there's a trade magazine devoted specifically to the subject. Complete with news that's important to talk-radio hosts and station owners, *Talkers Magazine* features a classifieds job board, so you can find the exact talk genre that suits your style.

Finding Work and Knowing Your Industry: Party and Event DJs

The Web has become indispensable for people in this profession because of the growing number of people who look online to choose a DJ to enhance their events. DJs responded by launching sites that highlight their skills. People or businesses needing a DJ for an event can come to your website and find out about you, the style of music you play, where you've worked before, and so on. It's your chance to spin your business just right.

The same website that gets you party work can also land you club work. For club work, use the Internet to target clubs you wish to work for (this works well in larger cities, but you may need to use your phone book as well to get a broader list of clubs). Get contact information off the club's site, and if there's an e-mail address, send the club your information. Remember, good e-mail presentation is just as critical as a good cover letter via regular mail, so keep it professional and include your Web address so the club's management can find out more about you. If there's no e-mail address, get the club's postal address off the site and send a cover letter along with any press kit you may have about your business, and make sure to include your website address.

There's a lot of help for aspiring DJs online—not just information resources, but networking opportunities. Here's a peek at four organizations you should check out (see Part Four for full reviews).

@ **American Disc Jockey Association (www.adja.org)**
This association seeks to represent the needs of the professional mobile and night DJs and KJs (karaoke jockeys). The site features a job board accessible to members only. To become a member, simply fill out the online membership form and provide credit card information to cover the fee.

@ **National Association of Mobile Entertainers (www.djkj.com)**
This organization has specific membership requirements to ensure that its members meet certain standards of professional conduct. To join, potential members submit client and business references as well as a copy of their client contract, which in turn is scrutinized by the membership committee. Once a member, you

become part of the searchable database available to party and event planners. You can begin your application process by using a secure online form at the site or via regular mail.

@ **Online Disc Jockey Association (www.odja.com)**
This is another association that seeks to help party planners find reliable entertainment professionals. Membership is free to those who qualify; there's an online form you can submit to see if you meet the requirements.

@ **DJ Cafe (www.djcafe.com)**
There's also a great community available with DJ Cafe. This site offers training articles and several message boards for those just starting out or already established.

Can I Find It on a Generic Job-Listings Site?

No. Mobile DJing is such a local industry that you're not going to find those opportunities on a typical job board. And for radio station DJs and hosts, those ads stay confined to the trade papers and station websites.

The Jobs That Make the Music Sound Great

If you've ever read the fine print to a CD, you've seen the people behind the music: recording engineers, sound engineers, mixers, editors, and mastering technicians. These jobs are found everywhere professional music recordings are made. That doesn't necessarily mean you're going to have to work in a giant record label–owned production house. Most radio stations hire these positions as well, as do small production houses that work on commercials, jingles, and voice-overs, as well as CDs made by those looking to "make it" as singers and musicians.

To find the places with these jobs, do a search for "music production facilities." You'll find companies offering audio duplication, mastering services, full production services, and recording studios, as well as some related video production. You can narrow the field by adding a city or state name to your search criteria to find what's near you.

To break into the business you can snag an internship or work through an education program, which will help you start the all-important networking process. Check out these sites to further your research.

@ **Holland Sound Studio (www.hollandsound.com)**
This production facility, founded in 1983, offers instruction and internships that put you into a recording studio environment. There is a fee for this program, and you've got to give them a phone call to register.

@ **Audio Engineering Society (www.aes.org)**
This trade organization offers a full educational program, with both its own instruction as well as links to other education resources that benefit audio professionals.

@ **ProSound News Online Daily (www.prosound.com)**
This site is part of the Creative Planet network and offers those in the professional sound industry daily news updates, plus classified ads that include employment opportunities.

The music production and engineering professions require you to get out there and get involved in the industry to get hands-on experience with equipment that is by and large too costly for the average person to own. While some music is indeed mixed and engineered on the computer, it would be very difficult—and costly—for you to get professional-grade equipment on your own.

If your passion is sound, find the job that lets you be around it, even if it's working as an assistant in a studio. Once you're there, ask to sit in on sessions during your nonworking hours. Get to know the engineers and form relationships with them. Remember: Don't just ask them for a job your first time sitting in. Be interested in how and what they're doing. Get yourself into a mentoring relationship and absorb everything you can.

As mentioned earlier, there are recording facilities in almost every town. Use the Internet to find the studios nearest you and go for it.

Case Studies in Music/Radio

Here are some movies that feature music and radio careers to give you an idea of what goes on in the industry. Keep in mind that even the parodies have some basis in truth.

Music Industry

@ *A Star Is Born* (us.imdb.com/Details?0075265). The 1976 Barbra Streisand remake looks at how a modern star can be groomed for success.

@ *Grace of My Heart* (us.imdb.com/Details?0116442). A little-seen 1996 film about a singer/songwriter trying to break into the business.

@ *Nashville* (us.imdb.com/Details?0073440). The definitive country/ western movie that rose to critical acclaim in 1975.

@ *That Thing You Do!* (us.imdb.com/Details?0117887). Okay, this 1996 film focuses on a band trying to make it in the 1950s, but it shows that things really haven't changed all that much.

Radio

@ *Talk Radio* (us.imdb.com/Details?0096219). This 1988 movie focuses on the host of a talk-radio show who is getting ready to go national.

@ *Pump Up the Volume* (us.imdb.com/Details?0100436). This 1990 films stars Christian Slater as a frustrated teen who starts his own pirate radio station.

@ *Private Parts* (us.imdb.com/Details?0119951). Howard Stern's shot at movie stardom was based on his best-selling autobiography.

Media

There's more news media today than ever before. Television is replete with twenty-four-hour news channels, newsmagazines, and locally produced news and talk shows. And there are thousands of magazines and newspapers on the stands. In magazines there seems to be a title for every interest, from *Acoustic Guitar* to *Zoetrope: All-Story*, a short-story magazine run by Francis Ford Coppola.

There's radio, too, with news updates on music-centric stations as well as the entire talk-radio genre. On the Internet there are more media sites than any one person could ever look at, from print and TV news sources with their own sites to publications created for the Web like Salon.com, which covers entertainment, news, people, life, politics, and sex.

All this news and information takes an army of people to keep it flowing and timely. Gone are the days when people were content reading the daily paper or merely watching the evening newscast. Now it's all about real-time, up-to-the-minute information. Weekly magazines such as *Time* (www.time.com) and *Entertainment Weekly* (www.ew.com) use websites to offer daily news updates to supplement their magazines. Updates are made to *The New York Times* (www.nytimes.com) and *USA Today* (www.usatoday.com) as news happens throughout the day. Don't overlook radio and television with the many all-news channels that deliver news and opinions, updated twenty-four hours a day.

What this means for the job seeker is plenty of opportunities to produce and present this nonstop flow of information in any of its forms. Unlike some of the entertainment-based jobs mentioned earlier in this book, media jobs are plentiful and easy to find on the Net through job boards and sites that belong to the media outlets. That's true no matter what the position you're looking for, be it writer, editor, broadcast engineer, camera operator, or graphic artist. The Net is the perfect place—and in some cases the preferred place—to research companies, network, and sift through job listings.

Journalists

As news has grown to become a leading form of entertainment, journalists, broadcasters, and other news presenters are becoming celebrities in their own right. The advent of all-news television, pioneered by Ted Turner with the launch of CNN in 1980, made media figures (and their aura of entertaining) increasingly a twenty-four-hour presence on television. As news items developed into prime-time features, the media industry feeds itself as journalists from other genres cross over to spin the news yet again. It's no longer a surprise when the editor of *Vogue* or a writer for *TV Guide*, for example, appears on a talk show or program like *Access Hollywood.* Reporters and editors have gone from "Don't shine the spotlight on me, I'm not the news" to grabbing their own fifteen minutes of fame.

The Internet has brought a sea change to journalism. Unlike the days of the daily newspaper where news came out only once a day (or maybe twice if you lived in a city big enough to warrant two editions), today news can be updated anytime in the instant publishing world of the Net. And, just like on television, there is the scramble to get it right and get it first to scoop the competition. This means that the morning paper now often carries news that many readers already have seen, heard, or read elsewhere. To ensure the continued viability of print publications, writers and editors now not only report the news, but also work to analyze the news and offer an angle that's different from the competition in other media.

Sometimes the ability to publish instantly leads to errors. In June 1998, for example, the death of Bob Hope was announced on the Associated Press's website (www.ap.org). The "news" reached the House of Representatives, where Bob Stump, a Republican from Arizona, announced Hope's passing to his colleagues. Only problem was that Hope wasn't dead. The AP was doing routine updating of Hope's obituary, a common practice among news organizations so that when a celebrity dies, there's an obituary ready to go. Unfortunately, the person updating the future obituary published the piece to the Web. ABC Radio then ran the same erroneous information because it took Stump's announcement as fact. Oops.

Even with the mishaps, the Web has opened a lot of opportunities for journalists. Granted, the dot-com bust during early 2001 saw sites go under or reduce their staffs. CNN, for example, trimmed its online staff as it became harder to sell advertising on the Net. That's where the Internet economy doesn't differ much from the old-school economy. If you can't sell ads to cover the costs, you will go out of business. What this meant for a lot of sites attached to successful companies, like CNN, is that the site stays inside the corporate family, where it can thrive as part of the larger operation, instead of a spin-off that has to earn its own way.

The good news for journalists is that there are still many opportunities to grab writing assignments for news and information sites, as well as in the rest of the media.

Get Your Foot in the Door

Journalism internships are abundant, especially in traditional print media and at smaller-market television stations. You'll likely start as an assistant; however, if you have done work on your high school or college newspaper or a modest community publication, you can get started as a beat reporter or general-assignment reporter. Keep in mind that job titles vary in responsibility at different publications and television stations, and an assistant at one could be equivalent to a beat reporter at another. Don't get yourself hung up on a title. As long as you're writing and soaking up writing tips and tricks from those around you, you've landed the right job.

Finding opportunities to write and report is as easy as selecting your favorite magazine, newspaper, or TV or radio station and traveling to its website to see what's available. You can search for those using a search engine by simply naming the publication or TV station. You also can broaden the search to things like "newspaper internship" or "broadcasting internship."

Here's a look at both some internship opportunities and organizations that list them. The organizations are also good networking opportunities to contact others who have the interest and expertise you are developing (see Part Four for full reviews).

@ **The American Society of Newspaper Editors (www.asne.org)**
This site features an extensive list of newspaper internships broken down by state and application deadline. This site also has a traditional job board as well as some tips on preparing for a newspaper career (www.asne.org/kiosk/careers/jcartxt.htm).

@ **Magazine Publishers of America (www.magazine.org)**
There is a full career center on this site, which lists both internships and regular magazine jobs for all positions at a magazine, including journalists and writers as well as production and sales staff.

@ **Radio and Television News Directors Association (www.rtnda.com)**
This organization promotes excellence in the profession via ongoing training, which is held at regional seminars around the country. The site has a wealth of information about the radio and TV industries as well as a job area. You do have to be a member of RTNDA to use the job board. For students and new professionals (designated as two years or less out of college), there is a discounted membership fee so that you can get started with the organization right away.

@ **JournalismJobs.com (www.journalismjobs.com)**
This is possibly the biggest one-stop site for internships and journalism jobs that cover all media from traditional print though Internet media. It even includes freelancing opportunities, which is a good way to build your clips portfolio.

@ **Associated Press (www.ap.org/apjobs/)**
This large news-gathering wire-service organization, with bureaus in many states and countries around the world, offers many employment and internship possibilities in print and broadcast positions. The site features listings for open jobs as well as internship information.

@ **United Press International (www.upi.com/careers)**
UPI is another wire service and has a limited job board, offering only the ability to e-mail its human resources department for more details.

If you're still in school, remember to check with your career-placement office as well. It has connections with local media and can help you get placed. Some colleges and universities have an online component to these offices. Even if yours doesn't, you can still research the job prospects online as a way to become familiar with the companies you might apply to.

Get Involved

There are a number of worthwhile journalism organizations, many of which you can join while you're still a student and/or getting started in the business. These provide important networking opportunities that can lead to story or career ideas. You'll want to interact with all levels of editors and reporters, as these are the people who hold the keys to your employment. Remember, however, that the critical part about networking is that you're trying to build a relationship, not just hit people up for work.

Here are some organizations you should look at on the Web.

@ **The Society of Professional Journalists (www.spj.org)**
This organization's website, called the Electronic Journalist, is full of information for journalists no matter what medium. Especially good for young journalists is the section on ethics, which can help provide the bedrock for the way you behave throughout your career. Also check out the Regions section to find a local SPJ chapter near you so you can become involved with your local peer group.

@ **Online News Association (www.journalists.org)**
Formed in 1999 and boasting a membership of more than 600 journalists, this news organization seeks to establish editorial integrity, independence, and excellence on the Web. Its board is made up of members from the Chicago Tribune, C|Net, and other news organizations with a presence on the Net.

@ **National Conference of Editorial Writers (www.ncew.org)**
This organization of editorial writers is very active in the realm of public-opinion journalism and offers networking opportunities through an e-mail discussion forum. It's a great opportunity to contact a possible mentor.

@ **National Press Club (npc.press.org)**
This prestigious group, formed in 1908, has the mission "to promote social enjoyment among the members, to cultivate literary taste, to encourage friendly intercourse among newspapermen and those with whom they were thrown in contact in the pursuit of their vocation, to aid members in distress, and to foster the ethical standards of the profession." The site is well worth the visit, and you can decide if you'd like to join. It's especially handy if you're in the D.C. area, where the Press Club is located.

There are a number of networking chances within niche groups of journalists, which can help foster your growth with a more select group of peers. Organizations like these include the Asian-American Journalists Association (www.aaja.org), National Association of Black Journalists (www.nabj.org), National Federation of Press Women (www.nfpw.org), and National Lesbian and Gay Journalists Association (www.nlgja.org). To find an organization for you, use your search engine and key words such as "journalism organizations" along with the words that describe the niche you're looking to join. You should also look for regional organizations that you want to connect with.

Another opportunity to network, learn the business, and connect with various job listings is through the journalism unions. These include the National Association of Broadcast Employees and Technicians (www.nabet.org), a union for news writers and announcers in television and radio as well as private video and film companies; and the National Writers Union (www.nwu.org), which covers all sorts of writers, from journalists and fiction writers to poets and cartoonists. Also worth browsing is the Communication Workers of America (www.cwa.org), which represents a variety of workers in cable TV, broadcast media, and newspapers. In addition, there's a sister organization, the Newspaper Guild (www.newsguild.org), which serves specifically to increase awareness and benefits for newspaper workers. Even if you're not a member of these unions, the sites provide a good look into the industry that will help your job research.

Self-Promotion

No matter what, do what it takes to start earning clips. Whenever you write something for a publication, make sure to get permission to post the clip to your website. You can scan the clippings and transform the file into either Adobe PDF files (for information about PDF creation, check Adobe's website at www.adobe.com/epaper/main.html) or graphic files using either the JPG or GIF formats (see Part Three for a comprehensive explanation of these formats).

Remember that you don't own the copyright on that clip even though you wrote it, so permission is very important. It's likely the publisher or editor will grant you permission to use the clip on your site as part of your portfolio. Plus, you'll make a good impression on employers who look at your site and see that you indicate "reprinted with permission" on the clip. You should do the same thing if you're using video or audio clips that were broadcast. Get permission and indicate you have the permission on the site.

If your article is already online, you can link to that. Be careful here as well; sometimes websites change the URL or articles as they age, or some, like *The New York Times*, place older articles into an archive that requires payment to view the article. Periodically check the links to your clips to make sure they're still active and free. You don't want prospective employers to come to your site and find dead links or that they have to pay to read your material.

In addition to clips you'll earn the traditional way, consider starting your own news site, filled with your own take on the news as a way to show off your writing and reporting skills. Even if you're writing only opinion pieces, you're displaying good writing skills for employers to see. If broadcast is more your thing, the ease of digital video allows you to take a stab at writing, shooting, and editing video news features that can be published online.

Consider contributing to the discussion boards of sites you visit. Jonathan Frank, who is profiled in the music section earlier in this book, is also a writer. He is a frequent visitor to Talkin' Broadway (www.talkinbroadway.com), a news and information site devoted to theater. He was frequently posting on its discussion board and his posts caught the attention of the site's editors, who asked him to start writing reviews of Broadway touring companies visiting the Seattle area. He proved himself doing that and now he also does celebrity interviews for the site.

You can get ideas from what others have done by searching with key words like "journalism résumés," "writer résumés," and "reporter résumés," and you could narrow it further adding media types like "newspaper," "radio," "Internet," or "magazine." You'll find a variety of online résumé and portfolio presentations from industry newcomers as well as more seasoned professionals, allowing you to see what your competition is doing.

Your Growth Path

Just as actors want to go from bit parts to star status and production assistants aspire to be in charge of productions, journalists tend to work toward the title of editor. What type of editor you want to be is up to you—research the editorial possibilities online by browsing mastheads, often linked as a Who We Are or About Us section, to see what different media outlets offer as their top positions.

For example, at a town newspaper, your field of choice initially could be reporting about the local courts as a beat reporter. Over time that can lead you to work at a larger paper, where you may become the legal editor. You may then move up to a national publication, such as *The New York Times* or *Newsweek*, continuing to focus on legal issues and becoming that publication's legal editor. As you continue, you'll have to consider how to use your specialty. Do you want to always stay focused on legal issues and work to a top position at a legal journal? Or do you want to take a more general path and use the skills you've gained to work your way to the top editorial position of a more general-interest newsmagazine? If you're good at the job of editor, you'll find that you can move between genres of publications because a good editor is a good editor no matter what the subject. Your chances of becoming a good writer, editor, or reporter are limited only by the depth of your contacts and the success with which you can position your work in front of the right people. Eventually you may get the chance to move into the publisher's role if you have a savvy mix of journalism experience and insight into the publication's market and audience.

You could even find yourself jumping from print over to television and becoming part of the editorial team at something like Court TV or MSNBC. Of course, you'd be fighting for that job with people who followed a similar path as you, but did so by coming up through the radio and/or television ranks from local to larger outlets. You can use the Internet to monitor job listings with these companies, through their websites as well as the regular job boards.

Also, if you work for a magazine that has a TV outlet (for example, *Time* and CNN have the same corporate parent) as well as an Internet site, you could just as easily end up cross-populating media. If you do get a shot at TV or radio, make sure you get a copy of the broadcast so you can start building a "reel" of your appearances. You can add that reel to your portfolio so you'll have something to give to producers who are considering putting you on the air. Getting a TV or radio gig is, again, accomplished almost entirely through who you know. Few media outlets are going to take the chance on an unknown. Build up your contacts and wait for the right moment to strike to begin your fifteen minutes of fame in a new outlet.

Broadcast Media Technicians

Just as film crews require lighting, sound, and other technical positions, you'll find many of the same jobs in the broadcast television media. All those sets for morning talk shows, evening news, or live programming done outside the station need lights, camera, and sound, and the people on the air need makeup artists. Television news sets and live productions, such as sporting events or on-the-spot news broadcasts, have similar requirements to prepare for broadcast as movie and television entertainment programs. You can read about those careers in the film and television crew section of this book.

There are some broadcast media–specific technical positions, such as operating a radio or television station's control board, which processes the signal going over the airwaves. If you've watched much live television or shows that are about making television shows, you've probably seen the inside of the control room. David Letterman, for one example, often sends cameras into his control room as part of his shtick.

Granted, if you choose to enter a career here, you may not be making comedy with Letterman, but you will serve critical functions within the television and radio industries. Among the people in the television control room are the master control switcher, who switches between cameras, video playback units, satellite receivers, and any other programming sources the station uses; an audio technician, who is responsible for the audio quality going over the air; a video technician, who takes care of the video quality and makes sure any videotapes are ready to roll; and a graphics operator, who is responsible for superimposing the graphics on the screen. In radio, the number drops down, usually just to a master switcher (who switches between the music, recorded segments, telephone callers, and live mics in the studio) and possibly an audio technician. Sometimes the switcher and the audio tech are one and the same.

If you're working in a control room, you're part of the team keeping the station on the air. During the TV broadcast day you'll air the programs and commercials, and go back and forth between a network signal and the local signal. During local news you'll transfer between the anchors in the studio and those in the field doing live reports, plus you'll feed in the prerecorded news segments. It's just as fast in radio, where you can find yourself playing the music, blending in the live DJ, airing commercials, making sure the news updates have field reports inserted, adding in all the recorded station IDs, and airing a listener's phone call. Both radio and television control rooms are fast-paced and precise operations.

The ultimate thrill for the broadcast technician is involvement in any sort of live sporting event, concert, or other large-scale production, on either television or radio. Your skills are pushed to the limit to keep up with the rapid pace of covering the proceedings as they happen, with little or no rehearsal in advance and no idea what may come next (even the evening newscast goes by a script, so there are few surprises).

There are no "do overs" for the broadcast technician. That's the primary difference between these jobs and the crew jobs on the taped entertainment programs. If something goes wrong with the audio while shooting *NYPD Blue,* they can stop shooting and fix it. If something goes wrong during a live football game, the problem gets fixed on the fly while millions of people are watching.

If your desire is to work in this field, you'll be studying extensively in the broadcasting school of your local college or university and working at its television or radio station. You'll learn how the broadcast equipment operates and, if you're in a program that operates a live station, you'll get thrust into the action.

Find Your Peers

Being on the technical end of the media operation means working with cutting-edge technology, such as the changeover happening at local TV stations because of high-definition television (HDTV). HDTV, because of the higher video resolution, changes how television is shot and transmitted. Besides reading the trade journals like *Broadcasting and Cable* (www.broadcastingcable.com), *Multichannel News* (www.multichannel.com), and *BE Radio* (industryclick.com/magazine.asp?magazineid=135&SiteID=15), you should network with your peers to make sure you're up-to-date. Several organizations, accessible online, exist to help you with this.

@ **Society of Motion Picture and Television Engineering (www.smpte.org)**
This organization focuses on television technology present and future, and is an invaluable learning resource. Between the discussion boards and the connection to local—and even student—chapters of the membership, this site provides a good networking opportunity.

@ **National Association of Broadcast Employees and Technicians (union.nabetcwa.org)**
Just like television and radio journalists, this is also the union for you once you have qualified to join. All it takes to qualify is to become employed in the industry, fill out the proper forms, and pay the dues (the forms and dues vary by local chapter, so you'll have to contact yours by phone, fax, or e-mail, which you can look up online, for specifics). The best thing this site can offer you is the chance to hook up with your local chapter as well as some discussion boards.

@ **Society of Broadcasting Engineers (www.sbe.org)**
This group serves engineers in television and radio as well as associated fields such as recording studios. From here you can locate other members and keep up on news and find job listings.

Pushing the Right Buttons

With jobs as technical as these, your first, best step into broadcasting, beyond obtaining the bachelor's degree in the field, is through an internship. Much the same as with TV and motion picture crew jobs, internships in the broadcast media pave the way toward knowledge and critical industry contacts.

Finding internship information is as easy as going to your search engine with key words such as "broadcasting internship" or "broadcast engineering internship" and substituting the word "broadcasting" with either "radio" or "television" for further results. You should look at the television and radio outlets in your own community. Use the Internet to find their Web pages and explore the employment information.

If no internships are listed, find the station's contact information and e-mail or call to find out if there are opportunities. Use the station's About Us or Staff page to identify those holding positions in the engineering and technical departments. If the site doesn't list all of the staff, make your contact with the head of broadcast engineering. Be ready to make your case about why they should consider you for an intern or assistant position. Let them know any experience you've had in college, your desire to further learn the field, and what your ultimate job goals are. Be ready for the question about why this career interests you. That answer is often what sets you apart from others, and you should give it serious thought. Is it the thrill of the live broadcast? Is it your love of technology? Were you inspired by the control room energy on Comedy Central's *Sports Night*? Whatever it is, be ready to give it all you've got so you stand out among the others who want these same jobs.

In addition to leads found through local stations, check the opportunities on these sites as well.

@ **TVJobs.com (www.tvjobs.com)**
This site specializes in TV jobs, and not just for engineers (although they are well represented). There are separate boards for internships and regular jobs, plus industry news.

@ **PBS (www.pbs.org)**
PBS has a number of different types of internships that begin at varying times of the year. Check the main PBS site as well as those of member stations, most of which also maintain active internship programs.

@ **National Public Radio (www.npr.org/about/nextgen/)**
NPR offers training programs and internship opportunities to bring the next generation of engineers into the fold. The programs change slightly each year, but since the mid-1990s, NPR has been training students in many professions within the radio industry.

@ **National Association of Broadcasters (www.nab.org/bcc/jobbank/Scholarships/)**
NAB has a large listing of organizations that offer internships and scholarships in the broadcasting field—both television and radio.

For these jobs, there's no replacement for job experience. There are no computer programs that simulate the experience and there is no way to professionally engineer a radio or TV broadcast from your home. You need to get out there and find a job to start doing it.

Case Studies in Media

Here are some movies in which journalists are working hard to uncover the truth.

- @ *All the President's Men* (us.imdb.com/Details?0074119). The 1976 film about the journalists who broke the Watergate scandal is an excellent look at investigative journalism.

- @ *The Insider* (us.imdb.com/Details?0140352). It's a 1999 film, but it's based on a true story about the tobacco industry that aired on *60 Minutes* in 1994.

- @ *Network* (us.imdb.com/Details?0074958). An Academy Award–winning 1976 film about network television and the blurring of news and entertainment.

- @ *The China Syndrome* (us.imdb.com/Details?0078966). This 1979 film is just as timely today. Here a TV news crew is tipped off about safety concerns at a nuclear power plant and find their reporting hampered by the plant's owners, who want to keep the story under wraps.

A Career That Transcends All Categories: Graphic Designers

Entertainment and media outlets require graphic designers to create the visual environments and support elements to make other content come alive. Newspaper and magazine design varies as widely as the number of markets served. Simply look at the differences in design between *Wired* and *Martha Stewart Living*, for example. The former is busy, boldly colorful, and at times, even hard to read because of the design elements. The latter is the polar opposite, with bright, airy pages and easy-to-read text with distinctive graphics that convey the Martha Stewart style. Every publication has a design team, headed by an art director, to produce an identifiable look consistent with its brand image.

The worlds of television and film also need graphics, such as those displayed behind anchors during the evening newscast and stylized special reports to the "bumpers" that lead into commercials, and even graphics that might adorn pieces of the set. The Internet combines elements of print and broadcast media into its graphical treatments, and must consider issues like software compatibility, load time, and bandwidth as it walks the fine line between what can be designed and what the end user can successfully experience.

Anything that needs a "look" most likely requires work by a graphic designer— and that means that there are many jobs for graphic designers in the entertainment and media fields. You can work directly for a company that produces some form of media and entertainment, or one that specializes in graphic design, or you can strike out on your own as a freelancer with any number of specialties.

Create Your Own Personal Style

The Web is the perfect place to express all the elements of your graphic style and make them accessible to potential employers. A website does away with the need to haul around portfolio cases and allows employers to evaluate your work at their convenience.

Your homepage is the gateway to your portfolio and says a lot about your design style. Is it clean and sleek or bold and daring? Is it black and white or full of colors? There are no right and wrong answers here. You may work well in a variety of styles, and you should show that, too. Whatever your style, show it off to the best of your ability. If you have a variety of styles you like to design in, you should represent those.

You should also show off any special skills you have. Are you a good photographer? Can you do something that's extra special in Adobe Photoshop or Illustrator? Can you make amazing Macromedia Flash animations? Use your site to show everything. The more you show, the more likely you are to stand above the rest of the designers. Keep in mind that with the easy availability of programs like Photoshop, many people fancy themselves as designers simply because they've got the technical know-how required to operate the software. Realistically, though, not everyone has a good design eye; there's a huge difference between being able to use Photoshop and being able to use it as a professional designer. Make sure all your work stands out so you come across as the professional you want to be (see Part Three).

If you're just starting out and haven't done work for clients yet, load up your portfolio with materials you've created. Do mock magazine page layouts, newspaper layouts, Web page designs, an ad for a huge movie release, and any other types of graphic treatments you'd care to create, such as logos, typefaces, and even business cards.

Make sure, however, that you're showing work that is wholly your own. Employers will check you out—both before they hire you and while you're doing work for them. If deception is ever uncovered, you'd likely be fired. You've got the talent, so sell yourself honestly.

At the same time, remember that artists are protected by their right to artistic expression. This means the artist can incorporate an existing work into a new derivative or evolution of it. To understand your rights as an artist, consult with a copyright lawyer and the associations that exist to protect artists' rights (you'll read about these associations in the following section). To learn how to copyright your projects, visit the U.S. Copyright Office website and read the document on visual-arts registration (www.loc.gov/copyright/fls/fl115.pdf). From that site you can also read the copyright law surrounding the visual arts (www.loc.gov/copyright/title17/circ92.html) and do a text search within the document for "visual art."

Associations to Expand Your Network

A graphic artist can take advantage of many networking opportunities to meet others in the profession and strike up relationships that can help better your skills, gain an understanding of how to break into the business, and possibly even land a job.

Here are some hookups you should make on the Net.

@ **American Institute of Graphic Arts (www.aiga.org)**
AIGA defines itself as the place design professionals exchange ideas and information, participate in critical analysis and research, and advance education and ethical practice. Its regional offices in select cities enable you to do both online (through a membership

directory) and in-person networking (at regional events). You can also search for jobs here.

@ **Graphic Artists Guild (www.gag.org)**
GAG is a national organization that offers very active discussion boards to meet and chat with Guild artists, who must earn half their income from graphic design work to be eligible for membership. You can also look at portfolios of Guild members, a good education when designing your own, or perhaps contact an artist to talk about mutual interests. Information available from local chapters offers information on events you can attend for some in-person contact.

You can also find niche organizations based on profession, gender, ethnicity, and more, such as the National Association of Photoshop Professionals (www.photoshopuser.com), Organization of Black Designers (www.core77.com/OBD/welcome.html), and Society for News Design (www.snd.org). You can find more of these by using your search engine and key words like "graphic design association" or "graphic design organization" along with the type you're looking for, such as "news" or "black."

Finding the Job—And Yes, You Can Find It on a Generic Job-Listings Site

Some of the Web resources listed above have job boards with an array of full-time and, in some cases, internship opportunities. The Web is the perfect place to look for graphic design positions within the entertainment and media fields. Why? Because the people hiring know that, along with the journalists mentioned earlier in this book, it's the graphic artists who are most familiar and comfortable with the computer.

When you use a search engine and search for "graphic design internship" or "graphic design job," you're going to find a lot of results. Narrow the results a bit by adding the type of medium that interests you.

Finally, if you're still in school, check your job-placement office—either on the Net or in person—to see if there are openings for designers within the fields you want to pursue.

A couple of great places to look for jobs are

@ **Creative Hotlist (www.creativehotlist.com)**
There are several job categories here for graphic artists in the media. The site lists not only jobs, but also paid and unpaid internships.

@ **AOL Time Warner (www.timewarner.com/careers/)**
Few companies have the demand for graphic artists that this company does, since it operates in every facet of entertainment and media. Typing "graphic designer" in its search interface yields a slew of opportunities, from onscreen graphics for its many websites to design needs for its magazines titles and set graphics for TV networks and shows. Every position from junior designer on up to creative director is represented.

An important avenue of opportunity not to overlook is a graphic design firm in your immediate area. You can find these by doing a search for "graphic design firm" or "graphic design business" and adding your city and/or state name to see what comes back. Unsure if they all have websites? Grab the Yellow Pages and see what else you find.

You should also try to get some freelance jobs. Maybe a friend has a website you could design, or someone you know is starting a business and you could design their entire look, from their logo to letterhead to brochures. Getting real client work is a major benefit to your portfolio and employment chances. Many sites on the Web are clearinghouses for freelance jobs. To find them via a search engine, the magic key words are "freelance jobs." A couple of specific sites to focus on are Guru.com, which maintains a large database of freelance opportunities (or gigs, as the site calls them), and eLance.com, which features a database of projects that freelancers can bid on to be considered by employers. For more on the freelancing experience, check out *Job Surfing: Freelancing*, which is devoted solely to freelance careers.

"Desk" Jobs

Many jobs in the media and entertainment fields don't involve being in front of or behind the camera, or even behind a computer creating the words to fill a page. They require you to be in the office making the true behind-the-scenes work happen, whether it's making the deal, paying the bills, doing the marketing and public relations work, or running the whole show.

Agents and Managers

It's these people's job to get their clients—actors, dancers, directors, screenwriters, musicians, singers, playwrights, etc.—into the right job to further their careers. Sometimes the performer hires both an agent and a manager, and sometimes only one. What's the difference between the two titles? An agent generally handles deals, contracts, and all the negotiations therein. The manager, who is usually the day-to-day overseer, looks at the career as a whole: Are the projects right? Is the publicity right? Are the best deals coming in? Is the client's hair right? Is the audition material right? You'll discover that some agents are also managers, and vice versa. A performer might have many agents, depending on the agent's specialties, such as theater, commercials, music, or film.

Trying to break in as an agent or manager still starts in the mailroom, or at least in an assistant's position. If you want to see if you've got the stuff to be a power player, check out the William Morris Agency (www.wma.com), one of the largest talent agencies in the business. This agency has several training and assistant programs to groom future agents. The training program can last from two to five years, with positions available in television, music, film, and new media. These programs are mostly for postgrads (as opposed to some of the other careers here that you start while in school).

For a huge resource of talent agency listings, look no further than the talent unions. Screen Actors Guild (www.sag.org), Actors' Equity (www.actorsequity.org), Writers Guild (www.wga.org), and Director's Guild of America (www.dga.org) all have agent lists on their sites. You can also use your search engine to find agencies using key words like "talent agency" or "talent management." Many firms listed have divisions for film, theater, commercials, music, and the other crafts listed in this book.

However, some agencies are not listed in search engines and some don't even have websites. One of the largest agencies, Creative Artists Agency (www.creativeartistsagency.com), maintains a single Web page with its contact information and nothing else, even though it has one of the largest training programs for future agents. You may find more contact information through the unions than standard search engines. After you get the contact information, you will need to pursue the agency through old-school means of cover letters and résumés along with phone calls. The agency world has, thus far, been slow to embrace the Web.

Through the Association of Talent Agents (www.agentassociation.com), you can learn more about the world of the talent agent. This group helps member organizations and independent agents with issues surrounding length of representation contracts, commissions, conflict-of-interest issues, and dispute resolution. The ATA also maintains communication with the talent unions and guilds to make sure agents are fairly treated and that agents treat the talent fairly. There's a job board here that doesn't require membership to view.

Can I Find It on a Generic Job-Listings Site?

No, unless you're looking at very small firms. Even then, listings are few and far between. But you will find many agency and manager listings on EntertainmentCareers.net, between its postings of internships and a help wanted section devoted to agency/management work.

Accountants

Would you like to be one of the people hired to prove that even though a movie grossed $300 million, it didn't make a profit? Or would you like to help a star manage his or her personal finances? How about guiding a magazine toward profitability? If you're already an accountant, or thinking of being one, by reading this book you're taking the right steps to become one who works in the entertainment or media world.

Search the major studios, production companies, publishing houses, and music studios, which you can easily find through a search engine, and check out what's posted on their employment pages. Accountant jobs will be there when positions are open, as well as related positions like tax manager, financial analyst, controller, and even chief financial officer.

There are a couple of professional organizations that can teach you more about accounting and the myriad of jobs available. The American Institute of Certified Public Accountants (www.aicpa.org) is filled with information about accounting, such as tax laws, audits, managing retirement funds, and ethics. The other major accounting organization is the National Society of Accountants (www.nsacct.org), which offers details about professional development, legislative news, and other information that impacts the industry.

Can I Find It on a Generic Job-Listings Site?

Yes, standard job boards carry these listings, as do the sites for the industry trade papers and EntertainmentCareers.net. Finding these job listings is pretty easy. Finding the exact position and company that suits you, then getting them to notice you—that's the challenging part and where the entertainment- and media-specific job boards will be beneficial to you.

Attorneys

Oh, my, does the entertainment field need attorneys. Someone is always suing somebody for something. Studios and production companies have attorneys, stars and directors have attorneys—everyone's got an attorney. Just like accountants, if you're on track to be an attorney, you're on your way to making the jump to an entertainment lawyer. You'll have to bone up on certain aspects of the law, such as copyright and trademark management, licensing, contracts, and other things in the realm of entertainment law.

The Web can give you an excellent feel for the scope of law covered in the entertainment field. Seek out your favorite law schools and see what's offered in their entertainment-law programs (normally combined as sports, entertainment, and media law). Harvard Law School even has a student committee on the subject (www.law.harvard.edu/studorgs/professional.html#sports).

In the media field, the focus is a bit different because you'll be dealing with issues like copyrights and things like libel and slander. There's a whole world of telecommunications law out there to be discovered. You can learn more about it at sites such as the Michigan Telecommunications and Technology Law Review (www.law.umich.edu/mttlr/).

The American Bar Association (www.abanet.org) has two forums that are of interest to lawyers in these fields. The Forum on Entertainment and Sports (www.abanet.org/forums/entsports/home.html) breaks the entertainment field down by movies, music, literary, visual arts, and media. The Forum on Communications Law (www.abanet.org/forums/communication/home.html) focuses on print media, electronic media, and telecommunications in general. The goal of both forums is to promote an exchange of information between practitioners in the respective fields.

Can I Find It on a Generic Job-Listings Site?

Yes, you can, although EntertainmentCareers.net has a section devoted to entertainment law where companies and firms post listings to find people interested in these specific positions. If you're headed into law school and think you want to travel down this path, keep an eye on EntertainmentCareers.net so you can see who's hiring; that way you can aim your clerking efforts there as well.

For those interested in media law, you should look at publishing houses, as well as radio and television stations and networks, which will need your expertise to navigate FCC and other media laws.

Like any field of law, competition for spots in prestigious media and entertainment firms is extremely competitive.

The Marketing/Promotions/Public Relations Machine

The 2001 movie *America's Sweethearts* offers a small glimpse into the world of film publicity and marketing. That movie focuses on a single weekend of a movie junket, coordinating star appearances, placating the media, and dealing with every little thing that could go wrong—and since this is a romantic comedy, many things do go wrong.

Of course, there's more to it than that. The publicity machine extends to every facet of the entertainment and media industry, no matter how big or small the scale. Even down to cable access and the smallest of community theaters, there's some marketing and publicity that goes on; otherwise, no one watches the production. Keep in mind that for major film releases the marketing budget can nearly match the production budget, and for large summer releases that can mean a marketing budget upwards of $80 million.

Opportunities also exist to become a personal publicist to a star, director, producer, or anyone else looking to elevate and preserve their status in the public's and industry's eyes. Behind every magazine cover and television interview, there's a publicist making sure his or her client gets on the right cover and is on the right TV shows—and is shot in the best light. Of course, the publicist must do his or her best work when the client is having trouble. That's all about spin control, whether you're working with an actor who has gone into rehab or dealing with a film that's tanking at the box office. The Net becomes a barometer of the state of a publicist's clientele. A good publicist masters the art of monitoring all the avenues of information in order to know exactly how a client is being portrayed.

On the other side of the coin, in the media field there's just as much for publicists, marketers, and public relations people to do. You've got to get the word out about the articles in the weekly and monthly magazines you work for; you've got to hype that the nightly news or newsmagazine on your channel is the one to watch. Pulling eyeballs in is your job.

Again, a basic education or previous job experience in these fields can gain you entry into a firm that specializes in entertainment- and/or media-based marketing, public relations, and publicity, or into a company that handles its own duties. And if you get a job at a larger firm, studio, or publishing, network, or producing organization, you'll be dealing with things on a worldwide level as well.

To get guidance about these specific careers, check out their associations. The Public Relations Society of America (www.prsa.org) seeks to provide members with a set of professional standards as well as professional development. Among the goals of the American Marketing Association (www.ama.org) is to empower marketers through information, education, relationships, and resources to help them perform their jobs better. Sales and Marketing Executives International (www.smei.org) seeks to constantly improve the job skills of those involved in sales and marketing. Each of these organizations offers not only a job board onsite, but also a connection to local chapters so you can do some of that all-important in-person networking.

Can I Find It on a Generic Job-Listings Site?

Very much so. Focus your searches with key words like "entertainment marketing," "public relations," or "publicity." EntertainmentCareers.net has a focused job board for these positions, including internship opportunities. Media companies tend to post on the more mainstream job boards, as well as the trade publications like *Broadcasting and Cable*. Make sure to also check the sites of companies you'd like to work for to see what they're posting on their own job boards.

Sales

Entertainment and media, at their most fundamental level, exist to sustain viewers between advertisements. Those fourteen minutes of advertising in a sixty-minute TV show are there to ensure that the network recovers the cost of making the show and makes a profit. It's the same for magazines and websites, too; sales make the money that finances the content. From selling ad space on television stations and networks to ensuring product placement in shows and movies to sealing a deal for an advertorial in a magazine, there are many opportunities for sales, and each requires a professional to facilitate them.

You'll need all the skills to construct great deals that benefit both the company you're pitching and the company you work for. Remember that someone thought up the idea of advertising a movie on a rocket that was being launched into space, so no idea is too crazy—too expensive, maybe, but not too crazy. Your education in sales is just the beginning.

Can I Find It on a Generic Job-Listings Site?

Of course—as if you haven't caught on to that trend in this section yet. EntertainmentCareers.net helps, too, as do the media trade publications, such as *Editor & Publisher* (www.mediainfo.com). Plus, if you know you want to work for a certain company, check its site and see what it's offering right now. Internships are available in this area as well.

The Top Boss

Ah, to run your own entertainment conglomerate—something along the lines of AOL Time Warner or Disney/ABC or Viacom—or to run something hot enough to get gobbled up by one of those behemoths.

Of course, if you're an entrepreneur, you could build it yourself. It would be a whole other book to tell you how to build your own entertainment or media company. Good examples of this initiative are Oprah Winfrey's Harpo Productions (www.oprah.com), which produces not only Oprah's show, but also her TV and theatrical films and magazine, *O*. Martha Stewart is her own empire as well with Martha Stewart Omnimedia (www.marthastewart.com), covering her books, magazines, TV shows, and website.

The top boss in this case means jobs like CEO of a studio, publisher of a magazine, and general manager of a television station. It could also be defined as jobs holding the title of vice president or above.

Suffice to say, there's enough information resources out there on the Web that you could do it—line up the right staff, commission the right projects, and have just the right combination of magic and luck strike, just as Oprah and Martha have done over the past decade.

Can you find a job running a company or division on the Net? Sure. Will you find one just as you graduate? Very unlikely. You're going to need to start off in one of the myriad of jobs covered in this book and work your way up the ladder, making good contacts and impressing people with your talent and work ethic in a few years—maybe as few as five to ten if you're really good (there are thirtysomethings in prime positions throughout the industry today) maybe as many as ten to thirty, depending on your goal.

If you want to bone up on what you're going to need experiencewise to land in the big chair, keep up with the executive job postings on sites like EntertainmentCareers.net, Variety.com, BroadcastingandCable.com, the National Association of Broadcasters (www.nab.com), and *Editor & Publisher* (www.mediainfo.com). Unions do not cover top brass in most companies, so union sites won't be much help in your information search.

Chapter 5
The Future of It All

What does the Internet crystal ball have in store for the entertainment and media industries, and those seeking careers within them? The answer depends on the eventual outcome of myriad factors that may validate the predictions of eternal optimists and naysayers alike. The Internet may develop faster and roll out exotic technologies to deliver more and more information, entertaining or otherwise, but will it all draw a larger share of the time and money the public spends to be entertained? Will the technology and bandwidth be available to enough people, at an affordable enough price, to make the existence of these new media forms viable? In the end, traditional market conditions will emerge as factors that shape the public's information and entertainment consumption habits; prosperous times breed new high-tech toys that people can afford to buy, while lean economies force industries to supply better value for the dollar.

So there may not be the kind of mushrooming market again that spurred Net-enterprising ventures such as Mike Ovtiz's Artists Management Group (AMG). Ovitz, once the head of Creative Artists Agency and later the president of Walt Disney Co., attempted to build a media empire. By forming AMG in late 1998, Ovitz was able to return to his roots as an agent, where his clients included stars like Robin Williams. More importantly and lucratively—at least to conventional thought of the time—he also took on television production through sister company Artists Television Group; invested in Scour Inc., which developed Napster-like file-sharing technology; invested in the production company that funded theater shows such as *Ragtime* and *Fosse*; and financed an attempt to bring an NFL franchise to Los Angeles. By September 2001, the only part of Ovitz's empire still standing was his management group. The rest of it fell apart. Scour filed for chapter 11 bancruptcy, after finding the file-sharing business to be both unfriendly and unprofitable, the NFL bypassed L.A., the theater company went under, and the TV group produced shows that, for the most part, bombed. Ovitz isn't the only big name to flounder here. Steven Spielberg backed the ill-fated Pop.com, and Time Warner's Entertaindom also tanked during 2001.

These companies all found that their great ideas hemorrhaged money and couldn't be sustained. Regardless of what happens to online entertainment-delivery systems, however, the Internet will remain an unprecedented leveler of the proverbial playing field for career seekers. A media or entertainment company may or may not have a robust online division teeming with employees, but it will always be represented, reachable, and researchable via the Internet. With a strong foundation of skills and the best information at your fingertips, you have as much access to the data you need to cultivate the career you want as anyone, anywhere.

Cabaret singer and writer Jonathan Frank feels that as people who grew up with the Internet move into positions where they are doing the hiring, the Internet will become further integrated into our "infotainment" habits. That time will arrive in the very near future. People age thirty-five and younger who got their first exposure to the Internet during college already use it extensively in both their work and personal lives. Meanwhile, people twenty-five and younger represent the *true* Internet generation. On the upper edge of this age group, they may remember a time before e-mail. Once you hit twenty and younger, you're looking at people just as comfortable and familiar with wireless pagers and Web design as their parents were with telephones and typewriters.

Within the next five to ten years, the first batch of those people intrinsically comfortable with the Net will be moving into positions where their willingness to innovate can impact the ways the Net is used to find actors, directors, designers, and all types of talent for projects. The ability to do these things effectively will develop concurrently with the growth and improvement of Internet technology. When technology evolves to the point where broadcast-quality broadband video is mainstream in the homes of most people, the worlds of entertainment and media will begin evolving exponentially. Corporate Intranet servers already host high-speed T1 and T3 connections with live video streaming to employees' desktops. For those with a DSL or cable modem—as well as those with dial-up connections—video capabilities online are still relegated to small-scale, limited-motion productions.

Broadband video, when it becomes a baseline accessible by the masses, will allow a director to audition actors and preview music samples all via the Internet. How soon will this happen? Until more of the country is wired for high-speed access (making broadband video cost-effective for its producers), there will be no hurry to go down this path. When will high-speed access hit a critical mass? It was already supposed to have happened. Current predictions put its arrival more in the 2004–2008 time frame.

Another hurdle to overcome before the Internet's full potential can be realized is the trust factor. People have to be willing to put their faith in the Internet. Many companies still don't view it as a good way to do business because of security threats, as well as the difficulties in gauging audiences and deriving revenue streams from them. On the consumer's side is a wariness of information's legitimacy in the online environment, where it remains too easy to commit fraud. In an example of the sometimes dubious nature of Internet information, a Texas day trader was found guilty of stock fraud in 2001 for posting a phony profit warning for Lucent Technologies on a Yahoo! stock message board. To make the posting seem real, it was formatted to look like a news release from PR Newswire with language from an older profit warning. The posting was made some twenty times on the board over a two-day period, during which Lucent's stock price dropped 3.6 percent. The trader faces up to ten years in jail.

Why Not Make It All Up to Get Hired?

It can be just as tempting for prospective employees to utilize the Net to manufacture an identity that cannot be backed up in person, leaving the employer wary of faith in an Internet presentation. It bears repeating: Keep anything you post on the Net rooted in truth. Don't become part of the myth that what's on the Net isn't to be trusted. It could eventually cost you a job and perhaps a career.

2010: Career by Career

Considered career by career, the future of the Internet is quite diverse. More jobs will be created with new ways to find them. Here's a look at what you may find by 2010 in the media and entertainment industries.

Actors/Dancers

Nothing will ever replace the in-person audition as the way for an actor or dancer to get a lock on the job. However, as Internet video technology gets better, a first audition could be passed with nothing more than a video clip on your website. One can envision a director surfing through and viewing headshots, video clips, and more, looking for actors, dancers, and other performers to cast a production.

Performers looking for work will benefit as the Internet gets better at pointing the way. As casting directors, especially those looking for new talent, harness the Net to get the word out more effectively, you'll be able to find more performing jobs. And, with sites like EntertainmentCareers.net and TVJobs.com already leading the way, the emergence of sites that act as clearinghouses for audition and casting notices is not far-fetched. Online tools such as these will be ideal for the underrepresented performer.

Directors

Directors will benefit from better video quality on the Internet, enabling them to direct films and put them on the Web with less worry about poor presentation quality of their work. In addition, as the creative members of the film and television industries continue to form online communities (through sites like CreativePlanet.com), directors will benefit as they find people faster to staff up their projects. This benefits up-and-coming directors most, but you can imagine a director of any type of production relishing a way to discover talent in a far more efficient manner.

Directors will also benefit from an expanded online community of their peers and colleagues, allowing them to find collaborators, problem solvers, and other support, including mentor opportunities with other directors. Certainly all directors currently in their teens and twenties grew up on chat rooms and used them as a way to solve problems, and they will bring that into their professional lives as well.

Crew Jobs

With such an entrenched community already in place, it's difficult to say if the current process of gaining employment in these crafts will make the transition to the Web. The ability for nationwide and worldwide connections, together with some of the groundwork already laid by sites such as CreativePlanet.com, makes it seem likely that more of the technical crews will be chatting over the Internet as a mode to connect to jobs within the next few years.

For production crews, the more networking they can do to find jobs, the better—a perfect match for the power of the Net. Imagine a gaffer on location in some area of the country he's not worked in before. Suddenly, he needs more crew people. The Internet can come to the rescue by showing qualified workers available in the area and displaying contact and reference information. The gaffer can have a crew member on the way with just a few mouse clicks.

Screenwriters & Playwrights

If two major Web projects currently under way—Project Greenlight and Storybay—are successful, look for more Web endeavors in the same vein to bring opportunities to screenwriters. Both projects are going to have to yield movies that are well received to stimulate further development along the same lines. If they fail, however, look for other ways for writers to work on the Web. Nothing like this exists for playwrights yet. As more Internet-savvy playwrights come up through the ranks, the landscape will change, with sites offering resources and services equivalent to those such as Storybay for screenwriters.

The Net will continue to evolve as a good research tool for writers crafting scripts. From the home or office, volumes of easily searchable research material exist online for reference and inspiration. Collaboration is accomplished more easily over the Net with its ability to transmit an entire script via e-mail with virtually no wait time between point A and point B.

Producers

The role of a producer is among the least likely to change with the Net. Producers will continue to put together all the elements of the production and fund it to completion. What gets easier for them is finding the talent and possibly the story they want to tell. Only if the writers' resources take off (as mentioned above) will producers be able to use the Net to find new projects. It's more likely that producers will continue to have in-person pitch meetings for many years to come. Producers who are tied to major studios or production companies, on the other hand, can use the resources of their deep-pocketed partners to find talent, through programs like the ABC/Disney Writing Fellowship.

Singers and Musicians

The Net has already improved the ability of singers and musicians to promote themselves, a trend that will continue. It will be safer, too, to have songs online as the recording industry continues to work toward a Digital Rights Management (DRM) system that will safeguard songs from being so easily copied and traded on the Internet. DRM technology places a silent digital code in songs; when a song is copied without permission, the resulting copy will not play. Under one DRM scheme under development, you'll still be able to trade song files, but will ultimately pay for it before you can play it (how *that* exactly works is still being researched). The end result of DRM, however, is that artists will no longer have to worry about their work being pirated. If you want to keep track of what's happening with DRM, check out InterTrust.com, one of the leaders in DRM technology. It includes a primer for everything you need to know about DRM (www.intertrust.com/main/metatrust/whatsdrm.html).

The Net continues to improve the ability for artists to showcase themselves and their work. More sites like GarageBand.com will rise to help artists get in front of potential consumers faster and easier. Might you be the next founder of such a site?

Songwriters

Like those for screenwriters and playwrights, tools for songwriters are very much in their infant stage online. Sites such SongLink International, which allows songwriters to connect with singers and musicians looking for new songs, have shown the way to the future. Yes, collaboration will become easier with the power of the Internet to facilitate quick sharing of documents, but with songwriting being a very personal process, how much songwriters will avail themselves of Net communities remains to be seen. The music publishing, royalty, and union sites are transforming themselves into better services as well. BMI already allows members to register their songs on the Net, so ASCAP should follow that lead. As for the unions and guilds, they will become more powerful information resources to keep members plugged in about the industry, especially copyright issues and, along with their singer/musician counterparts, the DRM advances.

DJs

Radio DJs use the Net to find work. The resources in place today are excellent in helping DJs plan their career moves. Streaming audio technology helps DJs get their sound bites into the hands of potential employers faster than ever. Forget about mailing a tape or CD; just offer up your URL and your work can be heard with minimal hassle for prospective employers. And make no mistake: Ease for them bodes well for you.

For club and party disc and karaoke jockeys, the Net will become a bigger and better Yellow Pages as search engines continue to make it easier for users to browse options in different music genres. More comprehensive listings will allow party DJs to go from being listed solely in large "DJ" listings, where *everyone* is listed, into categories that can define music preference, event specialties, and geographic regions. With more event planners using the Web, these types of directory breakdowns will make their searches more efficient and effective.

Sound Engineers

The Net's key resource for sound engineers, both professionals and those looking to break in, is the amount of technical information available online. As recording technology improves, engineers must stay ahead of the curve to keep themselves viable in the job market. Anytime a new sound format arrives, such as Dolby Digital did in the late 1990s, sound engineers must be ready to adapt so that they can keep producing the best-sounding audio possible. Companies like

Dolby and LucasFilm's THX will continue to battle it out to introduce the "next best thing" in sound technology for movie theaters as well as home theaters. It's a field that's constantly on the move, and the only way to stay on top is through the industry publications (such as ProSound.com) and trade associations (such as www.aes.org).

Journalists

While every media and entertainment company struggles with the breadth and depth their online presence requires, the Internet will continue to be the premier place for journalists to showcase the work they've done for future employers. Already gone are the days when you sent in photocopied clips of your stories. With the skills detailed in this book, you can make the future into the present, building a site with relatively complex functionality to allow your clips to be browsed by potential employers. The capabilities available to the junior journalist trying to get his clips seen by more coveted companies continue to evolve in ways that empower the seeker to make a positive introduction and reach a wide audience.

Finding work using the Web continues to be easy for journalists. This profession, along with graphic designers, is the easiest to find on job boards today and should remain so over the next decade. The number of jobs also will increase as the public remains insatiable in its appetite for news and information. There's a reason that there are a half-dozen all-news networks; people can't get enough.

Broadcast Media Technicians

This is another profession that uses the Web to stay up-to-date on technology. Broadcast technology is undergoing a revolution with the arrival of high-definition television (HDTV), which is already debuting in major cities like New York, Los Angeles, and Seattle. It's supposed to be nationwide by 2006, although few believe that it will have penetrated into consumer homes enough by then to warrant the shutting-down of the traditional analog signals we've all grown up watching. HDTV, however, means new equipment in the control room, translating to new equipment to learn how to operate. You can learn more at *HDTV Magazine* (www.hdtvmagazine.net).

Radio technicians face new challenges, too, as satellite radio launches, a push that began in the middle of 2001 with a new consumer advertising campaign by XM Satellite Radio (www.xmradio.com). Loads of research for these technologies are available on the Net, too, especially trade groups like the Society of Broadcast Engineers (www.sbe.org) and magazines like *Broadcasting and Cable* (www.broadcastingandcable.com).

The broadcast-technician trade is such a niche field that the existing resources of trade magazines and trade associations are the best places to find help wanted notices. In the quest for knowledge and networking opportunities, these people will gravitate more toward Internet discussions to help each other with the technology advances.

Graphic Designers

Graphic designers' resources will continue to evolve online with more options for designers to publish portfolios that stand out, through general search engines as well as through sites designed as clearinghouses for their work. Graphic artists possess perhaps the greatest ability to change the Net in the coming years as their cutting edge—or, who knows, maybe retro—designs push the Web to new levels of slickness. Websites will continue to get more stylized as graphic designers find new ways to make graphics come alive on the Net in synchronicity with the bandwidth the public can experience their work on. Web design, of course, is just one small piece of what graphic designers do. There'll be no end of work for them designing graphics for movies, TV, live productions, magazines, and newspapers, for both the traditional delivery methods of these media and their online counterparts.

Artists continue to rely on the Net as the best way to find work. Already their jobs are very computer-centric, and that makes the Net a perfect way for companies to reach out to designers with employment opportunities.

Agents and Managers

The Net has such possibilities for agents and managers. As creative types become more savvy in using the Web to promote their careers, agents and managers will see a better sampling of talent without leaving their computers.

For their own careers, agents and managers will use the Net to discover ways to make their jobs easier—from getting new clients to exposing their clients to the right people to getting them employed. The surface has only just been scratched with the relatively few sites that are up now, such as The Casting Site (www.thecastingsite.com). The fact that some major talent agencies, notably Creative Artists Agency, have yet to launch sites is an indication that the industry isn't sure about the best tactic yet.

The ability to get employed as an agent or manager using Net resources should also improve. Realistically, with more entertainment opportunities and companies producing, more talent gets employed; that means more agents and managers are needed to handle the talent. But, just like today, the "superagents" will do everything possible to own the top A-list talent, doing whatever it takes to bring the next Julia Roberts to their agency. Talent agencies must learn to get with the times, however, as more of the new talent, both performers and the next generation of agents, is Net savvy. Agencies must get their messages onto the Net to attract the new talent pool.

Accountants, Attorneys, Marketing, Public Relations, and Sales

With innovation comes litigation. Issues involving copyrighting, plagiarism, breaches of contract, invasions of privacy, mergers, and Internet legislation will give rise to more work for lawyers in media and entertainment than ever before. Work for accountants, too, will increase with the Internet's coming-of-age for entertainment and media. Those in the accounting fields will stay busy managing business plans employed by new entertainment and media companies to get off the ground, working on the budgets for individual projects, and providing personal money-management services to individuals within the business.

Sales professionals have the potential to use the Net to a greater degree as well, especially in the research area; the Web can be a fantastic tool to investigate companies and the marketplace before making any kind of sales pitch. Public relations and marketing professionals will also use the Internet in much the same way, seeking to inspire a great deal of buzz surrounding media and entertainment projects on the Web.

For jobs, these fields will continue to be among the easiest to find on the Web because the traditional job boards are already used. If the Net economy improves, there could even be specific job sites created for these fields, much as the creative community has EntertainmentCareers.net.

The Top Boss

Here's a job that could really change the Net. The people in the uppermost levels of entertainment and media have the potential to wield the most influence over the rest of the professions in this book. These are the movie studio, record company, and TV network presidents; magazine and newspaper publishers; CEOs of media conglomerates like Viacom and AOL Time Warner; and all staffers directly under them, such as vice presidents in charge of motion picture development, programming directors at TV networks and radio stations, and editorial directors of news outlets. When the economy cycles back upward and the growth of the Net continues, it's these people who will make key decisions and fund the new startups—either inside the companies they run or by investing in outside opportunities. By 2010 there will be "top bosses," those people in their forties who know all about Internet communities, the power of Web marketing done well, and the speed and ease with which the Net can deliver information.

The top bosses in 2010 will have lived through the dot-com crash of 2000. That experience positions them better to create the next Net economy and, hopefully, avoid the pitfalls of the first. They'll have the know-how to harness their staffs to create Web experiences that are more substance than flash and actually meet a business need rather than perceived need. Top bosses remembering these criteria will be able to help shape an Internet that provides information and entertainment while also turning a profit. In turn, that will make a better world for those working inside the media and entertainment professions.

One of those people may very well be you!

Part Three
Online Tips, Tools, and Tricks

Chapter 6

Be Prepared: Computer Skills You Will Need

So, what do you need to get started with this job-surfing stuff? A pocket protector? A virtual surfboard? A $3,000 computer system? One thing *not* to get is overwhelmed. First of all, don't think of job surfing as a technical task. Think of it as a life-improvement project. Like a home-improvement project, you just need the right tools and a little know-how to be successful. Think of this section as your personal Bob Vila, a strong foundation for both your job search and your presentation to prospective employers.

Your Tool Kit

The two most important items to have in your tool kit are

@   A computer (and the know-how to use it)

@   Access to the Internet (and the know-how to use it)

Need Some Help?

If you're an accomplished Net surfer and e-mailer who already utilizes the power of the Internet, this book will help take you to the next level. But what if "the know-how to use it" parts of the tool kit seem daunting to you? Perhaps you're not particularly computer-savvy. Don't feel bad; even Bill Gates once knew nothing about computers. The fact that you're reading this now proves that you're motivated—maybe not quite as motivated as Mr. Gates, but you certainly have enough gumption to become a proficient job surfer. The world of online computing may seem intimidating, but actually, it's relatively easy—that's why it became so popular so quickly. With only a minimal amount of effort, you can make effective use of this book.

There are many options available to improve your knowledge of computers. Depending on your personal preference, you can choose from one of the six methods below.

Courses

A good place to receive computer instruction is at any local college or university. Call and ask about continuing education or adult education courses. Many colleges and community centers have programs under these (or similar) names offering night and weekend classes in a wide variety of subjects, including basic computer and Internet skills.

You don't need to be enrolled in a degree course in order to sign up for these classes, and they can be surprisingly inexpensive. You might be able to make them even more inexpensive by asking about available financial aid. (You may be eligible for such aid and not even know it.) Also, if you're already employed, some employers may pay (or, more likely, reimburse you) for all or part of the cost of such courses.

If you decide to enroll in a computer course, try to find one that has a good student/instructor ratio. Large classes will likely teach you more about why large classes are a bad idea than they will about computers. It also helps to find a class that offers a reasonable number of total course hours (ten to fifteen hours should be sufficient for an introductory course) and is taught by a trained, reputable instructor. Be careful—there are a number of substandard operations that could leave you highly dissatisfied. Stick with accredited institutions. If you don't know whether an institution is accredited, ask. Then, be constructively paranoid and double-check to make sure that the accrediting agency is legitimate; you can do so by consulting the Council for Higher Education Accreditation (www.chea.org).

Even classes at prestigious colleges can be disappointing if they're taught by inexperienced or undertrained instructors. Try to check out the instructor's credentials before signing up; many institutions publish their instructors' course-related experience.

Professional computer training companies, which can be found in the Yellow Pages, are another source for computer courses. These companies are usually geared toward training professionals on specific software, but they may be well suited to training you as well. Training companies can vary widely in the quality of their instruction; looking for ones that offer "Novell certified" or "Microsoft certified" training is a good call—this usually indicates a general level of competence in all of the company's instruction.

Video

You might find that you're most comfortable with your best friend, the television. In this case, watching a videotape on computer instruction might be right up your alley. There are some good computer video-instruction series available, but here you need to be particularly wary of shoddy products. Some good ones are produced by EduPro Systems (www.eduprosystems.com).

Tutoring

Many people find that they learn most quickly when they get intensive, one-on-one tutoring. Professional or semiprofessional computer tutors can easily be found by inquiring at local computer stores and computer repair shops. Tutors may also advertise in local newspapers and on community bulletin boards.

Private tutors can be pricey, but there are ways of economizing. Ask around among your family and friends; you may find that someone knows of a computer whiz who would be willing to teach you for a reasonable fee. What amateur tutors lack in teaching experience, they make up for in bargain pricing. You may need to swallow your pride, though: It's quite likely that an inexpensive and informal tutor of this sort will be younger than you are. On the plus side, the younger they are, the cheaper they are. Go young enough, and you'll be able to pay them off with pizza and Game Boy cartridges.

Help from Your Computer

Most new computers come with built-in help—tutorials and help files on the computer itself that will help you learn how to use it. A well-designed computer will say "Howdy" (in one way or another) and offer to help you learn how to use it the very first time you turn it on. When buying a new computer, ask about the availability of this kind of help on the models that you're considering.

Help on the Web

Once you're online and surfing proficiently, you will find that the Internet itself is probably the best single source of information about computers (or pretty much anything else, for that matter). A simple Web search is often the best way to begin to educate yourself about a particular topic.

Let's say, for example, that you type in a Web address only to be confronted with the mysterious words "404 not found." Is this some strange code phrase? There's a simple way to clear up the mystery: Go to a Web search site, such as www.google.com, and type in "404 not found." You will instantly be taken to a page of links to websites that discuss and explain the "404 not found" phenomenon.

This simple strategy of using Web search sites, or search engines, will work with almost any topic. And there are more of these search engines that you can shake a stick at: Go to www.searchenginewatch.com for a near-definitive list, complete with reviews and rankings.

Books

You've already equipped yourself with one important tool: this book. Nice going—you have excellent judgment. This particular tool will take you through all of the basic information that you need to get online and ferret out exciting job opportunities.

While you were shopping for this book, you probably noticed that there are a lot of other books for sale. Once you're finished reading this book, you might want to look at some of them. You may want to learn more about designing websites, for instance, so that you can create an online presence that will truly leave potential employers gasping with admiration. Or you might want to develop some computer skills that will be useful in your work. There are books out there that can teach you all this and more. Other than the Harry Potter series, we can't recommend any books in particular, but do keep in mind that the printed word can be an invaluable resource as you continue your journey through the online world.

Completing Your Tool Kit

If you have computer and Internet skills in your tool kit, then all you need to complete the kit is a computer and an Internet connection. (We'll address these items in the next two sections.) Once your tool kit is complete, you'll be able to use your tools to embark upon your job search. As you begin this journey, keep your goals in mind. As a job surfer, your primary goals should be

@ To learn how to use a computer to create and print a professional-looking résumé

@ To learn how the Internet can help you to find a job

@ To learn how to create Web pages so that you can put your résumé and portfolio online

While using your tools to pursue these goals, keep in mind that your tool kit is never really complete. You will most likely find, at some point, that you need an item or skill that you hadn't anticipated. For instance, a freelance photographer might discover that a piece of hardware called a slide scanner needs to be added to the tool kit. This sort of thing will come up all the time, but don't panic: Armed with a computer, an Internet connection, and the knowledge of how to use them, you can harness the Internet as a research tool to find out exactly what you need and how it works.

Chapter 7

Past, Present, and Future: The History of the Internet

Even if you've been living in an underwater cave for the past ten years, you've probably noticed that the Internet has become quite a big deal in an extraordinarily short amount of time. Less than twenty years ago, personal computers were the latest technological novelty, and almost no one had heard of the Internet. Less than ten years ago, the Internet was still the near-exclusive playground of computer scientists and hard-core techno-geeks. It was completely lacking in graphics—a text-only world. And then, in the short span of six years, one area of the Internet, the World Wide Web—armed with dazzling multimedia capabilities—evolved from an interesting invention into a major sector of the economy and, in one overused phrase, "the repository of all human knowledge" (and, of course, of endless pictures of Anna Kournikova).

The Origins of the Internet

A long time ago—before MTV, even before the Beatles broke up—the U.S. government was fighting the Cold War, and among the tools in its mighty arsenal were gigantic, refrigerator-size computers—and the doughty, inventive scientists who ran them. As U.S. tax dollars poured out of Washington, D.C., to fund the high-tech number-crunching of these scientists, some of the money landed on college and university campuses, where it was used to develop these "supercomputers," which were about as powerful as a modern pocket calculator.

Many of these scientists were working with these supercomputers on large projects in collaboration with one another. To be more efficient, they needed to be able to share data with their coworkers—people who might be working on a campus on the other side of the continent. Sure, they could call one another and discuss the projects, and they could mail each other punch cards and printouts.

But there was a much faster way to share information—by networking these widely separated computers to communicate directly.

And so, in 1969, the Department of Defense's Advanced Research Projects Agency (ARPA) proposed a project called ARPANET, in which the government's far-flung research computers would be connected to one another via dedicated telephone lines (supplied by Ma Bell).

ARPANET had a unique decentralized design—it was specifically designed to survive a nuclear war. This requirement dictated that there be no single essential component of the network; if a nuclear strike took out, say, Stanford and the University of Utah, destroying their ARPANET-connected computers, the ARPANET computers at UCLA and the University of Michigan would still be able to communicate unimpeded.

One consequence of this decentralized design was that, once ARPANET was up and running, it was remarkably easy to hook a computer up to this expanding network. All you needed was a way for your computer to speak the computer-networking language, TCP/IP (Transmission Control Protocol/Internet Protocol), and a physical connection (usually a dedicated phone line) to the network. There was no way that a central authority could prevent someone from connecting to the network, and there was no way to control the content of the network. The seed of the Internet was planted.

The Infant Internet

Fast-forward to 1991. Thanks to the invention of the silicon chip, computers have become small enough to fit on your desk and no longer require air conditioners. They have keyboards and monitors instead of punch cards and Teletype-style printers. And ARPANET no longer officially exists. Its decentralized, easy-to-connect-to nature has caused it to evolve into something much larger: the Internet, to which more than 100,000 computers are connected (mostly on college and university campuses). The users of the infant Internet seemed to be coming up with new and creative operations for it every day.

In the next few years, the network spilled out of the academia and stormed the mainstream of American society. The darn thing was just so (relatively) easy to use, and it allowed all sorts of convenient communications between computers.

By the early 1990s, a large number of Americans were using personal computers, and most universities and large businesses were using mainframe (large, shared) computers with terminals. The Internet allowed the users of these computers to, among other things, swap computer programs using a system called FTP, or File Transfer Protocol; send messages using a system called electronic mail, or e-mail; and play text-only games using a system called Telnet.

One of the most popular areas of the Internet was a system called Usenet, which consisted (and still consists) of text-only bulletin boards on which Internet users could post messages on various topics, from microbiology to cartoons. To access Usenet, you would fire up a piece of software called a newsreader (the bulletin boards are called newsgroups). Nowadays, Usenet is more easily accessible via the website groups. One of the earliest topics pursued on Usenet was employment, both seeking and offering. Because Internet users were almost exclusively scientists or some other sorts of techies, the job postings were almost all for scientific and computer-related jobs.

The Dot-Com Gold Rush

A decade ago, the Internet had its great leap forward: Between 1989 and 1991, a interesting new use for the Internet called the World Wide Web was developed in Switzerland. It allowed Internet-based information to be displayed on Web pages, which could be accessed using programs called Web browsers.

In 1993, Mosaic, a graphics-capable browser for the Web, was written and released. The following year, the author of Mosaic, Marc Andreesen (at age twenty-two), founded Netscape Communications Corporation. Suddenly, the Internet was no longer a text-only environment; the addition of the World Wide Web's graphics capabilities made the Internet much richer, easier to understand, and more fun to look at. Most important, this rich graphical environment was interactive—it allowed Web surfers to send information, such as addresses and credit card numbers, to websites. It was clear that it was (at least theoretically) possible to make a lot of money in this new Web environment. The gold rush was on.

This sense of expansive opportunity led to a frenzy of Wall Street investing. A lot of Internet entrepreneurs and the investors who financed them made a lot of money during the next few years—and in those same few years, the Internet became a major financial and cultural phenomenon. Most Americans had never heard of the Internet before 1994; by 2001, most have done at least a little Web surfing, and millions have Internet access in their homes.

Most of these millions of Internet newcomers tend to think of the World Wide Web and the Internet as being the same thing. But old-timers who were on the Internet before 1994 know that text-only areas of the Internet such as e-mail and Usenet were around for many years before anyone ever clicked on a link to buy a book at Amazon or make a bid on eBay. The old-timers did not always welcome the massive tide of Internet newcomers, who were lured in by the millions by the World Wide Web's ease of use. These old-timers often complained that the "newbies" were technologically ignorant and lacking in "Netiquette," the honor code of manners that (in theory at least) guided online interactions. But no one could stop the stunningly swift expansion of the Internet because of its anarchic, easy-to-connect-to nature. Like most things on the anarchic Internet, job-board websites started out as small-scale, nonprofit ventures. But with the dot-com investing boom on Wall Street, job-board sites became slick, commercial, and very heavily trafficked as employers desperately sought qualified employees and workers sought to cash in on the boom.

The Dot-Com Bust

By the summer of 2000, the dot-com bubble began to burst. Greed—or, if you prefer, irrational exuberance—had driven the stock values for Internet-related firms far higher than could ever be justified. When a large number of heavily financed Internet startup companies continued to fail to show profits, investors began pulling back, triggering a chain reaction that brought the high-flying Internet financial juggernaut back to Earth. Employment-oriented Internet ventures were not spared; although no major jobs website has actually gone out of business, many had to resort to layoffs in 2001.

The crash of the Internet companies—massive layoffs, bankruptcies, etc.— has perhaps led to an excessive backlash against the Internet in the public mind. Unfortunately, such is the nature of our hype-driven culture; depending on whose hype you encounter, the Internet is either a dangerous digital swamp full of pedophiles and scam artists or the greatest American invention since television, guaranteed to lead us into a future of unlimited economic growth. The truth, of course, does not lie at either extreme. The Internet is anarchy, and humanity's worst and greediest impulses find easy expression there. But the expansive possibilities of the Internet as a commercial tool are still just as present as they ever were; it's simply become apparent that it may not be quite so easy to make fast, easy cash from these extraordinary possibilities. Fortunately for you, it appears that there will always be a market for jobs-related websites, no matter how many millions are lost or won on Wall Street.

The Future

What's next for the Internet? If present trends continue, bandwidth (the speed at which information can travel over the Internet) will continue to increase. What does this mean for job surfers like you? Well, in just a few years, it may be quite common to conduct job interviews via the Internet as it becomes more feasible to transmit high-quality video and audio. It will become much more common for people to have their own Web servers in their homes instead of paying for space on commercial servers. This will allow job seekers to store a lot of personal information, including extensive interactive portfolios, on their home computers and will allow people to access this information via the Internet.

Clever people will continue to find new ways to apply the Internet's ever-increasing bandwidth to the tasks of sharing information, collaborating, playing, working, and communicating. And the Internet-using public, the final judge of such matters, will decide for itself which of these new applications it wants to use. There's one thing you can count on, though: The Internet will continue to become a more powerful tool for many aspects of our lives. As a job seeker, you will need to understand this tool and know how to use it effectively. This won't necessarily make you a geek—it'll be much more likely to help put you on the path to a satisfying and well-paid career.

Chapter 8

Getting Wired: Obtaining Internet Access

If you, like millions of Americans, already have access to the Internet, then you may be tempted to skip this section. Not so fast, hotshot:There are a number of issues we'll cover here that you've probably never considered. For instance, do you know what ADSL is? GHz? No? Then consider this:At some point in your job-surfing endeavors, you may need help resolving a problem with your computer or your Internet connection. If only to prepare yourself for intellectual combat with the arrogant techies who often staff the computer help desks (they will sadistically try to humble you by slinging acronyms), you should read this section.

Although there are many factors to consider when trying to get connected to the Internet, it's quite simple. All you need are

1. A computer

2. A connection from the computer to the Internet

3. TCP/IP software (software that allows the computer to communicate on the Internet)

4. Internet software

Note that the most important piece of Internet software you'll need is a Web browser, which will allow you to access World Wide Web pages.You'll also need other Internet software (e-mail software, for example), which we'll discuss in more detail in the next section.

For the sake of argument, let's assume that you have none of these things at the moment, and let's look at each of them in turn.

A Computer

If you want to take full advantage of the Internet, then you should have a fairly modern computer. You wouldn't try to drive on an interstate with a Model T, right? Well, given the progress of the computer industry, a computer bought five years ago is basically a Model T by today's standards. As of 2002, there are certain specs that your computer should possess at the minimum. The recommended computer features listed below are comparable to the sensible family car. See pages 143–146 for a more detailed explanation.

- @ 10 GB hard drive
- @ 128 MB RAM
- @ Built-in Ethernet and modem
- @ Pentium II processor or higher, 500 MHz (PC)
  G3 processor or higher, 400 MHz (Macintosh)
- @ CD-ROM drive

There are dozens of features and specifications with which you'll be confronted while you're shopping for a computer—different kinds of graphics cards, sound cards, RAM, and more. You don't have to worry too much about these things (or even what they mean). As long as your computer meets the requirements we outline for you, your Internet-navigating experience will be a smooth one.

Buying or Upgrading a Computer

Have you decided that you need a new computer to help you land that perfect job? Who knows, maybe you'll even use it for work-related tasks once you're hired. Well, you have two basic options if you really need your own modern system: upgrading your old computer (if you've got one) or buying a new one.

Upgrading an Older Computer

On the following pages, you'll find a list of specifications—all the stuff that your computer should have if want to have a good job-surfing experience. If you currently own a computer but it doesn't measure up to these specifications, you could try to have it upgraded. There are many ways to upgrade an older computer, such as to add RAM, a bigger hard drive, or even a better processor. This process can be expensive, though, not to mention tricky: Some computers are not upgradable, some can be only slightly upgraded, and some can have only some basic features upgraded.

To find out whether your computer is upgradable, you can do any of the following three things:

1. Get the computer's model number. Sometimes this is clearly printed on the front of the computer, but it's usually on the back or the bottom. The model number should be near the computer's serial number. The model number, like the serial number, is usually some arcane series of numbers and letters. On most computers, this information should be fairly easy to find. If it's not, you can call up the manufacturer's help desk and yell at them.

2. Contact the computer's manufacturer. If you're armed with the model number, tech support should be able to tell you what's upgradable on your machine.

3. If you have no luck with method 1 or 2, take your computer to a local computer repair shop. They can help you figure out if you're able to upgrade.

Before taking the final step of paying for upgrades, it's important to evaluate cost versus benefit: unless the total cost of the upgrade is significantly lower than the cost of a new computer, you should buy a new computer. Putting money into an old computer is like putting money into an old car: You may keep it on the road for a bit longer, but who knows what will break or become outdated?

Buying a New Computer

Hopefully you have good self-esteem, because shopping for a computer can be a humbling experience. First you wade through oceans of maddening acronyms to try to figure out what you need, then you buy an expensive machine that you hope you'll understand how to use, and then, a few weeks later, you see an ad for a computer that's much cheaper and that seems much better than the one you've got. You've got one advantage on your side, though: this section. Read it thoroughly and you'll be able to avoid the most annoying aspects of this process.

Choosing an Operating System (OS)

One thing to consider when buying a computer is which operating system (OS) you would like to use. An OS—also referred to as the computer's system software—is the software that gives a computer its particular personality. Different operating systems give you different ways to access your documents and folders, run programs, and change the computer's settings. The OS basically controls the computer, so it's pretty important to choose the right one.

There are many different personal-computer operating systems available today for you to choose from (see sidebar). Keep in mind that choosing an OS for your computer will forever dictate what software and hardware you buy for your computer, because they have to be compatible with your computer's OS.

You may already be familiar with a particular OS listed in our sidebar, so you may already know which you would want on a new computer. If you are undecided, however, be wary of the commonly heard advice that one OS is "the only one to use" or "much better than all the rest." Each OS has its strengths and weaknesses, and you should choose the one that you like best. You might want to go to computer stores and try out the different ones that are available. Don't obsess over it *too* much, though—pretty much any OS that you can buy today will meet your needs as a job surfer.

The Lowdown on Operating Systems

Windows

There are many flavors of Windows available—so many that it's downright confusing. The best way to cut through this confusion is to choose one of the most recent versions of Windows; you'll avoid many potential problems (software incompatibilities chief among them) by doing so. As of this writing, the most recent versions of Windows are

@ Windows ME: A reasonable choice, especially for older machines or for machines that just barely meet the specs listed above in the "A Computer" section.

@ Windows 2000: This is the best choice in the Windows family, especially if you share your computer with others. It's more stable (meaning it crashes and freezes less) than other versions of Windows.

@ Windows XP: Looks promising from a user-friendliness standpoint, but it's a bit risky to commit to an OS that's so new—there may still be bugs that will be worked out in updates. Check on its progress in the next couple of years.

Macintosh

Apple aficionados have an easier time figuring out which OS to choose because they're consecutively numbered. As of this writing, your two Mac OS choices are

@ Mac OS 9: Remarkably easy to use. However, many PC games and some Windows-compatible software do not have Mac OS versions or equivalents.

@ Mac OS X: Combines Mac OS 9–style user-friendliness with Windows 2000–style stability. Very promising, but it's also very new—make sure that there is enough software available for it.

Linux

Linux is the most stable and most flexible of all the major operating systems, and it will run on almost any kind of computer. However, it's really only for hard-core technophiles. Mostly used for running Web servers and similar tasks, Linux requires an in-depth knowledge of computers, and it takes a long time to set up.

Tips on Purchasing a Computer

Sure, you can just go out to the nearest computer shop and buy yourself a new machine, using the specs listed later in this chapter under "Computer Specs." However, given the rapid advancement of the computer industry, this will probably work only within a year or so of the publication of this book. Beyond that point, the computer industry will surely have come out with computers that are twice as fast, are probably a bit cheaper, and incorporate features that don't even exist at this writing. So how do you figure out which computer to buy if things keep changing? If you crack open a computer catalog, the choices may seem overwhelming. You don't want to buy an enticingly inexpensive machine that turns out to be a lemon, nor do you want to saddle yourself with a mega-expensive, top-of-the-line computer that has many accessories you'll never use.

There is a rule of thumb that can help you through this thorny problem: In general, look at computers that are not quite top-of-the-line (i.e., not quite the most expensive). Computers that fall at this price point tend not to be packed with unnecessary features yet are powerful enough to last you for a few years.

But don't just use this rule of thumb to quickly choose a computer! Instead, get detailed specifications for models at that price point, and then

- Comparison shop. Try to find models by other reputable manufacturers that have the same (or very similar) specs, and see if the price is better.

- Look for special deals. You may find a similar model offered bundled with additional RAM, a color printer, a scanner, or even a digital camera.

Dirt-Cheap Computers

In the past few years, many extremely low-cost Windows-based computer systems have become available on the market, often costing less than $500. Why are they so cheap? Because they are built around certain kinds of non-Pentium processors, which are significantly less expensive than Pentiums—and significantly slower. If this is all that you can afford, then you might be able to get by with one of these super-cheap computers. Just don't expect such a machine to be fast or to last you a long time.

Warranties and Tech Support

Before purchasing a computer, find out what sort of warranty and technical support are included in the price. A computer with a very limited warranty and pay-per-use tech support may not be as good a value if you intend on using the tech support frequently. Novice computer users should probably pay for a computer with slightly lower specs but with a better warranty and free tech support.

How Long Will It Last?

One of the most frustrating things about buying computers is how quickly they become obsolete. It would be ridiculous if a five-year-old car were not drivable, yet that's essentially the situation with computers.

You can expect a top-notch new computer to be useful for about three years. This limit can be stretched another year or two if you make sure you buy a computer that's easily upgradable; ask the retailer if the processor and other components of the system can be upgraded in the future.

Save a Few Bucks

If you can't afford a new computer, look for a secondhand machine. It shouldn't be too difficult to find one that meets the minimum specifications outlined below. You can look in the for-sale ads in your local newspaper, in computer stores, and in computer repair shops. It also doesn't hurt to ask around among your family, friends, and colleagues.

You can, of course, also find used computers online, assuming that you can get online to do so! Auction sites such as eBay are good places to find used computer equipment.

The main advantage of getting a new computer rather than a used one is that new computers come with warranties and (usually) free telephone technical support. Also, a new computer's hardware and software should be in pristine condition—something that you cannot count on with used computers.

Another cost-saving option available to you is a refurbished computer. These are computers that were returned to the manufacturer for one reason or another. Usually returned because they were broken, they have been fixed and are now being resold at a lower cost. Refurbished computers are often sold without a warranty, but refurbished computers with warranties can be found.

Shared and Public-Access Computers

If these cost-saving tips are still beyond your means, then you should take advantage of public-access computers. If you're a student, then your school might have Internet-connected computers that you can use outside class time.

If you're not a student, then your workplace (if you're employed) might have Internet-connected computers that you can use. Unfortunately, most companies have policies against using company computers for personal Internet browsing. It can't hurt to check with your employer, though. Your company might allow its employees to surf the Web during specific nonbusiness times. Just be careful not to job-surf at work. Whatever your workplace's policy, you don't want to lose your present job because you were surfing for a new one!

Another option for cheap access to the Internet is a public library. Most public libraries offer the use of Internet-connected computers. Unfortunately, old and malfunctioning machines are, sadly, quite common in public libraries. If you're fortunate enough to have access to a public library with good Internet services, be sure that you understand their policies. You may need to reserve time on a computer and agree to time limits and other restrictions.

Finally, you could contact your state or local employment office—look under Employment in the government listings section of your phone book. Some of these offices have Internet-connected computers that they will make available to job searchers under certain conditions. They may also be able to direct you to other publicly accessible Internet-connected computers.

Computer Specs

The most important things to focus on when shopping for a computer are its specifications, or specs. (The color of a computer shouldn't really be a factor, so we won't cover that. Personally, though, we like translucent yellow.) The most important specs are outlined here.

Hard Drive Size

A hard drive is a disk inside the computer. All of the computer's programs and files, as well as its operating system, are stored on the hard drive. Hard drives from the 1980s and 1990s were measured in megabytes (MB), which are millions of bytes. Now that technology has increased the efficiency of hard drives, drives today are measured in gigabytes, or GB (there are a thousand megabytes in a gigabyte). A 10 GB drive is our recommended minimum. Watch out, though: as program sizes get bigger, this requirement is climbing fast. Soon we'll be measuring hard drives in TB—terabytes, or 1,000 gigabytes!

RAM

Do these computer acronyms make you nauseous? Don't worry. You don't really need to know what it stands for. (But if you're curious, RAM stands for random access memory.) What you *do* need to know is that RAM is the memory of your computer. The RAM is what helps you run several programs at once without slowing down your whole computer. RAM consists of little chips inside your computer, and the memory on those chips is used to run programs and store temporary information.

Don't confuse RAM with hard disk space. If your computer ever tells you that it's "out of memory," that means it needs more RAM, not a larger hard drive. RAM is measured in megabytes, or MB. *We recommend at least 128 MB of RAM for your computer.* If you plan on working with graphics and layout, you probably want to upgrade to at least 256 MB. Of course, it wasn't too long ago that even a few megabytes of memory was a lot, but today's programs are bigger and more complicated, and they demand more RAM. Therefore, it probably won't be too long until we measure memory in gigabytes; try to stay on top of what's required of your system and purchase a bit more memory than you'll need. That should keep your computer from becoming obsolete for at least a little while.

And the Keyboards Were Made of Stone

> "640K [of memory] ought to be enough for anybody."
> —Bill Gates, 1981

> "64 megabytes (MB) of RAM recommended minimum;
> more memory generally improves responsiveness."
> —Windows 2000 system requirements,
> as listed on Microsoft.com

Note: There are 1,000 kilobytes (KB) in a megabyte (MB). Therefore, we can see that Windows recommends at least 100 times the amount of RAM that Gates had deemed sufficient only nineteen years earlier!

Networking and Modem

A modem connects your computer using a phone line; networking hardware connects you directly to a network. (High-speed Internet connections such as DSL and cable, discussed later in this chapter, fall into the network category.) You'll need to use one or the other of these to connect to the Internet.

There are a number of different ways to connect to a network. By far the most common is with a system called Ethernet, in which the computer is connected directly to a network using Ethernet cables. Ethernet cables, also referred to as 10BaseT, 100BaseT, or Cat 5 cables, look like thick phone cords and use an RJ-45 connector (which looks like a phone jack connector, only slightly larger).

Wireless Ethernet networking—which uses radio waves, rather than cables, to connect your computer to a network—is just beginning to become competitive with cable networking. Wireless Ethernet uses a communications standard called 802.11 (Apple Computer calls it "Airport"), and it allows users to create a cable-free Ethernet network within a limited area, usually a single building. At the moment, very few computers come with wireless Ethernet built in, but this will probably become more widely available in the near future.

Networked computers connect to one another via a hub and to the Internet via a router. Make sure your computer includes a modem and Ethernet capability.

Processor Type and Speed

The processor is the heart of a computer, and it's the chip that operates all of the commands that pass through the computer. Computers can have a wide variety of processor types.

Processor speed is a very important spec, but it must be looked at in comparison to the computer system at hand. Processor speed is directly comparable only within a single processor type. For example, a 900-MHz Pentium II is faster than a 700-MHz Pentium II. However, a 700-MHz Pentium III is significantly faster than a 766-MHz Celeron.

In 2001, computer-chip makers created the first 2-GHz computer (2,000 MHz). This means that computer processor speed will soon be measured in GHz rather than MHz.

Removable-Media Drive

Computers can be outfitted with a number of different kinds of media drives. Drives can help you store and transport information easily using portable disks.

The most important kind of media drive is a CD-ROM, which stands for Compact Disc-Read Only Memory. A CD-ROM contains about 650 MB of data, which can easily be used to store just about any type of computer software you could use. In fact, most software today needs to be installed from CD-ROMs.

Ready to 'Ware

Hardware is your computer and any other physical stuff (printers, etc.) that's connected to it. Software refers to the programs that you run on your computer. Software is "soft" because it's ephemeral—it can crash, but it won't leave any broken glass on your floor.

There are many different kinds of drives that can read CD-ROMs; the most common kind right now is the DVD-ROM drive. This is a drive that can play

DVDs (CD-size disks that contain movies) as well as CD-ROMs. Other kinds of removable-media drives include floppy disk drives and Zip drives.

Other Specs

There are a number of other, less important specs for computers that you should probably know about. A semicomprehensive list follows.

Expansion Cards

Expansion cards (often referred to as PCI cards) can greatly expand a computer's capabilities. These cards generally serve to allow you to attach external devices, such as scanners and external disk drives.

This spec is becoming less important with the growing popularity of USB and FireWire ports (see next section), which can perform the same functions.

Ports

Computers are connected to other devices using ports. A computer might have several kinds of ports, such as parallel, serial, networking, USB, and/or FireWire (a.k.a. IEEE 1394). Just like expansion cards, these ports are used to connect devices such as printers and scanners.

USB and FireWire are the most advanced and convenient types of ports available. It's a good idea to find a computer that has them or (if you already have a computer and it doesn't have these kinds of ports) to look into buying USB and FireWire PCI cards.

Graphics Cards

Graphic design professionals and computer-gaming enthusiasts are particularly interested in the specifications for a computer's graphics card, which connects the computer to a monitor. The better the graphics card, the better the image on the monitor—especially animated images.

There are a wide variety of graphics cards that could come with any given computer, but don't sweat this particular spec too much—the card that comes with your computer is probably just fine for your job-surfing needs. If you are involved in a graphics-intensive career such as digital video or online animation, then you might want to invest in a higher-powered graphics card. If you're a computer-gaming aficionado, then you might also want a top-of-the-line graphics card so that you can slaughter aliens and mutants in rich, vibrant color. Note, however, that this is unlikely to contribute in any meaningful way to your job search.

Sound Cards

Sound cards can provide different levels of amplification and richness of sound, as well as different kinds of sound input. Just as with graphics cards, you'll find that the sound card that comes with your computer should be sufficient for your needs. If you're involved with digital music editing (or, again, if you want to blast aliens with extraordinary realism), then you'll need a high-quality sound card.

Other specifications are limited only by the ingenuity of the computer industry. There will no doubt soon be features available that we can't even imagine now.

The important thing to remember when buying a computer is that the specs should fit your needs. Don't be bowled over by sales pitches for computers with features that you don't need or don't understand.

An Internet Connection

This is the trickiest item on our list of Internet access requirements. That's because the Internet service provider (ISP) industry is in a constant and often very confusing state of flux. In most parts of the United States, there are several options for connecting to the Internet. Usually, you will find that there are several ISPs to choose from—perhaps one or two local ISPs and then as many as a half-dozen regional or national ISPs. Once you've picked an ISP, there are still several physical methods of connection to choose from. This section aims to help you find your way through this plethora of choices.

Until about 1999, if you were considering your Internet connection choices, you would have been thinking about modem speeds and a second phone line. In the past couple of years, however, there has been a high-speed Internet access revolution, and there are now several ways of getting "high-speed always-on" Internet connections that do not require a traditional modem. These services allow you to use your telephone while you're online and (in most cases) to remain connected to the Internet whenever your computer is turned on. If you plan to be spending a lot of time online (and in order to effectively use the Internet to find employment, you will need to do so), then a high-speed (also called broadband) Internet connection is for you. While such connections are not cheap, their prices are competitive with traditional modem connections, and they are likely to become more affordable in the near future.

Internet Connection Options

Before you choose an ISP, you may wish to consider what kind of Internet connection you need. Here are the different kinds of connections that are currently available.

Modem

A modem connection allows your computer to connect to the Internet via a regular telephone line (using an infernal cacophony of clicks, beeps, and whines). This option is not going to give you the speed and convenience that you should have in order to effectively job-surf (or download porn, if that's your bag). However, in many parts of the country and in most of the world, a modem is the only option.

Despite the galloping speed of the high-speed Internet revolution, which is rapidly making modems obsolete, most computers still come with built-in modems. These modems are the fastest available: 56kbps (kilobits per second), also known as 56k or v.90. If a modem connection is your only Internet connection option, make sure you are using a 56k modem. Modems slower than 56k are responsible for those super-slow load times; unless you really enjoy watching Web pages take thirty to sixty seconds to load, we recommend never, ever using a modem slower than 56k.

Cable

Also known as a cable modem connection, this type of connection comes into your home via a television cable line. The cable line then gets split in two; one segment goes into your television (for regular cable-TV service) and the other goes into a cable modem box, which connects to your computer.

If a cable modem connection is an option for you, this is probably the best kind of connection that you can (relatively cheaply) get. If cable Internet connections are available in your area, you can usually buy the connection from your local cable company. Recently, however, the federal government has been putting pressure on cable companies to allow other ISPs to use their cable lines to provide Internet access. As a result, there may be some added competition in the cable modem sector soon, and you'll be able to choose between your cable company and other ISPs for a cable modem connection.

DSL

A digital subscriber line (DSL) Internet connection comes into your home via a regular phone line; the line then gets split between your telephone and a DSL modem box, which in turn is connected to your computer. Despite the fact that DSL uses your phone line, you will still be able to use your telephone while online.

DSL is the most complex Internet connection option. For technical reasons, you need to be within a few miles of a central office (a telephone switching station) in order for it to work, so DSL is rarely offered in rural areas. And although many DSL installations work smoothly, there is a much higher probability of running into problems when trying to get it installed than with other types of Internet connections.

There are two main factors that make DSL installation so complicated.

@ Most phone companies are now also ISPs, and most offer DSL access. However, the equipment that these companies are using is complex and often alarmingly antiquated by technological standards (it may be older than you are), and well-trained technicians who understand the equipment are in short supply. As a result, it can take a long time to set up a DSL line, and there are serious problems with reliability.

@ Other ISPs are allowed to use the phone company's lines to provide you with DSL service—but in order to do so, they need the phone company's help. The service problems noted above make coordination difficult. And, it must be said, the phone companies often seem reluctant to provide fast, quality service to other ISPs—who are, after all, competing with them to offer you ISP service.

When shopping for DSL service, you may hear the term *ADSL*. This stands for asynchronous DSL—the kind of DSL service that's generally offered to residential customers. Other flavors of DSL tend to be significantly more expensive (though also faster) and are intended for business customers.

Satellite

Internet access via satellite dish is, in many rural areas, the only option for high-speed Internet access. While not quite as fast as DSL or a cable modem, it's significantly faster than a traditional modem.

Until recently, satellite Internet access had one major Achilles' heel: It only allowed you to download (receive information) from the Internet at high speed. In order to upload (send information, such as e-mail), you had to be simultaneously connected via a traditional modem. For most users, who do a lot more Web surfing (which generally involves only downloading) than uploading, this still provides acceptable speeds. However, you're still saddled with the inconvenience of a modem connection.

Recent satellite ISPs don't require a phone line to upload files. While the upload speed is still slow, at least you don't have to have a second phone line installed in order to use your telephone while online.

There are still several serious drawbacks to satellite Internet: The speeds are slower than other cable modems or DSL; the initial installation cost is high; and there is a longer "lag time" while your data bounces back and forth from Earth into orbit, making applications such as online gaming or instant messaging annoyingly slow.

Wireless

Wireless Internet access is just normal Internet access via a specially designed dedicated cell phone. While this provides an incomparable measure of freedom—especially if you're a laptop user—it does have some drawbacks: It's slower than other high-speed options (only four times faster than a modem); availability is limited to major cities (and is spotty even there); and it's pricey.

T1 and Ethernet

This is the sort of Internet connection that many schools and larger businesses have. A T1 is a high-capacity dedicated phone line that allows many computers to access the Internet at the same time. Ethernet is the networking system that distributes this connection to individual computers. A few places in the world (such as the Blacksburg Electronic Village in Virginia: www.bev.net/project/brochures/about.html) offer this sort of high-speed connection in apartment buildings. This arrangement is likely to become more common in the future.

Choosing an ISP

Once you've figured out which kind of connection best fits your situation, you can go shopping for an Internet service provider.

A-O-(HEL)L?

"So easy to use, no wonder it's number one!" America Online's ubiquitous ads, and junk-mailed installation CDs, have helped to make it by far the largest ISP. AOL is a good choice for newcomers to the Internet because it's designed entirely for beginners. The worldwide availability of the service and twenty-four-hour technical support are also powerful advantages.

AOL does have disadvantages, though: More than any other ISP, it's saturated with advertising, which you must wade through or past to get to your online tasks. AOL also requires that you use its unique Internet-navigation system, which is a far inferior product to either Microsoft Explorer or Netscape Navigator. While this is fine for many people, AOL users miss out on the richness and flexibility of the Internet experience.

Also, AOL mostly offers traditional modem connections, though it has begun to branch out into broadband connections.

Local and Regional ISPs

Not too long ago, local and small regional ISPs dominated the market that was left over from AOL. In recent years, however, larger ISPs have bought out these smaller players at an alarming rate, reducing competition.

Fortunately, many of these smaller ISPs are still surviving. Look in your Yellow Pages under "Internet." Or, if you can get online, do a search on www.yahoo.com for "ISP directories" for a list of several websites that can help you search for an ISP.

Although local ISPs are more likely than national ISPs to be bought out or go out of business, they tend to offer friendlier, more accessible customer service and can generally be more flexible.

Larger ISPs

While large regional or national ISPs may keep you on hold longer than local ISPs, they often have longer tech support hours, and you can move to another part of the country without switching ISPs.

Specialty ISPs

You might find that there is an ISP that offers exactly what you want from the Internet. Some ISPs specialize in providing Internet access to corporations only; some specialize in a particular kind of connection, such as satellite; and at least one (www.speakeasy.net) specializes in providing Internet access to online gaming enthusiasts.

Free ISPs

Beware of free or extremely cheap Internet access. A number of companies offering this sort of access appeared in the late 1990s, but many of them have gone under in the dot-com bust, and there is no guarantee that the remaining ones will not do likewise. In any case, just like so many other places in life, you get what you pay for: These bargain ISPs generally require that part of your computer screen be taken up by advertisements, and the services are not noted for their high speeds or reliability.

AOL

Web address: aolplus.aol.com/highspeed/

Modem? Yes

Cable? No

DSL? Yes

Satellite? No

Wireless? No

Monthly cost: $43.85

Installation/equipment charges: $0

Earthlink

Web address: www.earthlink.net/home/broadband/

Modem? Yes

Cable? Yes

DSL? Yes

Satellite? Yes

Wireless? No

Monthly cost: $49.95

Installation/equipment charges: $100

MSN

Web address: essentials.msn.com/access/broadband.asp

Modem? Yes

Cable? No

DSL? Yes

Satellite? No

Wireless? No

Monthly cost: $39.95

Installation/equipment charges: $99

Verizon

Web address: www.verizon.net

Modem? Yes

Cable? No

DSL? Yes

Satellite? No

Wireless? No

Monthly cost: $49.95

Installation/equipment charges: $50

DirecPC

Web address: www.direcpc.com
Modem? No
Cable? No
DSL? No
Satellite? Yes
Wireless? No
Monthly cost: $49.99
Installation/equipment charges: $690

Time Warner Cable

Web address: www.roadrunner.net
Modem? Yes
Cable? No
DSL? Yes
Satellite? No
Wireless? No
Monthly cost: $39.95
Installation/equipment charges: $100

Wireless Web Connect!

Web address: www.wwc.com/products/anywhere/
Modem? No
Cable? Yes
DSL? No
Satellite? No
Wireless? No
Monthly cost: $59.95 (additional telephone charges may be applied; see website for details)
Installation/equipment charges: $300

All prices are for basic residential DSL service, with the exception of DirecPC, Time Warner Cable, and Wireless Web Connect.

Keep in mind that this information is changing all the time—even month to month and week to week! You might consider updating this chart yourself by visiting the websites of the ISPs listed and seeing what their current offerings are.

A Checklist for ISPs

When choosing an ISP, there are a number of factors to keep in mind.

Connection Type

You should first determine what kind of connection you want, based on the choices available in your area. Ideally, you want the fastest and most reliable connection available, but cost must naturally be taken into account. Of the most common types of affordable residential Internet connections, these are kinds to look for, in order of desirability: cable, DSL, and satellite. Modem connections should be used only as a last resort.

Customer Service

The best Internet connection in the world is useless if no one can help you to set it up and use it. Before signing up with an ISP, check out its telephone support hours. Call the customer service line and ask about services. Are the customer service people polite, and do they appear to be well trained? Find out if you might ever have to pay extra for telephone tech support; ideally, it should always be free!

E-mail

When you buy Internet access, your ISP will provide you with an e-mail account. Since e-mail may now become your most important communication tool with potential and future employers, you should review the details of an ISP's e-mail offerings before signing on. Here are some things to look for.

IMAP compatibility
With most e-mail systems, you need to always check your e-mail from a single computer. If you move around from computer to computer, you'll be able to access only messages that you haven't read yet; none of your older messages—ones that you've already read—will be accessible. IMAP-compatible e-mail systems allow you to move around from computer to computer while retaining access to your entire e-mail collection. If you plan to commonly use multiple computers, this could be an important consideration.

In order to use IMAP, you will need -to use an IMAP-compatible e-mail client, such as Eudora or Netscape (Netscape includes an e-mail program in its Web browser package).

@ **Attachment size limits**

Most ISPs have restrictions on the maximum size of a file that can be sent or received as an e-mail attachment. If this size limit is too low—I MB, for example—this could be a problem if your work requires you to send and receive large files, such as image files. Word processing files will usually fall far below any attachment size limit. However, if you have attachments (such as pictures) on your word processing résumé, you might not be able to send them.

@ **Webmail**

Many ISPs will offer Web-based access to your incoming mail—a very convenient feature if you are often away from your own computer. Note, however, that this feature does not give you access to e-mail that you've already read.

@ **Extra e-mail accounts**

Many ISPs offer extra e-mail addresses for free or for a small fee. Don't confuse this with having multiple Internet access accounts (which you don't need)—think of it this way: one Internet access account, multiple e-mail addresses.

For job surfers, having multiple e-mail accounts allows you to separate your business-related e-mail from your personal e-mail. This will help you avoid overlooking business-related correspondence, which can easily happen if you receive a lot of personal e-mail.

Free Webmail

If your ISP does not provide you with extra e-mail accounts, you may want to use a Web-based e-mail service, such as Yahoo! or Hotmail. These services are free, and they do not require that you use special e-mail software; the mail system is accessed using a Web browser. An enormous advantage of these services, as with IMAP, is that you don't have to be at your computer to see your e-mail; you can get into your e-mail from any Internet-connected computer.

Web Space

Does the ISP offer free Web space, and if so, how much? Can you pay extra to get more space? Will they help you to register a domain name (personal Web address) for your Web space? These will be important considerations when it comes time to publish your online résumé and/or portfolio.

Contract

Are you required to sign a time-specific (e.g., one-year) contract with the ISP? Is there a penalty for canceling the contract?

There are a couple of online resources that help evaluate an ISP, so find some time on an Internet-connected computer and check out www.dslreports.com. Although this site is geared toward DSL consumers, it also provides information on other kinds of connections and on ISPs in general. The Community Forums section features lively discussion of the merits and sins of many ISPs. Another terrific resource is www.cnet.com/internet/0-3761.html. This page, on the technology-industry site cnet.com, offers a number of interesting links related to the ISP industry.

Now Go Get It!

Okay—you've chosen your ISP and connection type, and you're ready to get connected to the Internet at (hopefully) a blazing-fast speed. The next step is to contact that ISP and tell them what you want. The ISP's customer service department should take it from there, sending you all of the information, hardware, and software you will need in order to get connected.

TCP/IP Software

TCP/IP is the language that computers on the Internet use to communicate. (TCP/IP stands for Transmission Control Protocol/Internet Protocol. Use this little-known fact to amaze and delight people at parties.) Fortunately, all personal computers made since 1995 that came with Microsoft Windows (including Windows 95, Windows 98, Windows NT, Windows 2000, and Windows ME) or the Macintosh OS (any version) have TCP/IP software built in.

You *will* need to configure the TCP/IP settings on your computer, however. When you sign up with an ISP, you will receive instructions on how to do this. Sometimes you will receive a CD-ROM that contains a software installer that will do the TCP/IP configuring for you.

A typical TCP/IP configuration dialog box for Windows looks like this:

A typical TCP/IP configuration dialog box on a Macintosh looks like this:

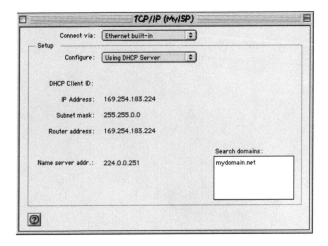

The actual numbers that appear in these boxes may be quite different on your computer.

This process can seem very technical, but it's usually quite easy. Every computer that's connected to the Internet needs to have a unique IP address; configuring the TCP/IP settings on your computer will give it such an address. Think of an IP address as being like your street address: In order for information to reach your computer from the Internet, your computer needs to have an address.

Internet Software

Any new computer should come preloaded with some Internet software. In fact, Windows comes preloaded with Microsoft Internet Explorer, which is a very competent Web browser. Netscape Communicator, the second most popular Web browser, can be downloaded for free from www.netscape.com.

As a job surfer, you'll need some software in addition to the Internet software to help you find your dream job. This software includes a word processor, an e-mail program, an FTP program, and a Web page editor. We'll discuss how to acquire and use this software in the next chapter.

Chapter 9

Sharpening Your Tools: Basic Internet Software and Skills

Okay, here are just a few more little things before we go on to the really fun stuff like creating online résumés. Once you've got Internet access, it's time to get familiar with some of the basic software tools that you'll need to master the online environment. This includes not only the obvious and all-important Web browser but also a plethora of other programs that will help you to take full advantage of your Internet connection.

Web Browsers

The most essential tool for a job surfer is the surfboard: a Web browser. There are a number of Web browsers available today, and most of them are free. Netscape Navigator was the first mass-market Web browser, but in the late 1990s, Microsoft aggressively marketed its Web browser, Internet Explorer, which now dominates the market.

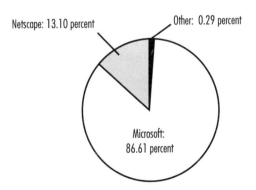

Netscape: 13.10 percent

Other: 0.29 percent

Microsoft: 86.61 percent

(Source: www.websidestory.com, February 2001)

Some folks prefer Netscape, others Internet Explorer. As you can see from the percentages in the pie chart, most prefer Explorer. In fact, Explorer is essentially the better of the two at this point—it's more stable and user-friendly than Netscape. On the other hand, Netscape has built-in e-mail, Usenet, and Web design software. The choice is yours. (Netscape wishes that you and other Web surfers had been given more of a choice in the past—the central issue in the antitrust lawsuits against Microsoft is the aggressive marketing techniques used to propel Internet Explorer's market share past Netscape's.)

Why would anyone use one of the browsers found in the 0.29 percent group? Because Netscape and Microsoft, in their brutal war for market share, have packed their browsers with numerous features and released new versions as quickly as possible. As a result, both browsers are somewhat buggy, take up a lot of disk space and RAM, and have features that you'll probably never use. The alternative Web browsers that make up much of the 0.29 percent, such as Opera and iCab, have tried to exploit these weaknesses by being smaller and more stable.

If you want to explore other Web browsers (not all of which are free), you can find a list at dir.yahoo.com/Computers_and_Internet/Software/Internet/World_Wide_Web/Browsers/.

Keep in mind that your ISP may provide support for only Netscape and Explorer, or possibly only Explorer. Check with your ISP to see which Web browsers they support. If you use any others, you'll be on your own if you run into trouble.

Using Your Browser to Stay Organized

As you find effective job sites that help you meet your job-searching goals, you'll want to bookmark them for future reference. Bookmarking is a feature available in all Web browsers that allows you to save sites (usually in a pull-down menu). It may have different names in different browsers; Internet Explorer calls it Favorites.

You should also familiarize yourself with the history feature of your Web browser. This feature gives you a complete list of all the websites that have been visited by the browser—up to a limit that's predefined in the browser's preferences. This feature is particularly useful when you want to return to a job site that you've forgotten to bookmark, but remember: Any *other* site that you may have visited within that specified time is also public domain.

Web Add-Ons

Internet Explorer and Netscape Navigator can deal with most Web content (text and pictures), but they need a little help with the fancier online sounds and animations. For example, to hear high-quality music or see video clips, you'll likely need an add-on to your Web browser. In fact, your Web-surfing experience will be much smoother if you outfit yourself ahead of time with the most commonly needed plug-ins. Our brief list below shows a few of the essential plug-ins. As you surf the Web you may discover that you need another plug-in. You'll be told what you need and where to get it on the website, so installation should be a snap.

WinZip (for Windows users only)

Many files that you get from the Web will be zipped, which is just a fancy way to say compressed. (The file's size gets shrunk so that it can be downloaded more quickly.) WinZip allows you to decompress these files so that you can use them. This program, unfortunately, is not free, even though it isn't expensive by computer software standards.

This nifty piece of software is available at www.winzip.com. You should also download and install the WinZip Internet Browser Support Add-On, available at www.winzip.com/ibrowser.htm.

A note for Mac users: You don't need software of this type because all Macs come with a program called Stuffit Expander, which performs the same function.

Shockwave

This oft-used bit of Internet software allows you to view complex, beautiful, sometimes interactive Shockwave animations. As more sites use its animations, the plug-in becomes even more essential to have. It is available for free at www.macromedia.com/shockwave/download.

Adobe Acrobat Reader

Acrobat Reader allows you view and print PDF (portable document format) documents. This format is often used for downloadable forms, and you're likely to need it at least once or twice in your job hunt. This free software is available at www.adobe.com/products/acrobat/readstep.html.

Windows Media Player, QuickTime, and RealPlayer

These three fiercely competing packages allow you to view a wide range of video and audio content on the Web. As a job surfer, you should equip yourself with all three to ensure that your computer can handle almost all audio/video stuff that you'll encounter.

QuickTime and RealPlayer are available in both free and commercial versions; the commercial versions have more features, but the free versions will provide you with the basic playback that you need.

Media Player is available at www.microsoft.com/windows/windowsmedia/en/download/default.asp; QuickTime is available at www.apple.com/quicktime/download; and RealPlayer is available at www.real.com/player.

E-mail

Once you're fully online, you may find that e-mail will begin to replace the telephone as your most important communication tool. You'll need an e-mail program first, though. Fortunately, most new computers come with a copy of Microsoft Outlook Express preinstalled.

If you don't have Outlook Express on your computer, you can download this freeware program from www.microsoft.com/windows/oe.

Another popular e-mail program is Eudora, available in both freeware and shareware versions from www.eudora.com.

Using E-mail Effectively

There's more to using e-mail than catching up with your crazy uncle Morty, who just got connected. Using e-mail is not necessarily as simple as it appears, and there are a number of ways to use it more effectively. Here are some pitfalls to watch out for so that you don't make some embarrassing mistakes.

Don't Get Too Cute

See if you can guess which of the following e-mails is more appropriate to send to a prospective employer.

RK,
IMHO, prjt 4NYC is satis.
BTW, SOS ASAP b4 pm.
TTYL,
M.

Did you give up on trying to translate that? Your prospective employer probably did. Here's the translation:

Russell Kahn,

In my humble opinion, the project for New York City is satisfactory.

By the way, I could use some help as soon as possible before this afternoon.

Talk to you later,

Mark Dulgov

If you're still unsure which version is more appropriate, the answer is the latter.

@ Avoid being overly informal. Just because e-mail allows you to communicate with the world while wearing pajamas doesn't mean that you should use the same tone with your business correspondents as you would with your family and friends. It's generally acceptable to be slightly less informal than you would be in a business letter. Pretend that you're writing an interoffice memo. Use salutations and closings, and check your messages for spelling and grammar mistakes before sending them.

@ Do not argue or attempt to settle disputes via e-mail. It's easy to convince yourself that you're having a real conversation via e-mail, but e-mail lacks the often subtle visual and audible cues that are present in a real conversation—cues that communicate whether a person is angry or sarcastic, for instance. It's very easy to misread the other party's tone and to misinterpret his or her intentions; also, people tend to be less restrained via e-mail, because unlike a face-to-face or telephone communication, e-mail conversations lack the potential for immediate negative consequences. As a result of these factors, e-mail arguments can quickly escalate. As soon as a tone becomes strained, initiate personal contact to resolve the issue.

@ One of the most serious breaches of Netiquette (online etiquette) is spamming—sending out bulk e-mail to a number of people whom you don't necessarily know. Should you somehow get hold of e-mail addresses for a number of potential employers, you may be tempted to send job queries or résumés to them. Don't do this. Most people do not like to receive impersonal, unsolicited e-mail, and any potential benefit of this strategy will likely be more than offset by the annoyance you will cause.

@ If you want to contact potential employers, try using the telephone first; a personal contact will make a much better impression. If you must e-mail someone you don't know, keep the message brief, polite, and professional, and do not attach a résumé; because many viruses these days come in the form of attachments, an unsolicited e-mail with an attachment is likely to be immediately deleted.

@ Keep your e-mail organized. As we mentioned, one way that you can stay organized is to keep separate e-mail accounts for personal and business e-mail. Within an e-mail account, you should also organize your e-mail carefully: Create folders (or mailboxes) for different topics and/or correspondents, and keep your inbox empty.

@ Erasing a message will usually erase any attachments that came with it, so copy any important attachments to a secondary location.

Transferring Files on the Internet

The Internet is, above all, a communications device. Part of the communicating that you'll engage in as a job surfer will probably include sending and receiving files. In general, when you send a file over the Internet, it's called uploading; when you receive a file, it's called downloading.

Receiving Files

Web browsers make it easy to download files. If you want to download a file from the Web it will usually be fairly clear how to do so. For example, at www.snood.com, you can download the shareware game Snood by clicking on one of the links in the section labeled Download Snood. (For maximum job-searching productivity, however, you might want to wait until *after* you've found some work before downloading this insanely addictive game.)

Share and Share Alike

Most of the software that's available for downloading from the Internet falls into one of two categories: freeware and shareware. Freeware is software that you may download and use for no charge; shareware can be downloaded for free, but you are expected to pay a (usually quite modest) fee to the author if you use it. Although shareware licensing fees are essentially unenforceable, we urge you to be a good Netizen (citizen of the Internet) and pay your shareware fees—you will encourage the continuation of the generosity of the amateur programmers who write most shareware programs.

How can you tell if a particular program is freeware or shareware? There will rarely be any mystery to it; most shareware programs will frequently and prominently present you with reminders to pay the shareware fee.

After clicking on the right place, your Web browser will either simply download the program to your desktop or ask you where on your hard drive you'd like to have the file saved.

When you download a program, you will often be downloading not the program itself but only an installer of the program. Once the download is complete, you need to locate the installer (wherever it is on your hard drive) and double-click on it. The program will then be installed.

If an individual wants to send you a file, the easiest way to do this is via e-mail. Most e-mail programs have an attachment feature that allows you to do this.

Sending Files

Sending a file to an individual is also fairly straightforward; you simply e-mail the file as an attachment.

However, if you're going to be creating Web pages for an online résumé and/or portfolio, as described in the next chapter, you'll need to be able to transfer the Web pages that you create to a Web server (a computer that allows worldwide access to Web pages). To do this, you'll need FTP software. Yes, it's yet another scary-looking computer acronym, but it's actually quite easy to learn.

FTP stands for File Transfer Protocol, and FTP software allows you to move files between your computer and other Internet-connected computers, such as Web servers. You'll need FTP software if you want to publish Web pages, such as an online résumé.

There are many different FTP software packages to choose from. One of the most popular FTP programs for Windows computers is WS_FTP, which can be downloaded from www.ipswitch.com. It comes in both Pro and Limited Edition versions. The latter has fewer functions but is free under certain conditions. If you're a Macintosh user, download Fetch from www.fetchsoftworks.com. It's not free, but it does come with a cute little animated doggie.

Word Processors

We know, word processors are not actually Internet programs. Still, the word processor will become a major component of your online tool kit. Although you may deliver résumés, cover letters, and other business correspondence via the Internet, you will often create these documents using a word processor.

Microsoft Word is by far the most popular word processing program. Although you can choose to use any of a number of other word processors, you will guarantee maximum compatibility with the rest of the world if you get a copy of Word. (It often comes preinstalled on new PCs, which is a very easy way to acquire it!)

Like many other word processors, Word also has a convenient feature that allows you save any document as a Web page, ready to be published on the Web.

Web Editors

With its Save as Web Page feature, Microsoft Word can be considered a very basic Web editor. However, there are other, much better programs specifically designed to create Web pages. You'll find this sort of program helpful when you start building Web pages of your own, such as an online résumé and portfolio.

There are two types of Web editors: HTML assistants and WYSIWYG ("what you see is what you get") editors. HTML assistants are programs that help you with HyperText Markup Language, the programming language in which Web pages are written; toolbars and pull-down menus give you access to HTML tags so that you don't have to remember them. WYSIWYG editors allow you to design Web pages graphically, bypassing HTML entirely. The Web-editing software acts as the interface between the computer language and you. (You don't ever have to see it.)

Many HTML assistants are freeware or shareware programs; you can find a list by going to www.versiontracker.com and searching for "HTML assistant." The industry-leading WYSIWYG Web editors are the commercial products Macromedia Dreamweaver and Adobe GoLive.

In addition, many text- and graphics-oriented programs (like Microsoft Word, as we mentioned) have basic Web page editing or exporting features built into them.

Chapter 10
Online Résumés

If you want to be a truly efficient job surfer, you're going to need a well-made online résumé, which allows you to deliver your résumé to potential employers instantaneously. Instead of mailing a paper résumé, you can simply e-mail the address of your Web résumé. An online résumé also demonstrates your familiarity with the Internet. A proper online résumé shows a flair for design and a comfort level with the Internet. No matter what your career is, an eye for production and Web savvy are very desirable traits.

Before we show you how to create an online résumé, let's show you what else you must have before you can create this supplemental (and serviceable) second résumé.

One Résumé, Many Formats

You should create and maintain your résumé in the following formats:

@ **Microsoft Word**
Having a résumé in Microsoft Word allows for easy e-mailing. Most employers who accept résumés via e-mail require that the résumé be in this format.

@ **Plain Text (ASCII)**
Most word processing programs allow you to save your résumé in plain text, or ASCII, format. This is useful in several circumstances. Some employment websites ask you to type in an entire résumé; pasting your plain-text résumé will allow you to do this quickly. (Pasting text from standard Microsoft Word documents usually does not work correctly.)

Some people who receive résumés in e-mail attachments may have trouble reading a Microsoft Word attachment. (Maybe your prospective employer isn't very computer-literate.) In these cases, you can copy and paste your plain-text résumé into a regular e-mail message.

@ **PDF (portable document format)**
This format allows you to create documents that incorporate both text and high-quality graphics, yet are small enough to be easily delivered via the Internet. To read PDFs, you need the free product Adobe Acrobat Reader; unfortunately, to create PDFs, you need the rather expensive software package Adobe Acrobat.

This format is used extensively in computer graphics–oriented industries, such as advertising and design, and may make a good impression when seeking work in those fields. Keep in mind, though, that the person who receives your résumé may be a not-particularly-computer-savvy human resources staffer, and therefore may not be familiar with the PDF format.

Before using any of these formats to deliver your résumé to a prospective employer, make sure that the person receiving your résumé can read that particular format. In many ways, an online résumé is the safest of the formats, because most employers will have no problem accessing a Web page.

@ **Online (HTML)**
Making yourself visible as a prospective employee on the Web can be challenging. There are literally millions of other job seekers who already have online résumés, with thousands more coming online every week. Keeping that in mind, an online résumé is still a must-have. Although it may be challenging to make yourself stand out from the masses, a well-designed online résumé can be an effective and convenient way to communicate your abilities to prospective employers.

The Plain Text (ASCII) Résumé

If you insist on using plain text, your options are limited. That doesn't mean your plain text résumé has to be, well, plain. Here are five handy tips when creating a regular résumé, whether it's for e-mail or an online database.

@ Delete any special formatting. ASCII does not understand underlining, italics, bold, bullets, links, or colors. Make sure to eliminate any of these fancy formatting features before uploading your plain text résumé. You can use asterisks or tildes (~) in lieu of the standard bullets that you see in HTML (or a Word document).

@ Maintain a page width of sixty characters. Different e-mail readers will view your résumé differently. Therefore, you have to play it safe and assume that their screen can only view sixty characters per line. If you go over this limit, you run the risk of having your text spill over to the next line.

@ Eliminate abbreviations and symbols. Don't expect everyone to understand your career-specific abbreviations. Consider that many of the viewers of your online résumé will be human relations personnel or headhunters, and they won't understand your job lingo. On the same note, never use &, %, or + in your online résumé. Spell those characters out.

@ Remove all tabs. Any tabs that you have used to help format your résumé in regular text may show up as garbled gobbledygook. Replace your tabs with spaces, and your résumé will look the same regardless of who is looking at it.

@ Review your résumé first. If you're going to e-mail a résumé to a potential employer, send a copy to a friend or to yourself first. That way you can review it first for typos, grammatical errors, and layout before anybody important sets their eyes on it. This point can't be stressed enough.

The Online Résumé

The first instinctive act of most online job seekers is to post a résumé on one of the popular Web-based job boards, such as Monster.com or Hotjobs.com. These sites offer the tantalizing promise of near-effortless job searching: Post your résumé, and thousands of employers can view it. These sites are great—and we heartily recommend them—but you can take their usefulness to another level with your own HTML.

Some job sites allow you to post your résumé in HTML format, but very few require it. When given the choice, most people choose to send their résumé in plain text. However, we recommend taking advantage of any HTML option; that's your chance to stand out.

If you create a personal account at Monster.com (which you can do by going to my.monster.com) and choose to create a résumé, you will be led through a series of screens that allow you to create a very detailed résumé. It has some limitations, however: You are limited to the categories that Monster.com gives you; you can't make the résumé look particularly snazzy (from a graphic design standpoint, all Monster.com résumés look exactly alike); and you can't attach samples of your work. In other words, Monster.com makes it rather difficult for you to communicate a sense of your uniqueness through the use of graphic design and multimedia elements.

HotJobs.com's résumé feature is even more basic and less flexible than Monster.com's. Making yourself stand out from the many thousands of résumé-posters on the site is very challenging indeed.

If you do decide to post your résumé on a job-board site, keep an eye out for the "add a URL" feature; URL stands for universal resource locator. All it means is "Web address." Like many other job-board sites, Monster.com gives you a chance to put a personal Web address on your résumé. If you have a résumé and/or portfolio somewhere else on the World Wide Web, you can use these little boxes to post a link to a much more personalized, comprehensive, and (potentially) effective advertisement for yourself. Think of this as a side door out of their cramped résumé environments into the limitless possibilities of the Internet.

Creating an Online (HTML) Résumé

Before you can enter anything into one of those Your URL boxes, though, you need to have a résumé somewhere on the Web! If you already know something about Web design, then you're way ahead of the game. For the rest of us, though, let's learn how to create a basic (yet professional-looking) résumé Web page using HTML.

Web pages are written in a simple programming language called HyperText Markup Language, better know by its acronym, HTML. Web designers create HTML documents, which Web browsers interpret and display as Web pages.

There are ways to create Web pages without learning any HTML whatsoever. A number of specialized programs, such as Netscape Composer (which is free) or Dreamweaver, are designed specifically to help you avoid using HTML at all. However, it's a good idea to know at least a little bit about HTML. It helps you to understand the Web's limitations and possibilities, and makes it easier for you to solve problems with Web pages that you may create. In many cases, it's easier to fix a minor problem with a Web page by quickly editing the HTML code rather than using a Web editor program (like Dreamweaver or Composer) to try to fix the problem.

HTML Basics

HTML is a simple computer language used almost exclusively for the Internet. The language uses "tags" to assign colors, pictures, text, and formatting for your browser. In fact, if you click View on the top navigation bar of your browser and choose Source (in Netscape, choose Page Source) from the drop-down menu, a Notepad file will open up containing all the HTML code for whatever page you might happen to be viewing. You will see that each page is formatted in HTML using a < at the start and a > at the end for each tag. A slash is used to end a format. Take a look at the following examples of basic HTML tags:

If you type this in HTML:	It will look like this:
Joe Bloggs	Joe Bloggs
Joe Bloggs	**Joe Bloggs**
<u>Joe Bloggs</u>	<u>Joe Bloggs</u>
<i>Joe Bloggs</i>	*Joe Bloggs*

That's not too difficult, right? (We told you so.) Here are a few more important HTML tags to know to make the most of your HTML résumé:

<center>Joe Bloggs**</center>**
Will center the text.

<div align=right>Joe Bloggs**</div>**
Will right-justify the text in the tag.

**
**
Will add a line break. You need this to separate the text in your résumé.

<hr>
Will add a horizontal line across the screen. This is a nice feature if you want to divide the sections on your résumé.

<font size=+1>Joe Bloggs**</font>**
Will increase the size of the text in the tag. You can also make the font size larger (+2, +3, etc.) or smaller (–1, –2, etc.).

\<ul>

Creates a bulleted list (useful for listing job duties).

\<li>

Creates a single bulleted item in a list.

Two additional tags are important to know for creating a successful HTML résumé.

> Type **\<html>** at the start of the file, and put **\</html>** at the very end. This tells the Web browser that it's looking at an HTML file.

> When you're ready for the text of the résumé, type **\<body>**, and type **\</body>** when you're done.

Okay, so now you know the basics. Already you know more than 99 percent of the Web-surfing public. Before you get too cocky, there are a few more HTML tags that can really enhance your online presence. And before you get too attached to the way anything looks on your screen, consider which browser you are using to view the page.

HTML Headings

There is a neat feature with HTML programming called meta tags, which can help your résumé get noticed. These specialized tags allow you to put text in the file that won't actually be visible in the real résumé. Why would you want this? A brief description in your résumé will allow you to pop up on more employer searches. For example, look at the following two lines of HTML code:

> **\<META NAME**=Description**CONTENT** =Description I am a terrific worker.**>**

> **\<META NAME**=Key Words**CONTENT**= HTML, Quark, Adobe, workaholic**>**

Putting the above two lines at the top of your HTML file will automatically direct employers to you if they search for the words listed under CONTENT. You can put as many words in that description as you want. The more, the merrier.

Giving your HTML résumé a title will also help to get it noticed. The title is what you see in the top left corner of your browser's screen.

```
<title>Joseph Bloggs Résumé</title>
Will add a title to your page.
```

Since the title of your HTML résumé and meta tags aren't part of the body of the résumé, they go before the **<body>** tag. Instead, these heading codes have their own tag, which is **<head>** and **</head>**. A typical introduction to an HTML résumé looks like this:

```
<html>

<head>

<METANAME=DescriptionCONTENT=
Description I am a terrific worker.>

<META NAME=Key WordsCONTENT=
HTML, Quark, Adobe, workaholic>

<title>This is my awesome résumé!
</title>

</head>

<body>
```

Links

Links are one of the most convenient features of the Internet. They allow users to hop around the Web with a simple click of the mouse, yet they're incredibly simple to create. For your résumé, linking prior jobs to their respective websites is a professional and handy way to say, "Look where I've worked." A prospective employer should appreciate your effort to make his or her research as simple as possible. Check out the following two lines of HTML code.

```
<a href= "http://www.review.com">
Review.com</a>

<ahref="mailto:joe_bloggs@review.com">Joe Bloggs
</a>
```

The first line above links Review.com to its URL. The second line links to Joe Bloggs's e-mail. Just use **<a href=**http://www.x.com**>** before the text you want to link, and a **</a>** to complete the tag. Link as many companies and references as possible. The easier you make it for employers to learn about you, the better chance you have of getting hired. Always remember to add the **<**http:// at the start of a linked URL.

Tables

Tables are the jewels of simple HTML coding. They are a bit more complicated than the other coding tags, but learning them opens you up to whole new range of options. If you look at the most professionally designed Web pages (see www.review.com/career/car_wh_HTMLresume_bloggs.html), you'll notice that résumé information is justified on both the left and the right of the same line, creating an orderly layout that covers the screen—regardless of its size. This is done with a table.

<table COLS=2 WIDTH=100%>

The above tag sets up a table that looks like this:

Column 1	Column 2

The table, like the code says, has two columns and is the width of 100 percent of the screen. You can always add more columns or make the width smaller. It's up to you. You won't actually see the border of the table unless you type the word "border" (with no quotes) after the word "table." Play around and experiment with different border sizes.

You can enter information in either cell of the table separately, and then you can alter the text inside it without affecting the other information in the table. For instance, let's say you wanted to put your last job in the left box and the dates you worked there in the right. You start entering data in a table with a **<tr>** and end the data with a **</tr>**. Then the information in the individual boxes is marked with **<td>** and **</td>** tags. Check out the code below and the table that it produces.

```
<table COLS=2 WIDTH=100%>

<tr>

<td>Tenfold</td>

<td>August 1999–present</td>

</tr>
```

Tenfold	August 1999–present

Now, if you wanted to right-justify the dates of your last job, just type in the code for it before the text. To link to Tenfold, simply add the tags with the URL. Look at the HTML below.

```
<table COLS=2 WIDTH=100%>
<tr>
<td>
<a href="http://www.tenfold.com">Tenfold
</a></td>
<td><div align=right>August 1999–present</div>
</td>
</tr>
</table>
```

That's it. You've added justification and linked to your job. If you want to change the dimension of the cells, that's easy to do. If you want a cell to be 20 percent of the screen, just add **WIDTH=20%** as part of the **<td>** tag. Or if you want the cell to be 100 pixels wide, **WIDTH=100** will do it. Look at the code below.

```
<td WIDTH=30%><a href="http://
www.tenfold.com">Tenfold</a></td>
<td><div align=right>August 1999–present</div></td>
```

Your First Web Page

Believe it or not, you already know most of what you need to know to create your first Web page. Let's try it: First, locate a text editor on your computer. A text editor is a program that creates simple text documents. On a Windows PC, you can find a text editor named Notepad under Start Menu/Programs/ Accessories; on a Macintosh, you can usually find a similar program named SimpleText in the Applications folder on your hard drive.

Open your text editor and type in the following text (we explained what each of these lines of codes mean earlier in this chapter):

```
<html>
<head>
<title>
</title>
</head>
<body>
</body>
</html>
```

Between the **<title>** and **</title>** tags, enter a title for your résumé. Your full name followed by an apostrophe and then "Résumé" is usually a good bet. It'll look something like this when you're done:

> # Susan A. Jobseeker's Résumé

Between the **<body>** and **</body>** tags, type out your résumé using the format listed earlier (bullets, bold, tables, italics, different font sizes, and more!).

Line Breaks on Web Pages

As you begin to experiment with HTML, you'll notice something strange about blank lines. Viewed in a Web browser, a document that contains this code:

```
<body>
Hello there!
Hello again!
</body>
```

will look exactly the same as a document that contains this code:

```
<body>
Hello there!


Hello again!
</body>
```

Because HTML is such a simple-minded language, it doesn't recognize the line breaks that you enter into your text editor. When you want to create a line break, you need to use the HTML tag **
**. You use it like this:

```
<body>
Hello there!
<br>
<br>
Hello again!
</body>
```

Don't forget to save your document. Be sure to note where you're saving it. It's probably easiest to save it on your computer's desktop.

You can give your HTML document a wide variety of names, but there are a few hard-and-fast rules.

- @ The name must end in ".htm" or ".html" (the latter is preferred).

- @ The name cannot contain spaces or certain nonalphanumeric characters (such as slash symbols). If you want the name to have a space in it, use an underscore (_).

- @ Generally, the file name should be kept as short as possible.

You can now view your Web page using a Web browser.

First, locate a Web browser on your computer. Most computers come pre-equipped with a copy of Microsoft Internet Explorer and/or Netscape Navigator.

Use the Web browser's Open a Local File feature to open your HTML document. This feature has different names in different browsers, but it's usually called something like Open File.

Before you create your first Web page, you may want to use our sample résumés as guidelines. This will give you a head start on creating your own online résumé!

Sample Online Résumés

Take a look at the way a regular résumé can look in plain text—just the regular, standard résumé on the Web. Look below or at www.review.com/career/car_wh_htmlresume_bloggs_bad.html.

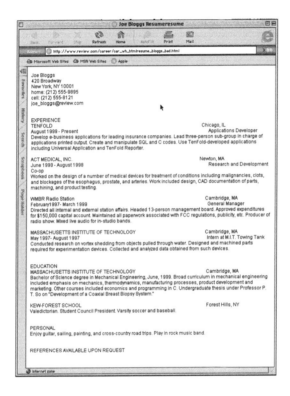

Now compare that plain (old) résumé with a polished online résumé. See below or at www.review.com/career/car_wh_htmlresume_Schmo.html. Notice how much more striking it is and how it fits the screen no matter what size you set it to. Check out the hyperlinks, which allow potential employers to learn about the companies you've worked for with one simple click. They'll appreciate the better presentation, and they'll value the ease with which they can research your background.

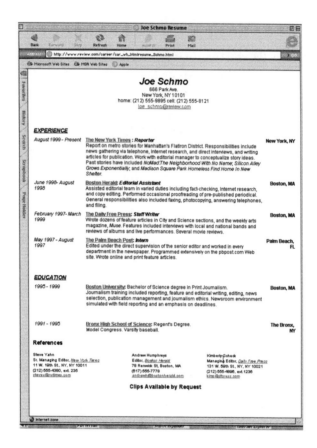

As you can see, the ability to apply advanced graphic design concepts can greatly enhance the inherent attractiveness of an online résumé. With a well-designed online résumé, it's possible to get the flavor of your personality across—and to provide a much more palpable sense of what you can offer potential employers.

Feel free to steal the HTML from the sample online résumé above. Put in your own information and pretend you did it from scratch; we won't tell. Be careful to copy this text very precisely; the smallest typo could drastically change how the page looks when you view it in a Web browser.

Take a look at how we've used the tags described earlier in this chapter. As you can see, these tags surround the text that you want to format. You'll soon see the dazzling results in your browser.

Getting Your Résumé Online

In order for you to share your résumé with the world, it needs to be copied onto a Web server—a computer that's connected to the Internet all the time and that's dedicated to hosting, or publishing, Web pages. There are two flavors of Web servers for you to choose from: free and commercial.

There are a number of popular free Web-hosting sites, including geocities.yahoo.com and www.tripod.com. An extensive list with reviews can be found at www.collfreewebhosting.com. These sites have the advantage of being easy to use, often requiring no knowledge of HTML or of FTP software. On the downside, most free Web-hosting sites offer only a very small amount of disk space—not enough to host a respectable portfolio. Also, advertisements will appear on every page that you create, and these sites can be excruciatingly slow to access. All in all, a free Web-hosting site may not communicate the most professional image, even if the price can't be beat.

Commercial Web servers allow you to buy Web space for a monthly or annual fee. Most ISPs offer Web-hosting packages. Some companies specialize in Web hosting and don't even offer Internet access. You can find hundreds of commercial Web-hosting options by doing a Web search for "website hosting."

Commercial Web-hosting sites are usually much faster than free sites and give you total control over the appearance and organization of your pages. You can also usually buy a cool personalized Web address (such as www.susansresume.com). To take advantage of these sites, though, you will need to learn some basic Web design and HTML skills, and you'll need to use FTP software. (If you remember from our Sending Files section on page 168, file transfer protocol software is free software that you can download from the Web and then use to send files to various places on the Internet—such as Web-hosting sites!)

Commercial Web space can be pricey, but you can economize by looking for hosting packages that offer only the features that you need: sufficient disk space (20 to 30 MB should be enough to begin with), the ability to affordably add additional space, and domain-name registration services. In regard to the last item, don't be fooled by sites that merely offer you a "personalized Web address"; you may wind up with an address such as myportfolio.bobswebhosting.com. You need real domain registration, which allows you to choose any available Web address you want.

Do You Already Have Web Space?

You may already have Web space and not know it. Many Internet access accounts include a small amount of Web space; the space can be increased by paying a bit more per month. Contact your Internet service provider to find out about this.

Beyond the Basics: Learning Intermediate and Advanced Web Design

Once you have your online résumé up and running, you will no doubt be tempted to tweak it, update it, and give it a more attractive look. This is a good thing, as long as you don't neglect other aspects of your job search! There are many things that you can add to your online résumé, such as striking graphics, which we'll discuss in the next chapter.

In order to spiff up your online résumé, you're going to need to build up your Web design skills beyond what we've taught you here. The best place to learn about Web design is—you guessed it—on the Web. Do a Web search for "Web design tutorial" or "HTML tutorial," and you'll find many sites that can help you in this area. One of the best (and most amusing) intermediate Web design tutorial sites is www.webpagesthatsuck.com.

Many commercial Web editors also have design tutorials and Web page templates built into them; Web design how-to books are another option for improving your Web design skills.

Finally, Remember What You're Selling

It pays to put some time and thought into the graphic design/presentation aspect of your online résumé. Clumsy or ugly Web design may make a worse impression than not having a personal Web page at all. Put yourself in the position of a potential employer. What would a poorly designed online résumé communicate to you? It's a bit like showing up for an interview in a stained suit that's two sizes too small.

Chapter 11
Creating an Online Portfolio

Once you've started your online résumé, you may want to add samples of your work for prospective employers to peruse. Adding a few samples can change your online résumé into an interactive online portfolio.

The purpose of an online portfolio is the same as that of a physical portfolio: to showcase samples of your work for potential employers. If you've ever worked in a creative or media-related field, then you may already have a handsome bound folder full of writing samples or a cumbersome, coffee table–size imitation-leather bag full of drawings and/or printouts. An online portfolio fulfills the similar function of a traditional portfolio but with several interesting and advantageous differences.

- @ You can include a variety of nonpaper-based media such as animation, music, and programming samples.

- @ You can easily present your work in different ways for different audiences.

- @ An online portfolio is much easier to carry—just put the Web address of your online portfolio onto your résumé and/or business card.

Don't assume that you can't compile a portfolio just because your work is not creative. If you've produced work that can be in any way printed, transferred onto videotape or CD, photographed, or put onto a computer, then you have material to include in a portfolio. It's almost always possible to include some graphically attractive representation of the work you've done, no matter what your work may be.

In perhaps the most exciting development of all, it is now possible to include a wide array of multimedia (animation, sound, video, etc.) elements in an online résumé. With a little bit of imagination and the right tools, you can include such elements in your online portfolio. If they're done well, these multimedia elements rarely fail to impress.

Gathering Your Materials

When deciding what to include in your online portfolio, you should keep in mind many of the same considerations that apply to physical portfolios.

- @ Decide on a specific focus for your first portfolio (you can compile additional portfolios later). Ask yourself what kind of work you would like to do and in what environment you'd like to do it. The resulting focus can be as broad as "television production assistant" or as specific as a particular position at a particular company.

- @ If you don't have enough existing material from school or previous jobs—and some of you might not have *any* such material—then create some. Be sure to dig through your archives, filing cabinets, and hard drives, and even contact previous employers if possible. You may have at some point in your career produced material that fits your focus.

- @ Cut your compiled material down to a manageable size. The goal is to keep your portfolio as concise as possible; include only your best work, and make sure it is small enough to be quickly evaluated but still effectively showcases your skills.

  This may mean different things in different contexts. You should include the pieces that you think will be most impressive to the particular companies or market to which you're targeting your portfolio. But the main point here is this: Don't just put *all* of your work into your online portfolio—don't force potential employers to wade through material that may be of little interest to them. People who are responsible for hiring are almost always very busy. Don't make them spend half an hour sifting through your portfolio, fascinating though it may be.

- @ Tailor your portfolio to the particular market in which you're seeking work.

The Internet provides remarkable flexibility and convenience in building a portfolio. Consider a person seeking work in both writing and photography.

This person could put up a single portfolio page, like this:

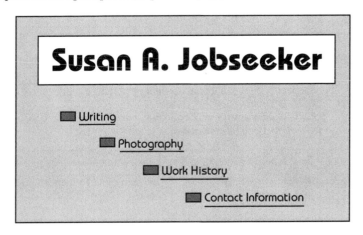

This method forces potential employers who are looking only for a writer to wade through the photography section of the portfolio—and for employers who are hiring only photographers to wade through the writing section. Not only does this waste employers' time—and the more time you make them waste, the more you risk losing their interest—but it also may give the impression that you are not wholly focused or specialized in one area. While some employers might consider multiple areas of expertise to be a selling point, others—perhaps most— might pass you over for someone equally qualified who specializes in the skill they're interested in.

The Internet gives you the flexibility to present multiple versions of your portfolio, each tailored to a specific market. For example, Ms. Jobseeker could create two versions of her portfolio, one for writing and one for photography. She could then direct potential employers to one or the other.

You will probably be tempted to include material that you are particularly proud of. But just because it's good work doesn't necessarily mean that it's the sort of work that your potential employer is looking for. When compiling your portfolio, try to put yourself in the position of a prospective employer, and ask yourself, "Would this particular piece convince me that this person is right for the job?"

Design and Organization

When laying out your online portfolio, there are a couple of tips to keep in mind.

- Make the portfolio easy to understand. Include an introduction, an index with the title of each piece, and comments for each piece (attach these comments to the appropriate pieces).

- If possible, include testimonials and recommendations related to the work that you're showcasing.

You may be tempted to include quotes of recommendation as part of your online résumé, testifying to the quality of your work and to your reliability and worth as an employee. Inclu

ding such generic recommendations is a bad idea. Potential employers are generally going to want to call your references anyway—and it's much better that they should hear words of praise directly from the source. By including these kinds of comments about yourself, you could make yourself seem immodest (and perhaps a bit desperate).

It can be very effective, however, to include specific comments about the work that's in your portfolio. If the people for whom you did the work can express their satisfaction with it—and, even better, be specific about how that particular work helped them to achieve their business goals—this can be a powerful selling point to others who may be in the market for your services.

Preparing Your Materials

Once you've decided what materials to include in your online portfolio, you need to prepare the materials for your website. If the material is already on your computer in one form or another, then you're halfway there. If not—if the material exists only in printed format or on videocassette, for instance—then you will need to digitize the material. That means you need to find a way to transfer it onto your computer.

Digitizing Text

If the material exists only on paper and you don't want to type the text in manually, then you'll need to scan the material into your computer. For text documents, you will need the following equipment:

@ A good scanner (600 dpi or better)

@ OCR (optical character recognition) software

Without OCR software, your scans will arrive on your computer as images, not as word processing documents. An image format does not allow for easy editing or for copying and pasting of the document's contents, and it's usually quite hard to read. This should definitely be avoided.

Once you've used the scanner and OCR software to get your documents onto your computer, you'll need to edit the documents, because OCR software is not 100 percent accurate. Depending on the quality of your scanner and which OCR software you're using, it'll be more like 98 percent—meaning that two words out of every 100 will be wrong. You'll need to track those words down in the document on your computer and correct them.

Also, OCR software usually does not deal very well with nontext elements on a printed page such as tables and graphics. This, too, will require editing in your word processor to correct.

Most OCR software has built-in features designed to help you get the best possible accuracy from your scans and to correct problems in the resulting word processing document. Read the software's manual carefully to learn about these features.

Digitizing Graphics

In order to transfer your noncomputer-based graphics work onto your computer, you will need

@ A scanner

@ Image-editing software

Since you are scanning only for the Web, a top-of-the line scanner is not required. Most scanners can handle only $8\frac{1}{2}$-by-11-inch or $8\frac{1}{2}$-by-14-inch documents. If you want to scan a larger piece, you have five options.

@ Locate a larger scanner.

@ Take a photograph of the work and scan the photo.

@ Take a digital photograph of the work and transfer the photo onto your computer.

@ Reduce the image on a photocopier and scan it (which will result in a loss of image quality, however, especially for photographic images).

@ Scan the piece in sections and reassemble the sections in Adobe Photoshop.

You will need Adobe Photoshop to edit your scanned document, because scans rarely, if ever, come out perfect. Photoshop is the industry standard for image-editing software, but you can use any such software as long as it allows you to save your images in GIF or JPEG format, which are the only two formats that are viewable with all Web browsers.

Digitizing Video

In order to transfer your work from videocassette to a computer, you'll need

@ An analog video capture card

@ Video-editing software

When selecting a capture card, keep in mind that you may want to output your computer-edited work back to videocassette; in that case, make sure that you get a capture card that has that capability.

If your work is in digital video format, then you'll need a FireWire (also called IEEE 1394) card instead of an analog video capture card. As with any other digitizing task, you'll want to edit your work once it's been transferred onto your computer.

Digitizing Audio

If your audio work is not already on your computer, you will need

@ A way to connect your audio device (minidisc player, DAT player, etc.) to your computer

@ Audio-editing software

Most computers have either an "audio in" or "microphone" ministereo jack, so all you will probably need to connect your audio device to your computer is a cable to connect to that jack.

If your audio work is on a CD, then (assuming that your computer has a CD drive) all you will need is CD-ripping software.

Optimizing Your Computer-Based Material

Once all of your portfolio pieces are on your computer, you will need to edit the material to make it presentable. When editing your material for uploading to your online portfolio, there are two major points to keep in mind.

@ You should make the material as attractive, impressive, and comprehensible as possible.

@ You should make the individual file sizes of your documents as small as possible. The less disk space your portfolio pieces take up, the less time it will take a prospective employer to download them. Try to keep your file size below 1 MB.

Finding What You Need

All of this digitizing and editing requires specialized hardware and software. If you can't find the appropriate tools, a sales associate at a good computer store should be able to help. Just don't let yourself get talked into shelling out big bucks. Educate yourself, evaluate your options, and decide what you really need. And keep in mind that copy shops and graphic service bureaus might be able to meet your needs more economically, especially if you need to use the services only once or twice.

Optimizing Text

If written material is going to be part of your portfolio, you have a number of different options for preparing it.

@ **Microsoft Word**

More likely than not, your material is in Microsoft Word format. If not, it's relatively easy to copy and paste the text into Word and save it as a Word document.

You can upload copies of your Word documents directly to your website, but this has several drawbacks. Not all prospective employers have a copy of Word or a compatible word processor. Even if they do, their version may be different than yours, which can cause strange things to happen when they try to open your Word documents. Also, Word documents are often replete with hidden codes and information. This may allow others to view, for instance, all of the deleted text and past revisions from your documents. Unless there is a compelling reason to use Microsoft Word format for your online text documents, you should choose one of the other options.

@ **HTML**

Word and some other word processors have an option to save any document as a Web page (or HTML document), which can then be uploaded to your portfolio site. Use what you've learned in chapter 10 to tweak your HTML document.

@ **PDF**

The PDF (portable document format) gives you total control over the fonts and general look of your documents; it's essentially like taking a snapshot of your document, except that those viewing the resulting PDF file can search, copy, and paste the text. If maintaining the exact look that your documents have on your computer's screen is important to you, then PDF is the best choice.

Virtually anyone on any kind of computer can read PDF documents. If you don't already have the necessary software, you can go to www.adobe.com and download it—it's called Adobe Acrobat Reader, and it's free. PDFs can be created from almost any kind of document, as long as the document contains only text and graphics. However, you'll need a copy of Adobe Acrobat (which costs several hundred bucks) to create PDFs.

Optimizing Graphics

If you're a graphic artist who works on computers, then most of your work will probably be in either Adobe Photoshop or Adobe Illustrator format. You could simply upload these files to your portfolio site, but there are two major drawbacks to using Photoshop or Illustrator files in your portfolio. First, the file sizes are huge compared to your other options. Second, anyone who wants to view them must have Photoshop or Illustrator. Instead, choose one of the compressed formats below. Photoshop, Illustrator, and most other computer graphics programs will allow you to save in these formats (or at least in the first two).

@   **GIF**
    This format is the best choice for line drawings, cartoons, or any graphic that does not contain a huge number of gradients of colors. (Photographs almost always contain color gradients.)

@   **JPEG**
    This format is the best choice for photos and anything with gradients of colors. When saving a document as a JPEG, you'll be given the option to set the "quality level"—usually from 1 to 10 or 1 to 100. The higher the quality level, the larger the file; the lower the quality level, the smaller the file, but the cruder it will look. This loss of quality will usually manifest itself in the form of fuzzy "halos" around the edges of objects; text usually becomes unreadable. We recommend choosing a quality level in the intermediate range.

@   **PDF**
    Once again, this is a great choice for complex compositions including both text and graphics. (This is especially useful in advertising and graphic design work.)

    Most Adobe products will allow you to save in PDF format directly from the product. When this is not possible, you will need to use the Adobe Acrobat software package.

Optimizing Video

If any of your work is already in the form of digitized (computer-based) video, then it's probably in one of the following formats:

@ QuickTime (.mov)

@ Video for Windows (.avi)

@ MPEG (.mpg)

Any one of these formats will be fine for inclusion in an online portfolio, but in general, QuickTime is your best bet. It is easily readable on both Windows and Macintosh computers (which are very common in creative industries) by downloading the free QuickTime Player from www.apple.com/quicktime. It also provides good image quality with relatively small file sizes.

If you're working on a Macintosh, Cleaner from Terran Interactive Software (www.terran.com/cleaner) is a great software tool for minimizing video file sizes while maintaining high image quality.

Optimizing Audio

If you have digitized audio files that you'd like to include in your online portfolio, the MP3 format is your best bet. It can provide CD-quality sound while keeping file sizes small. (The only exception to this might be in the case of electronically composed music, where the MIDI format is the industry standard.)

Optimizing Web Work

If you want to include Web design work that you've done, the simplest thing to do is to include a link on your portfolio website. Beware, though: Unless you have full control over it, work that you've done in the past may be taken offline or updated. To protect yourself, always keep a copy of Web design work that you've done.

If you haven't kept a copy on your computer, or if the online version looks better than your copy as a result of design work done by others, you can download your Web pages (including graphics and other content) using a program such as PageSucker.

If you choose to include Web pages that include work by others, you should first get permission from them. Then you should credit the collaborators in your portfolio.

Online Hosting Options

Once you have your material compiled, optimized, and ready to upload, you need to find a place to upload it. Choose one of three basic options: the free or commercial Web space discussed in the previous chapter or specialized portfolio-hosting sites.

You can upload your material to a site that hosts portfolios, such as www.elance.com or www.portfolios.com. These sites will charge you a monthly fee for this service. The advantage is that you usually don't need to know anything about Web design or HTML. The disadvantage is that you don't have total control over how your portfolio pages will look; usually, you will have to put your material onto pages that are predesigned by the website.

De-digitizing

As useful as online portfolios can be, there are still many circumstances in which you need a traditional physical portfolio. Perhaps the employer does not have Internet access, has a slow connection, or is simply not computer-savvy. Plus, physical portfolios are a requirement in some interviews.

When you're working on a physical portfolio, you may want to include computer-based material. Depending on the format of your work, you may have to create printouts, burn a CD, or output your work to videotape.

When "de-digitizing" your work, you'll want to achieve the highest-quality output possible. You will need specialized hardware and software to get the best results. Your local print shop or service bureau can help with some of this, and manuals included with the hardware can also provide guidance.

If you have computer-based work that you'd like to include in a physical portfolio, you should create a hard copy of your work. In the case of images, you will want to create high-quality printouts. If you don't have a high-quality printer, spend the extra money in a local print shop or service bureau; it's worth it. If you have access to a CD burner, you can also burn a CD of your work. (This presupposes that your interviewer is computer-literate.) When burning CDs, keep the same design rules in mind that you would use with an online portfolio. The CD needs to be easy to navigate, and the material needs to be well presented. You may want to include a Readme file explaining how to use the CD.

Unlike an online portfolio, a physical portfolio involves performing: Usually, you will need to present your physical portfolio in an interview. Be sure to practice presenting your portfolio first so that your presentation will seem natural, relaxed, and professional. And keep it short, or you risk losing the interviewer's interest!

Copyright Issues

The growing popularity of online portfolios raises a host of thorny copyright issues. Following the simple rules below will help keep you out of trouble.

Don't Rip Off Others

Make sure that you own everything you're including in your portfolio. In many cases, the employer for whom you produced a particular piece of work owns it. You'll need to get explicit written permission from the owner(s) of your work before uploading it to the Internet.

Don't Get Ripped Off by Others

If you are the owner of a piece that you're putting on your portfolio site, you'll want to protect yourself from potential thievery. Here are some tips.

- Incorporate copyright information into each of your pieces. It's easy to add copyright information to each of your Web pages. If you want to protect yourself, do it.

- Use the lowest quality digitizing that you can accept. For images, keep the image dimensions small and the quality less than top-notch; this will discourage theft.

@ Consider using small sample portions of your material instead of entire works. For example, if your portfolio includes video or animation work, you might include just a few seconds of the work—enough to show your talents—rather than an entire piece, which could be stolen.

@ Add watermarks to images. Watermarks are available in Adobe Photoshop and other image-editing programs; they superimpose a semitransparent, embossed-looking image of your design over an image. Your watermark image can be simply a text-only copyright notice or your name, or it can include graphic elements.

Compiling Multiple Portfolios

If you have chosen more than one focus for your job search, you will want to compile more than one portfolio. This concept seems simple enough when applied to physical portfolios, but how should you go about creating multiple online portfolios? The answer depends on which Web-hosting option you've chosen.

@ If you've chosen free Web hosting, the easiest thing to do is simply to sign up for multiple free accounts with different user names.

@ If you've chosen a portfolio-hosting site, you should be able to create multiple portfolios showcasing different areas of talent. Consult the technical support for the particular site.

@ If you've chosen commercial Web space, put each of your portfolios into a different directory. You could create separate directories for a writing portfolio and a photography portfolio, which would allow you to use two different Web addresses. For example, www.susanjobseeker.com/actor and www.susanjobseeker.com/director would separate the portfolios.

Get Help and Get Inspired

Remember that the best place to learn about computers and the Internet is on the Internet. Having trouble with scanning? Go to your favorite search engine and do a search for "how to scan." Want to learn how to transfer your work from videocassette to the Web? Search for "how to digitize video." And because one of the most powerful learning tools for any task is to check out how others have done it before you, try searching for "online portfolio." You will find thousands of existing online portfolios to inspire you.

Finally, keep in mind that, just like an online résumé, an online portfolio is not a magic key to a job—it's a tool to add to your tool kit of online job-search strategies.

Chapter 12
Attracting Employers' Attention

Once you have an online résumé and/or portfolio, the next issue is what, exactly, to do with it. You should not expect potential employers to find your online presence on their own. Instead, think of your online presence as an enhancement to your traditional résumé and portfolio. You wouldn't leave your résumé and samples of your work posted on bus stops and bulletin boards around your town, would you? No, you would probably try to get your résumé and portfolio into the hands of people who are interested in hiring someone like you. The strategy should be the same with your website: you should try to get its address into the hands of people who might hire you.

Getting Your URL into the Hands of Employers

When trying to get your Web address into the hands of potential employers, keep in mind that a personal contact, rather than an e-mail, is best. Don't believe that you can run your entire life (or even the job-searching part of your life) via the Internet. E-mail from a stranger can be lost, overlooked, or easily deleted; a personal conversation will be remembered. You're better off sharing your Web addresses verbally once you've established a communication with the other person.

It can be awkward to give someone your Web address verbally, however, unless it's a remarkably simple one (such as www.myportfolio.com); this is one reason why it's great to have a very simple Web address. Unfortunately, for most Web addresses, you may well find yourself reduced to spelling out the address character by character. This is usually an annoying experience for both parties ("Right after the L, you should put a forward slash—no, a forward slash, not a backward slash—it's on the same key as the question mark . . . "). Rather than putting yourself through this painful process, you should use a different method of conveying your Web address.

@ If you're in a face-to-face meeting, write your Web address down. Better yet (to avoid misinterpretation of handwriting), present a business card or a résumé with the Web address highlighted.

@ If you're communicating via phone, ask for an e-mail address to which you can send your Web address or a fax number to which you can send a résumé that includes your Web address.

Put It on the Network

Another way to disseminate your Web address is to show your site to friends, colleagues, and acquaintances. You never know who might be in a position to further your job search. This kind of networking can be one of the most effective methods of job searching. If your website is impressive enough, they may pass it on to a potential employer via word of mouth.

Are *They* Searching for *You*?

Prospective employers may try to find employees by using Web search engines—those indispensable sites such as www.yahoo.com and www.google.com that help you find stuff on the Internet. There are several things that you can do to make it easier for search engines to find your website. First of all, when you're creating your pages, be sure to use meta tags, as described on page 176. Search engines use meta tags to help people find your site. For example, if you have a Key Words meta tag of "photographer," a Web search for "photographer" should list your page.

There are a few rules of thumb to follow when adding meta tags.

@ In the Description meta tag, make your description as, well, descriptive as possible. The entire contents of this tag may be displayed on a search results page, so try to make your description as intriguing as possible to potential employers.

@ In the Key Words meta tag, make your key words as specific as possible. For example, if you're a comedy screenwriter, don't just put "screenwriter"; put "comedy, screenwriter, writer, scripts, screenplay, funny, play, hilarious, writing." The more key words you use, the more visitors you'll wind up attracting.

@ Make sure that you put meta tags on *all* of your pages, not just your main page. Some search engines will index every page of your site, which could either bring you higher up on the search results pages or give you more listings on those pages. Either way, the tags increase your chances of being found by a potential employer.

Adding meta tags alone isn't going to do the trick, though—it's like hoping that your business will flourish just because your phone number is in the Yellow Pages. So don't just sit there; go register your site with those Web search engines. By registering with a particular search engine, you guarantee that your site will show up (somewhere) on the results pages if someone does the right kind of search.

A good way to get started is to go to www.searchenginewatch.com. This useful site not only lists all of the major search engines but also gives you tips on how to register your site with each one. The process varies from search engine to search engine—it can be as simple as submitting your Web address, though most will ask for more extensive information. Just make sure that you read the site-submission instructions carefully (look for a link named something like Submit Your Site or Add a Site). Among other useful information, these instructions will also often tell you how long it will take for your site to be added to the search engine's database—a process that can sometimes take several weeks.

It's possible to purchase software that will do the grunt work of site submission for you, submitting your site to hundreds or even thousands of search engines. You should probably save your money for other endeavors; once your site has been submitted to the major search engines, other search engines will pick it up anyway.

Here's a trick that may help you show up more prominently on search engine results pages: Pretend you're an employer, go to a search engine site, and do a search for someone like you. Take a look at the top results. If you can mimic (without plagiarizing or misrepresenting yourself, of course) the content of these pages, then your site may also rise to the top of the results pages. Try looking at the HTML code for these top-ranked pages (most Web browsers allow you to do this) and see what meta tags they use.

Keep in mind that different search engines have different methods of generating search "hits" on your site. Some will simply use the information that you give when you submit your site; others will use your meta tags; some will index all of the words on your pages; some will use a combination of all of these methods. You can learn more about the nitty-gritty of how search engines do what they do at www.searchenginewatch.com/webmasters/work.html.

Another way to attract attention to your site is to submit your address to sites dedicated to your particular profession. For example, Playbill.com offers a site-linking service; if you're an actor, you should definitely avail yourself of it. Rather than fishing for attention from the entire online world, you're advertising your site directly to your peers. Check with your favorite profession-related site to see if they have a service like this.

Web rings can also give your site some exposure. Web rings are informal groups of subject-specific websites. In order to join, you register your site with a particular Web ring, and then place a link on your page to the Web ring. Although Web rings are generally fan-oriented, there are rings dedicated to acting, stagecraft, and other entertainment-related professions. Check out www.webring.org to register your site or to find out more about Web rings.

Don't forget to put your Web address on every piece of printed material that's related to your career: flyers, résumés, head shots, business cards, whatever. You'll probably be pleasantly surprised by the results—often, people who wouldn't learn more about you in the real world will take the time to check out a website.

Use Your Time Wisely

The process of submitting your website to search engines is time-consuming, and your time might be better spent on other aspects of your job search. There are also companies that will offer to submit your website to dozens of search engines for a fee or sell you software that purports to do the same thing. Some services will even assert that they can help you get a "high ranking" on these search engines—that is, that your website will show up near the top of results pages. Unless you have money to spare, don't waste your time with these services. No matter how high you rank in search engines, prospective employers rarely use search engines to shop for employees. See chapter 13 for more efficient job-hunting resources.

Chapter 13

Internet Job-Hunting Resources

The Internet is chock-full of resources for job seekers. There are sites that list open positions, sites that allow you to contact employers, sites that will give you general job-hunting tips, and even sites that provide real-time interviews. So where do you start?

Job Boards

Most people think of job hunting on the Web and immediately think of job-board sites, where employers post online help wanted ads. Think of these sites as more convenient versions of your local newspaper's help wanted section. Job-board sites have some significant advantages over newspapers. First, the job postings online are searchable, which saves a lot of time and effort. Second, online job ads are usually quite detailed because the Web does not impose the same kind of space constraints that newspapers do.

Job-board sites can give you a good sense of what the job market is like; you can easily see what sort of skills are being sought by employers, which industries are hiring in your area, and so on. Among the most popular general-interest job-board sites are

@ www.monster.com

@ www.hotjobs.com

@ www.jobsonline.com

@ www.vault.com

@ www.careerbuilder.com

@ careers.yahoo.com

@ www.americasjobbank.com

@ www.flipdog.com

@ www.jobbankusa.com

@ www.headhunter.net

Freelancers' Sites

There are a few sites that cater specifically to the needs of people who prefer contract work rather than full-time employment. Freelancing can be a great lifestyle if you have a skill that allows you to do it. Freelancers must deal with a number of complex financial issues that full-time employers take care of for their employees, such as setting aside money to pay income tax and securing insurance and retirement funds. And, of course, freelancers must search out contractors to give them work. In return for this extra effort, however, freelancers often enjoy the freedom of working wherever and whenever they want.

Freelancers' sites simplify the contractor-search aspect of a freelancer's life by offering online contract job postings. Two of the most popular freelancer's sites are www.elance.com and www.guru.com. But www.elance.com has one major drawback: Only subscribers get access to the higher-paying contract jobs; www.guru.com has no such restrictions.

Industry-Specific Sites

You can significantly narrow your job search by visiting sites that have job postings for the particular industry in which you're interested. The Sites section of this book, beginning on page 213, will cover this area in great detail.

Individual Employer's Sites

One efficient online job-search strategy is to target specific employers and visit their specific websites to get employment information. Not all employers have actual job postings on their sites, but it's definitely worth looking. If you don't know an employer's Web address, you can, of course, search for the company's site using your favorite search engine. If you still can't find it, you can always use that reliable nineteenth-century technology—the telephone. Call the employer's main number and ask if it has have a website.

For sites that don't have job postings, you can at least educate yourself about the companies that you're targeting.

Usenet

Before the World Wide Web exploded in popularity in the mid-1990s, Usenet was one of the hottest spots in cyberspace. It has now been pushed aside because the Web is easier to use and because Usenet is text-only—no graphics or multimedia elements.

There are a number of different ways to access Usenet, but the simplest way is via the Web at groups.google.com. Many of the hierarchies (the links beginning with "alt," "biz," etc.) have job groups in them. Try this:

1. From groups.google.com, click on the alt link.

2. From the alt page, pull down the menu in the upper left-hand corner, and select the alphabetical range within which the word "jobs" falls.

3. On the resulting page, click on the "alt.jobs" link. You'll be taken to a page that has job listings and (at the top of the page) further subgroups with even more job listings

Due to the somewhat esoteric nature of Usenet, its job postings are heavily slanted toward highly technical, and especially computer-related, jobs. Other jobs may be found here as well, however, so it's worth a look.

Support, Advice, and Job Training

Finally, there are sites that, while they may not offer actual job listings, will help you become a better job surfer. These sites offer job-searching advice and information, sort of like an online employment center.

Many job sites have features like this built into them; Monster.com's subsite content.monster.com is one example. Two good sites that specialize in support and advice are www.jobsmart.com and www.jobhuntersbible.com.

Chapter 14
Moving Forward

The rest of this book will help you use the Internet to advance your job search. However, you should continue to research non-Internet-based strategies. You're already pursuing one of them by reading this book. In this book, you'll find sites that will in turn suggest more real-world job-search strategies. By exploring this complex interrelationship between the real world and the virtual world, you'll be empowered to search for jobs in ways that you never imagined—and that will give you an edge over the conventional job searcher.

Keeping Up with New Internet Resources

Once you've taken your first steps toward being a successful online job searcher, remember that the Internet is constantly shifting. By the time you read this, there may be some great sites and useful resources that aren't in this book because they didn't exist at the time of its printing. In order to keep up with these new developments, you should do some creative surfing. Periodically search for job-related sites on www.yahoo.com and your other favorite search engines.

Part Four
The Sites

How to Use This Section

While looking through the website reviews in this section, keep in mind two important facts about this crazy thing we call the Internet: It is mind-bogglingly huge, and it changes every microsecond. As a result, this list gauges the quality and usefulness of sites with a proverbial grain of salt. While it cannot aspire to be either as comprehensive or as entirely up-to-date as a search you might do online at this very second, it can promise to be a tailor-made set of search results compiled just for you, the intrepid media/entertainment juggernaut in the making. Among the types of sites you'll find here are

@ Most of the very best websites for arts and entertainment–industry job surfers

@ A representative sample of most of the various different kinds of arts and entertainment websites that are out there

@ A sampling of unusual or hard-to-find websites that might be of interest to you

The sites are rated using a five-star system. A given rating is neither an overall evaluation of the worth of a particular site nor a commentary on its aesthetics; instead, the rating reflects our evaluation of how useful the site will be to you in your search from a both a research and a job-opportunity perspective.

There's no doubt that some of the lower-rated sites will improve at some point, just as it's true that the better sites may consolidate with others, lose quality, or disappear for some other reason. All prices for membership and services provided by the sites are subject to have changed since the time they were researched. Also, it's inevitable that sites that should be in here aren't—because they didn't exist as of this writing.

In a way, this all part of the fun—or at least, the wonder and mystery—of the Internet. As it constantly changes and grows, no one can claim (accurately, at least) to be an infallible authority on any aspect of it. To a certain extent, every Internet user is on his or her own, and must explore and sift to through it all to find coveted information. Let this set of reviews give you an edge.

Keep in mind, though, that the Internet is above all a communication device, and there are lots of people out there in cyberspace who will help you in your quest to find the best sites for your employment-search needs. Some of those people are your friends and colleagues—if you know people who are or who have been in a similar employment situation, don't hesitate to ask them which sites they have found to be helpful. Most of your helpers, though, will likely be people you've never met, such as the people who manage Yahoo!, Google, and other portal, search engine, and link sites. You and your unknown helpers, and all of us, are all part of the wired global village now—and that's exactly what makes it possible for you to surf for jobs in the first place.

Review Breakdown

Each listing is divided into the following parts:

The Pitch: The site's usually short, punchy motto.

They Say: The site's description of itself. Note that this is *not* written by us—it's taken verbatim from the site (that's why it's in quotes).

Wallet Impact: If you have to pay to access anything on the site, this'll tell you what you're paying for and what it'll cost you.

The Skinny: Our review of the site.

Rating: Nothing NC-17 here—this is our rating of the usefulness of the site to you in your job search. We use a five-microphone scale, with zero microphones being "completely useless" and five microphones being "visit it, bookmark it, use it."

Most Useful For: We know you're a busy person, so check out this line for a quick summary of what you might use this site for.

101 Hollywood Blvd.

@ ***The Pitch:*** "FREE Job Listings For Actors and Film Makers"

@ ***They Say:*** "If you're producing a movie or music video you can advertise here for free. If you're available to work on student films or small independent movies you can advertise here for free."

@ ***Wallet Impact:*** None

@ ***The Skinny:*** Very amateurish, rudimentary, not to mention relentlessly self-promoting (of the owner's film projects). Credible job postings and useful advice are pretty much nonexistent. "This board's a joke" is a typical posting.

@ ***Rating:***

@ ***Most Useful For:*** Finding out how many clueless people there are out there who would really like to be working in the film industry.

4entertainmentjobs.com

www.4entertainmentjobs.com

@ **The Pitch:** "Jobs, Internships, and Career Information in the Entertainment Industry"

@ **They Say:** "4entertainmentjobs.com is the premiere Internet-based employment source giving members access to hundreds of current jobs and internships from the largest names in the highly competitive entertainment industry. Our job listings cover a wide variety of fields, from Film/TV to Sports/Recreation."

@ **Wallet Impact:** $24.95/month (or $99.95/year) to access job listings and post a résumé

@ **The Skinny:** The site promises hundreds of job listings, but user confidence in the quality of the listings is adversely affected by the clunky design of the site; if the quality of the listings is at all similar to the quality of the design, then the service is overpriced. It also lacks extras such as industry information, career advice, and links to other sites. This may be part of a "no frills, job listings only" site strategy, but it suggests that the producers of the site are not trying very hard.

@ **Rating:**

@ **Most Useful For:** Finding an entertainment-industry job.

ABC/Walt Disney Studios New Talent Programs

www.abcnewtalent.disney.com

@ **The Pitch:** "A variety of programs to help aspiring individuals in the fields of writing, directing, and production"

@ **They Say:** "ABC New Talent Development is proud to provide a variety of fellowship and internship programs to help aspiring individuals in the fields of writing, directing, and production. We are searching to discover new creative voices and to employ culturally and ethnically diverse talent."

@ **Wallet Impact:** None

@ **The Skinny:** This site provides, clearly and briefly, details about the ABC/Disney scholarship, grant, internship, and fellowship programs in writing, directing, and production. These prestigious opportunities should make this a key site for anyone looking to break into these areas of the entertainment industry.

@ **Rating:**

@ **Most Useful For:** Finding out how to apply for a fellowship at ABC/Disney.

Academy of Television Arts and Sciences

www.emmys.org

@ **The Pitch:** "Devoted to the advancement of telecommunications arts and sciences"

@ **They Say:** "The Academy of Television Arts & Sciences— founded one month after network television was born in 1946—is a nonprofit corporation devoted to the advancement of telecommunications arts and sciences and to fostering creative leadership in the telecommunications industry."

@ **Wallet Impact:** None

@ **The Skinny:** Once you get past the orgy of self-congratulation that is the essence of the Emmys (and this site), there's some great information here about the Academy's other activities, including seminars and other educational programs. You may be particularly interested in this internship-info page: www.emmys.org/foundation/internships.htm.

@ **Rating:**

@ **Most Useful For:** Learning about the educational opportunities offered by this prestigious organization.

Academy of Video Arts and Sciences

academyofvideoarts.com

@ *The Pitch:* "Dedicated to the unity and betterment of the independent film and video maker"

@ *They Say:* "AVA stands for quality and integrity. Its primary goal is promoting the interests of the independent film and video producers of tomorrow. AVA is an information and communications source for the entrepreneur of film and video business, as well as for the newcomer and student of the industry."

@ *Wallet Impact:* None

@ *The Skinny:* This Wisconsin-based site has an earnest pro-indie-film agenda and an impressive-sounding name, but there isn't much here besides a manifesto and pitches for a book and a small film festival. Both are the brainchildren of the site's creator, semilegendary independent filmmaker Bill Rebane.

@ *Rating:*

@ *Most Useful For:* Finding out how to get your film entered into the Silver Street International Film Festival.

Actors' Equity Association

www.actorsequity.org

@ **The Pitch:** "The union of American theatrical actors and stage managers"

@ **They Say:** "Actors' Equity Association is the labor union representing over 40,000 American actors and stage managers working in the professional theatre. For eighty-eight years, Equity has negotiated minimum wages and working conditions, administered contracts, and enforced the provisions of our various agreements with theatrical employers across the country."

@ **Wallet Impact:** None

@ **The Skinny:** This should be one of the first stops on the Web for any working or aspiring stage actor or stage manager. The site has extensive (even exhaustive) information about the union and stage industry in general, and an unparalleled job list (the Casting Call section). Unfortunately, though the site is quite well designed, it seems to need a little help on the technical side: the Questions and Casting Call sections are periodically out of order.

@ **Rating:**

@ **Most Useful For:** Finding a stage job; learning about Actors' Equity rules and benefits.

AFTRA—American Federation of Television and Radio Artists

www.aftra.org

@ **The Pitch:** "The Official Website of the American Federation of Television & Radio Artists"

@ **They Say:** "The American Federation of Television and Radio Artists (AFTRA) is a national labor union affiliated with the AFL-CIO. Its headquarters are in New York City, and there are thirty-six local offices throughout the country. AFTRA represents its members in four major areas: 1) news and broadcasting; 2) entertainment programming; 3) the recording business; and 4) commercials and nonbroadcast, industrial, educational media."

@ **Wallet Impact:** None

@ **The Skinny:** This AFL/CIO-affiliated union represents (mostly) radio and TV broadcasters. The site doesn't offer much in the way of information on getting a job, but its information on benefits and rights could be invaluable once you do get some work.

@ **Rating:**

@ **Most Useful For:** Finding out about your union benefits.

Alt.SHO.com

@ **The Pitch:** "Alternative Media Festival™. Expose Yourself. Submit—You Know You Want To."

@ **They Say:** "Submit your Sho [this site's term for a short film, animation, or game]. Working on an animation short? An interactive game? Bring it on. If it's creative and you can upload it, go for it. You could win $30,000 and a chance to work with us."

@ **Wallet Impact:** None

@ **The Skinny:** This entertaining short-film-and-animation contest site has the serious cash and power of media behemoth Viacom behind it. Anyone can enter the contest; it doesn't cost anything to submit your work, and it appears that winning an award from this site could actually live up to its hype of being a stepping-stone to bigger and better things. Take a look at the past winners before submitting your work—this is quality stuff, so make sure that your submission is top-notch and well polished.

Women should note that this "alternative media festival" now includes a women-only awards category, "herSho: a 'digital diva' celebration."

@ **Rating:**

@ **Most Useful For:** Getting exposure for your high-quality digitized short film or animation work.

AOL Time Warner Careers

tw.tmphosting.com

@ **The Pitch:** "One of the most exciting career sites on the Web today"

@ **They Say:** "Here, at your fingertips, is an easy way to explore employment opportunities at the world's first Internet-powered media and communications company—AOL Time Warner."

@ **Wallet Impact:** None

@ **The Skinny:** As befits one of the largest and most powerful media companies in the world, this site features state-of-the-art design and functionality, and includes many hundreds of current job and internship postings for locations all across the country, in a wide variety of media-related job categories.

@ **Rating:**

@ **Most Useful For:** Finding a job at AOL Time Warner, whose holdings include America Online, HBO, New Line Cinema, Turner Broadcasting, Warner Brothers, and more.

Apple's iMovie Gallery

www.apple.com/imovie/gallery/

@ **The Pitch:** "The iMovie Gallery plays host to great iMovies [short films created using Apple's iMovie digital editing software] from all over the world."

@ **They Say:** "When we put the magic of Hollywood inside every Mac with iMovie, thousands of people used it to create their own movies. We're proud to present some examples of what they've done. We hope you enjoy these movies as much as we did."

@ **Wallet Impact:** None

@ **The Skinny:** Every new Macintosh computer comes with the easy-to-use video-editing software iMovie. Get yourself a digital video camera, and voila, you're a filmmaker. Submit your iMovie to Apple's iMovie Gallery and you could be a marginally famous filmmaker at the least; at most, who knows who might discover you?

@ **Rating:**

@ **Most Useful For:** Getting some high-class Web exposure for your best iMovie-edited film; getting inspiration from other amateur digital filmmakers.

ASCAP—American Society of Composers, Authors, and Performers

www.ascap.com

@ **The Pitch:** "The World's Most Visited Professional Music Website"

@ **They Say:** "ASCAP is a membership association of more than 120,000 U.S. composers, songwriters, and publishers of every kind of music and hundreds of thousands worldwide."

@ **Wallet Impact:** None

@ **The Skinny:** This elegantly designed site offers a wealth of information about the music business. It has especially useful features in the Inside Music and Your Career sections, including information on workshops and other development opportunities. If you're a professional musician, you should not fail to thoroughly explore this site.

@ **Rating:**

@ **Most Useful For:** Learning all about the music business.

Asian American Journalists Association

@ **The Pitch:** "A nonprofit organization [for Asian American journalists] with approximately 1,700 members"

@ **They Say:** "Our mission is three-fold: 1) to encourage Asian Pacific Americans to enter the ranks of journalism; 2) to work for fair and accurate coverage of Asian Pacific Americans; and 3) to increase the number of Asian Pacific American journalists and news managers in the industry."

@ **Wallet Impact:** None

@ **The Skinny:** Besides providing news and information about Asian Americans in journalism, this nonprofit site also provides details about the numerous scholarships, internships, and similar opportunities offered by the AAJA. Aspiring Asian American journalists should not fail to check this out.

@ **Rating:**

@ **Most Useful For:** Finding out about scholarship and internship opportunities for aspiring Asian American journalists.

ASIFA—International Animated Film Association

asifa.net

@ **The Pitch:** "The International Animators Home Page"

@ **They Say:** "The Association is founded in the firm belief that the art of animation can be enriched and greatly developed through close international cooperation and the free exchange of ideas, experience, and information between all who are concerned with animation."

@ **Wallet Impact:** $20–$33 per year for membership, which includes (among other benefits) Web space to showcase your work

@ **The Skinny:** This relatively new site has limited information about animated film festivals and access to some interesting short animated works. Unfortunately, the design of the site does not make it easy to find the animations or a reason to pay the annual membership fee, nor does it really get across exactly what it is that ASIFA does.

@ **Rating:**

@ **Most Useful For:** Getting relatively cheap Web space for showcasing your animation work; getting inspiration from the site's gallery of short animations (which are well hidden inside the Art Zone section of the site, under the title "stART Gallery").

ASIFA Hollywood

www.asifa-hollywood.org

@ **The Pitch:** "A California Nonprofit Organization Devoted to the Advancement of the Art of Animation"

@ **They Say:** "The International Animated Film Society: ASIFA-Hollywood is a California nonprofit organization established over twenty years ago to promote and encourage the art and craft of animation."

@ **Wallet Impact:** None

@ **The Skinny:** The designers and content editors at ASIFA's Hollywood branch website could teach the AFISA.net's developers a thing or two—the site is simple and direct, and includes useful features such as info about screenings and ASIFA-Hollywood's awards ceremony. It also features an excellent links section. Potential members are given clear reasons why joining this support/educational group could be a good thing. If you're an animator working in the Hollywood area, you should check this site out.

@ **Rating:**

@ **Most Useful For:** A variety of resources for animators in the Los Angeles area.

AtomFilms

@ **The Pitch:** "Get into our shorts"

@ **They Say:** "The Mission: To be a leading entertainment provider for businesses and consumers worldwide. The Company: AtomShockwave offers world-class entertainment, spanning games, films and animations, driving distribution across the Internet, mobile devices, television, airlines, and more. AtomShockwave is a pioneer and innovator in technology and content."

@ **Wallet Impact:** None

@ **The Skinny:** AtomFilms is one of the most ambitious and extensive short-film showcase sites on the Web. It's not merely extremely entertaining, but it is one of the best showcase opportunities on the Internet if you make short live-action or animated films. Strangely, the submission guidelines are well hidden; click on Help, then on Submit Films.

@ **Rating:**

@ **Most Useful For:** Getting an opportunity to present your work on one of the most popular short-film sites; getting inspiration from other filmmakers.

B-roll.net

@ **The Pitch:** "The Television News Photography Website"

@ **They Say:** "A full service page devoted to TV News Photography, we supply information, tips, and discussions on Photography, News, and the entire Television Medium. This is interactive, so we need your thoughts and opinions to make it work."

@ **Wallet Impact:** None

@ **The Skinny:** A near-perfect example of what a career-specific site should be. B-roll.net offers detailed technical advice, industry news, lively discussion boards, and a good job board.

@ **Rating:**

@ **Most Useful For:** Gaining access to much of what a working or aspiring TV news photographer would want to know; finding a job in this part of the TV industry.

BackStage.com

@ **The Pitch:** "The complete online performing arts resource"

@ **They Say:** "Performing arts professionals, from all disciplines, turn to BackStage.com every day to check out the latest news, casting notices, and editorial pieces from the best minds in the business."

@ **Wallet Impact:** None

@ **The Skinny:** This is the single best site on the Web for the acting profession. It is chock-full of news, advice, useful information, extensive job listings, and a lively discussion board. Featuring the combined resources of both *Back Stage* and *Back Stage West,* BackStage.com has become an unparalleled online performing arts resource, providing the most complete coverage of opportunities in the performing arts community.

@ **Rating:**

@ **Most Useful For:** Finding a way to succeed as an actor.

BareWitness

@ **The Pitch:** "San Francisco Improv Web Movies"

@ **They Say:** "BareWitness is a collective of filmmakers, actors and writers who combine their talents to create short, original, dramatic films that explore contemporary issues."

@ **Wallet Impact:** None

@ **The Skinny:** This site showcases movies made by an ensemble cast (most of whom are current or past students from the Phil Bennett Theatre Lab in San Francisco) using "small, lightweight, digital cameras and wireless microphones." It's a good example of people posting their work on the Web.

@ **Rating:**

@ **Most Useful For:** Inspiration for those desiring to create and Web-post short films.

TheBigChance.com

@ **The Pitch:** "This is YOUR Big Chance."

@ **They Say:** "Have you ever dreamed about getting your script produced or perhaps starring in a feature film? Maybe you just want to work in the Entertainment Industry? Are you convinced you have some real talent but have no clue how to get started? If this sounds like you, we may just have 'TheBigChance' that you've been looking for."

@ **Wallet Impact:** $50 to submit your script, music, headshot, etc.

@ **The Skinny:** The creators of this site promise that if you send them $50, they'll give you a shot at becoming a star—they say they will produce your movie or CD themselves. Afterward, they will present you with the Brooklyn Bridge as a personal gift. Everything about this site, including the fact that it hasn't been updated in more than a year, should indicate to you that signing up with them would be just like setting a $50 bill on fire, only more pathetic.

@ **Rating:** 0

@ **Most Useful For:** Getting an education in the fine art of separating naïve showbiz hopefuls from their money.

Billboard.com

www.billboard.com

@ **The Pitch:** "The number one newsweekly for the music, video, new media, and entertainment industries."

@ **They Say:** "Billboard is not a trade publication. Rather, Billboard is Billboard, a completely unique chronicle of the music, video, and home entertainment industries that invented its own job over a century ago even as it pioneered the concept and parameters of ethical trade journalism. Our mission is to provide maximum new information in the timeliest possible fashion to help our readers do better business. Moreover, since our audience includes a wealth of experts, we aim to offer them surprising and insightful advance knowledge they couldn't possibly locate anywhere else."

@ **Wallet Impact:** $14.95/month plus per-report charges to access in-depth content and databases, as detailed on this page: www.billboard.com/billboard/members/fulldetails.jsp

@ **The Skinny:** The online version of the leading music-industry magazine is a must-read in its free version and a comprehensive research tool in its pay version. Given the relatively high price tags on the pay features, you probably won't want to pay for them unless, for instance, you're a music reviewer who needs frequent access to information on the history of popular music—or your employer is picking up the tab. Once you do so, however, a large portion of the history of the music industry in America since World War II is at your fingertips in the form of sales charts dating back almost fifty years and articles from the magazine dating back about a decade.

@ **Rating:**

@ **Most Useful For:** Keeping up with music-industry news; researching the past and present of the industry.

Black Broadcasters Alliance

www.thebba.org

@ **The Pitch:** "One of the greatest broadcast organizations in the world"

@ **They Say:** "The BBA is comprised of owners and professionals who want to see equality and real opportunity for African Americans employed in the broadcasting industry and/or who are in pursuit of ownership."

@ **Wallet Impact:** None

@ **The Skinny:** This site does little to inspire confidence in the BBA—amateurish design and broken links abound, and there is surprisingly little content. The job board consists of nine links to various broadcasting companies' job pages.

@ **Rating:**

@ **Most Useful For:** Scratching the surface (but just barely) as a resource or history of African Americans in the broadcasting industry.

BlackTalentNews.com

@ **The Pitch:** "The Entertainment Industry Trade Publication"

@ **They Say:** "Blacktalentnews.com is the only website focused solely on black entertainment. From useful content, related resources, expert advice tips, and interactivity, it is the world's first website dedicated to bringing aspiring, beginning, and veteran black entertainment industry professionals together in a virtual community devoted to providing tools, access, information, opportunity, professional resources, and a networking forum for the exchange of ideas and information."

@ **Wallet Impact:** None

@ **The Skinny:** A good guide to what's going on in African American Hollywood; includes a one-of-a-kind black-film-oriented job board. Unfortunately, some of the promised features, such as the expert advice and a black theater section, are missing.

@ **Rating:**

@ **Most Useful For:** Keeping up with Hollywood news about, or of interest to, African Americans.

BFCA—Broadcast Film Critics Association

@ **The Pitch:** "The World's Largest Film Critics Group"

@ **They Say:** "The Broadcast Film Critics Association is the largest film critics organization in the United States and Canada, representing 142 television, radio, and online critics. Our collective membership is the primary source of information for today's entertainment consumers. The very first opinion a moviegoer hears about new releases at the multiplex or the art house usually comes from one of our members."

@ **Wallet Impact:** None

@ **The Skinny:** This site is oriented more toward the consumers, rather than the producers, of film reviews. Although there are a few (no doubt interesting) members-only message boards, these are off-limits for all but the high- (or at least medium-) profile film critics who make up the majority of the organization.

@ **Rating:**

@ **Most Useful For:** Finding out what the critics are recommending and getting a feel for the different criteria entertainment critics use when judging a film.

The Blair Witch Project

@ **The Pitch:** "You can't go forward . . . until you have gone back."

@ **They Say:** "Artisan Entertainment's Book of Shadows: Blair Witch 2 delves deeper into the legend of the infamous Blair Witch and the unspeakable evil wrought in the Black Hills near Burkittsville, Maryland."

@ **Wallet Impact:** None

@ **The Skinny:** This site originally served as the first hugely successful Web-based promotion for a major film release. The creators of Blairwitch.com used the site to stir up online interest in advance of the 1999 release of their $35,000 film, *The Blair Witch Project.* This strategy reaped remarkable rewards; it helped turn the film into one of the major box office successes of the year. Although the site now contains mostly a promotion for the video and DVD release of the 2000 sequel, *Blair Witch 2* (which was much less successful than the first film), some flavor of the original, intriguing content that lured horror fans to multiplexes in 1999 can be found in the Legacy section.

@ **Rating:**

@ **Most Useful For:** As an example of a successful independent-film promotion site, and a reminder that a sequel rarely is as good as the original.

Broadcast Careers Network

www.careersnetwork.com

@ **The Pitch:** "If you're interested in working in radio, college is a waste of time and money. . . .You need experience in commercial radio!"

@ **They Say:** "Broadcast Careers Network represents thousands of working professional broadcasters at radio and television stations from coast to coast who want to lend their knowledge and experience to train the next generation of broadcasters in certain belief that radio is taught best by working professionals in real operating radio stations."

@ **Wallet Impact:** It costs nothing to peruse the site, but it costs $3,950 to sign up for the apprenticeship program that it's advertising.

@ **The Skinny:** Although the apprenticeship program offered by this site sounds promising, the amateurish design, hard-sell approach, and lack of prestigious endorsements or affiliations would have to make one wonder whether the relatively high price tag is justified.

@ **Rating:**

@ **Most Useful For:** A place to begin the prudent practice of cautiously investigating the world of broadcast-career education.

Broadcast Education Association

www.beaweb.org

@ **The Pitch:** "Educating Tomorrow's Electronic Media Professionals"

@ **They Say:** "The Broadcast Education Association is the professional association for professors, industry professionals, and graduate students who are interested in teaching and research related to electronic media and multimedia enterprises."

@ **Wallet Impact:** None

@ **The Skinny:** This nonprofit organization's site is great for anyone involved in the teaching of broadcasting. It provides a wide breadth of information and services covering the academic side of the broadcasting world. Prospective broadcasting students should make a beeline for the Scholarships & Grants page at www.beaweb.org/injobs1.html. On the downside, the site apparently suffers from seemingly haphazardly scheduled updates—perhaps a symptom of its nonprofit status—and its academic, as opposed to professional, focus. The academic job-listing page is regularly updated, for example, while the industry jobs page is not.

@ **Rating:**

@ **Most Useful For:** Applying for a broadcast education scholarship; learning about the world of broadcast education.

theBroadcaster.com—The Broadcast Training Program

@ **The Pitch:** "A nonprofit 501(c)3 organization formed to provide training opportunities to minority college graduates in radio/television news reporting and news management"

@ **They Say:** "Selected applicants are placed in radio and television stations across the country as TRAINEES. Once they receive their training, we help them find permanent employment within the broadcast industry (although most are hired at the stations that train them)."

@ **Wallet Impact:** It costs $55 for students or "freshman journalists" to retrieve a list of trainee programs and receive numerous other benefits described here: www.thebroadcaster.com/MEMBER.html.

@ **The Skinny:** It's hard to imagine a website of more importance to minority college students or graduates who are interested in pursuing a career in broadcast news. There are a plethora of free services, including a good job bank. On the other hand, this site may unleash a plague of pop-up advertising windows on your computer, which, together with its desire to extract $55 from each student who uses its services, leaves it to the user to judge how user-friendly it really is.

@ **Rating:**

@ **Most Useful For:** Aspiring minority news broadcasters looking to break into the business.

Career Connection

@ **The Pitch:** "Radio TV Film Music Recording School: Career Connection, your job vocational training resource"

@ **They Say:** "Do You Want to Work in Radio, TV, Film, or Music Recording? Career Connection provides on-the-job training in major radio/TV stations, recording and film studios."

@ **Wallet Impact:** No cost to peruse the site, but you'll have to pay for this service—about $5,000, according to one article at www.career-connection-inc.com/recording/articles-spinrecords.html.

@ **The Skinny:** This apprenticeship program is intriguing, and the site comes with a boatload of testimonials. However, the site is so hype-heavy that it's reminiscent of an infomercial, and many important details about the program aren't available on the site—but the site encourages you to order a free video or CD-ROM "for more information."

@ **Rating:**

@ **Most Useful For:** Exploring a fee-based apprenticeship program.

CareerPage

@ **The Pitch:** "The Job Bank for the Broadcasting Industry"

@ **They Say:** "The National Job Bank serves broadcasters and those seeking employment in the industry. The members of BEDA, the Broadcast Executive Directors Association, are the managers and chief executives of state broadcast trade associations throughout the U.S. and Puerto Rico. We created this site to enable job seekers to find jobs in the exciting field of broadcasting, and to allow our member radio and TV stations to post their job openings at a central location."

@ **Wallet Impact:** None

@ **The Skinny:** This bare-bones site has one function only, to list broadcasting jobs. Given this narrow focus, one would expect to find more than the hundred-odd listings that are currently here. On the other hand, most of the listings are good and quite recent.

@ **Rating:**

@ **Most Useful For:** Finding a job in the broadcasting industry.

Careers in Music

@ **The Pitch:** "The world's largest independent music college and the premier institution for the study of contemporary music"

@ **They Say:** " An environment designed to provide the most complete learning experience possible, including all of the opportunities and challenges presented by a career in the contemporary music industry . . . in such areas as composition, performance, and recording/production, and . . . the informed business decisions necessary to career success."

@ **Wallet Impact:** None

@ **The Skinny:** This site is intended for the use of students at Boston's prestigious Berklee School of Music, but there's nothing stopping you from using it. It may be the most comprehensive site on the Web about music careers. While there are no job listings on the site, you'll find that and more on the sites in the links section (at the bottom of the Music Career Resources page).

@ **Rating:**

@ **Most Useful For:** Finding out about music careers; exploring music career-related links.

Casting Daily

@ **The Pitch:** "Empowering the Talent Community Since 1996"

@ **They Say:** "Since 1996 Casting Daily has been helping talent professionals take control of their careers. The Casting Notices members' area of Casting Daily provides the most up-to-date and comprehensive casting notices available anywhere."

@ **Wallet Impact:** $19.95/month to access listings

@ **The Skinny:** Casting Daily is one of the best actors' job sites on the Web. It has an attractive, professional design, and hundreds of job listings. The site offers portfolio and e-mail services as well. Given the quality of the site, the price for membership services is fair.

@ **Rating:**

@ **Most Useful For:** Finding acting and dancing jobs.

Casting Society of America

@ *The Pitch:* "Casting is extremely complicated."

@ *They Say:* "With over 360 members nationwide and in Canada, CSA is an organization of professional Casting Directors from all fields: feature films, television, and theatre. Our goal is to provide a standard and level of professionalism within our field on which the entertainment community can rely."

@ *Wallet Impact:* None

@ *The Skinny:* This site has some good information about the career of casting director, but the low-rent design of the site makes it look like a backwater of the entertainment industry.

@ *Rating:*

@ *Most Useful For:* Finding out about the career of casting director.

creativePLANET Communities

@ ***The Pitch:*** "Online Resources for the Film and Video Professional"

@ ***They Say:*** "The creativePLANET communities produce online resources for film and video professionals. Through news, interviews, feature articles, jobs, discussions, and directories, the websites connect the creative community."

@ ***Wallet Impact:*** None

@ ***The Skinny:*** CreativePLANET is the motherlode of quality, profession-specific, film-industry sites. All of its member sites are worth visiting, but the best of them are:

Cinematographer.com (for cinematographers)

DesignInMotion.com (for motion graphic-design professionals)

DirectorsWorld.com (for directors)

EditorsNet.com (for film and video editors)

PostIndustry.com (for post-production professionals)

VFXPro.com (for visual-effect professionals)

Each of these sites features a slick but easy-to-navigate design; lots of news, updated daily, of interest to the community that it serves; some fascinating, professionally moderated discussion groups; an excellent links section; and, best of all, a large number of current job postings (shared between the sites). And it's all free!

@ ***Rating:***

(We'd give it more if we could.)

@ ***Most Useful For:*** Finding a film- or video-production-related job; learning all about the careers covered by these sites; keeping up with career-related news.

Crewcall-Jobs.com

www.crewcall-jobs.com

@ **The Pitch:** "Nationwide film and television crew job referrals"

@ **They Say:** "Spend your downtime enjoying life, not constantly looking for work. Whether for union, non-union or breaking into the business, we provide links to a constant flow of film and TV work."

@ **Wallet Impact:** $39.99/month to access job listings

@ **The Skinny:** The amateurish design of this site sets the stage for its Crew Call service, in which subscribers can call a voicemail box and access crew job listings (or receive them via e-mail). The service promises "30-60+ job calls a month per category," which sounds good—but based on the subpar Web design, you should proceed with caution before investing in the service.

@ **Rating:**

@ **Most Useful For:** Finding out how to sign up for the Crew Call job listing service (after wading through bad Web design to find the information).

Crew Net

@ **The Pitch:** "The Most Trusted Film/TV Career Resource Since 1994"

@ **They Say:** "Welcome to Crew Net, the industry standard employment resource for the film and television industry on the Internet. Since 1995 we have been in the business of providing quality job leads to below-the-line [crew] professionals. If you currently work, or are looking to work in Feature Films, Commercials, Music Video's, or Television Shows, The Crew Net Job Hotline could be one of the most important career investments you could make."

@ **Wallet Impact:** $19.95/month to access job listings

@ **The Skinny:** The same people who run the Casting Daily site produce this site, which lists entertainment-industry crew jobs. Like Casting Daily, Crew Net has an easy-to-navigate, professional design, hundreds of job listings, and an e-mail service.

@ **Rating:**

@ **Most Useful For:** Finding a crew job.

D.Film

@ **The Pitch:** "Reinventing the medium"

@ **They Say:** "The D.FILM Digital Film Festival is a traveling and online showcase of films made with this powerful new filmmaking technology."

@ **Wallet Impact:** None

@ **The Skinny:** D.Film aims to promote the medium of digital film while entertaining the masses and inspiring and supporting those who want to make their own digital films. You can get started by making your own short film with the ultra-cool Macromedia Flash–based animation tool, D.Film Moviemaker. The site also sponsors a traveling digital-film festival, to which you can submit your work.

@ **Rating:**

@ **Most Useful For:** Learning about the world of digital film; getting Web exposure for your short films.

Disney Careers

@ **The Pitch:** "We are the dreamers and doers; a cast of thousands commited to making magic and making dreams a reality."

@ **They Say:** "Our people represent a broad spectrum of experience and cultural heritage, and we want to add to this diverse wealth of talent. So, come along and take a look at the jobs we have to offer. This is your invitation to explore Who We Are and start on the road to making your own dreams a reality at Disney."

@ **Wallet Impact:** None

@ **The Skinny:** The exemplary corporate-jobs site is easy to use—and the ever-growing Disney empire is always hiring, so you'll find a good number of jobs here.

@ **Rating:**

@ **Most Useful For:** Finding a job at the Walt Disney Company.

EIDC—Entertainment Industry Development Corporation)/ Los Angeles Film Office

www.eidc.com

@ **The Pitch:** "A precision machine"

@ **They Say:** "You need to film in L.A. That means you need to know what EIDC does. You have ten seconds. You read this. You keep your job. You still can't sell your script, but you know how EIDC, a precision machine, serves the industry you're a slave to. The entire process is laid out before your eyes—from film permitting to location assistance. You no longer care about your pathetic script. You've seen greatness at work. You venerate the EIDC logo; an icon of splendor."

@ **Wallet Impact:** None

@ **The Skinny:** This film commission site for the Los Angeles area offers a fascinating and comprehensive look at what goes into movie production planning: the permit, regulatory, traffic, and similar considerations. It also provides public records about L.A.-area shoots and an education program.

@ **Rating:**

@ **Most Useful For:** Learning about production planning in general; preparing to film in the Los Angeles area.

Electronic Media

@ **The Pitch:** "The broadcast, cable, interactive weekly"

@ **They Say:** "This is the website of Electronic Media, the weekly newspaper of broadcast, cable, and interactive media."

@ **Wallet Impact:** None

@ **The Skinny:** This is a good general-interest TV-industry news site, with the latest on executive job shifts, controversies in the industry, news on ratings patterns, and so on. It has a clean, professional design and a small job board, whose usefulness is somewhat limited by the fact that the listings don't include posting dates.

@ **Rating:**

@ **Most Useful For:** Keeping up with TV-industry news.

EntertainmentCareers.Net

www.entertainmentcareers.net

@ **The Pitch:** "Entertainment Jobs and Internships"

@ **They Say:** "Entertainment Jobs, Internships, and Career Information in the Entertainment Industry. Hundreds of job opportunities available."

@ **Wallet Impact:** None

@ **The Skinny:** This site doesn't have the slickest design or the most features, but it does deliver where it counts: it has a large number of job listings, and it's entirely free. It also has a good links section, and a nifty internships-only section.

@ **Rating:**

@ **Most Useful For:** Finding a job in the entertainment industry.

Entertainment Employment Journal

@ **The Pitch:** "Entertainment Jobs & Internships, Film, TV, Cable, Radio"

@ **They Say:** "Entertainment Employment Journal is a biweekly national career magazine focusing exclusively on careers in the creative, professional, production, and technical areas of the entertainment industry. Since 1992, it has featured over 12,000 industry jobs and over 170 career articles and interviews with industry professionals."

@ **Wallet Impact:** $39 for three months, $67 for six months, or $109 for twelve months; you can choose between an online membership or receiving the print version

@ **The Skinny:** Despite the ugly, unimaginative, and hard-to-read Web design, this is an entirely professional, straightforward, and useful site, brought to you by the publishers of the U.S. Directory of Entertainment Employers (see review later on in this section). It features from 100 to 200 job postings at any given time.

@ **Rating:**

@ **Most Useful For:** Finding a job in the entertainment industry.

EntertainmentJobsNow.com

www.entertainmentjobsnow.com

@ ***The Pitch:*** "EntertainmentJobsNow.com Posts Hundreds of Entertainment Jobs Daily!"

@ ***They Say:*** "Are you tired of searching endlessly for a great job in the entertainment industry? EntertainmentJobsNow.com provides you with hundreds of employment opportunities, thousands of industry contacts, discussion board, chat room, career advice, and news in every major area of the entertainment industry."

@ ***Wallet Impact:*** $29.95/month to access job listings

@ ***The Skinny:*** The Members Area features a large job list and some useful extras, including industry links, news, and career advice, but the substandard site design raises questions about the publisher's commitment to quality. Also, the price tag is high compared to similar sites.

@ ***Rating:***

@ ***Most Useful For:*** Finding a job in the entertainment industry.

Film Music Magazine

@ **The Pitch:** "The professional voice of music for film and television"

@ **They Say:** "*Film Music* magazine is the only trade publication specifically designed for professionals in the film, television, and multimedia music business."

@ **Wallet Impact:** None

@ **The Skinny:** *Film Music* magazine features industry news, pieces on both established and up-and-coming artists in the world of film music, investigative reporting specifically designed to serve film- and television-music professionals, and a calendar of events of interest to the film- and television-music community. Check out this site's FAQ section first for some serious resources of film-music information. The passage of several months between site updates may prompt you to subscribe to the print version of the magazine. Still, the Film Music Directory section has some useful information.

@ **Rating:**

@ **Most Useful For:** Learning about the film-music industry.

Film Music Network

@ **The Pitch:** "Bringing the film music community together"

@ **They Say:** "The Film Music Network, sponsored by Film Music Media Group, was established for professionals in the film music business. It serves to provide you with opportunities for one of the most essential ingredients of success in this business today—networking. The Film Music Network exists for only one purpose—to facilitate communications and networking among professionals in all aspects of the film music business. We are not an advocacy group, union, guild, or society—we are simply an organization created to improve communications and networking among film music professionals."

@ **Wallet Impact:** $14.95/month in order to access job listings and obtain other benefits

@ **The Skinny:** This site does a credible job of covering the film-music industry, and features news, discussion boards, and a job board. It's difficult to evaluate the usefulness of the members-only features, though, since no samples or other information are provided. Also, the site is difficult to navigate, and several links to free features are broken. On the other hand, there is an excellent and extensive Career Advice and Information section.

@ **Rating:**

@ **Most Useful For:** Learning all about the film- and TV-music industry, including how to break into it.

Film, TV, and Commercial Employment Network

www.employnow.com

@ **The Pitch:** "Auditions, Casting Calls, Resources, and Information for Actors and Production Personnel"

@ **They Say:** "The Film, TV, & Commercial Employment Network provides important information and resources [in the form of books and pamphlets] for individuals interested in pursuing a career in the entertainment industry. It's for beginners as well as seasoned professionals. Information and resources are provided for many areas both behind and in front of the camera."

@ **Wallet Impact:** A plethora of publications and services can be ordered at www.employnow.com/orderfor.htm.

@ **The Skinny:** The "resources" promised on the site's front page, whose design is not very professional, consist of various books and pamphlets about breaking into the acting industry. You can even buy pre-addressed mailing labels to talent managers and agents. Your money would be better spent at Amazon.com on non-self-published books about the acting profession. Nor does it seem prudent to join the seventeen brave souls who are paying $65 per year to post their portfolios on this site.

@ **Rating:**

@ **Most Useful For:** Evaluating the misdirected entrepreneurial spirit and poor Web design skills of this site's creators.

Filmmaker.com

@ **The Pitch:** "The Filmmaker's Home Pages"

@ **They Say:** "Simply put, this site is intended as an online resource for filmmakers on a budget."

@ **Wallet Impact:** None

@ **The Skinny:** This outstanding site for novice and independent filmmakers follows a format pioneered by the computer-technology site Slashdot.org—moderators working for the site post news items, and visitors can comment on them. Filmmaker.com also has some great extras, including reviews of film schools, some excellent links, and a section called DUMPS, which warns readers away from some typical student-film clichés and self-indulgences. The site is generally so useful and well run that it's puzzling more people aren't participating in its discussions.

@ **Rating:**

@ **Most Useful For:** Reading reviews of film schools; keeping up with news of interest to aspiring filmmakers; exploring interesting links; participating in discussions with other filmmakers.

Filmmaking.net

@ **The Pitch:** "The Internet Filmmakers FAQ"

@ **They Say:** "Reference and community for the new and independent filmmaker."

@ **Wallet Impact:** None

@ **The Skinny:** This site features handy how-to articles about the film biz, book reviews, equipment information, bulletin board discussions, and lots of useful FAQs. This is a good place to buy books, ask questions, and learn the laws of independent filmmaking.

@ **Rating:**  +

@ **Most Useful For:** But of course, the FAQs! This site is one of the best sources on the Web for learning about the craft of filmmaking.

Gameplan!

@ **The Pitch:** "The Sports Broadcast Resource"

@ **They Say:** "Welcome to Gameplan!—The Sports Broadcast Resource. Here, you'll find a vast array of sites, resources, and books that can help you succeed in the sports broadcast industry."

@ **Wallet Impact:** None

@ **The Skinny:** This crudely designed, homegrown little sports broadcasting page is essentially just a "jump site," listing links that are pertinent to the profession. As such, it could be a good place to start learning about sports broadcasting.

@ **Rating:**

@ **Most Useful For:** Exploring sports-broadcasting links.

Get A Mentor

@ **The Pitch:** "Get training in the real world."

@ **They Say:** "On-the-job, one-on-one apprentice and mentor training for a career in radio and TV broadcasting, recording arts, film, and television production."

@ **Wallet Impact:** It costs nothing to explore this site, but it costs up to $6,950 to enroll in the apprenticeship it promotes.

@ **The Skinny:** This broadcasting and production apprenticeship program is pricey, and the site's design is very unsophisticated, but the site is to be commended for its full disclosure—it provides clear and full details about the four- to nine-month program. Some professional endorsements or affiliations would help to inspire confidence, but they are unfortunately lacking.

@ **Rating:**

@ **Most Useful For:** Finding out about a broadcasting and production apprenticeship program.

Guru.com

@ **The Pitch:** "We connect quality talent with great projects."

@ **They Say:** "Founded in 1999, Guru represents skilled professionals who think about work in a different way—with an independent mindset. We're a new kind of home for independents. We provide them with job opportunities, career guidance, and support services—and we don't take a cut of their pay when we find them work. We help companies find great talent fast. And we charge them in a revolutionary way—one flat fee that's dramatically less expensive than the markups charged by traditional recruiters."

@ **Wallet Impact:** None

@ **The Skinny:** This exemplary freelancer's job-board site doesn't specialize in media and entertainment, but it does have some jobs available in creative areas. It's quite well designed, well run, and entirely free.

@ **Rating:**

@ **Most Useful For:** Finding contract work.

HBO.com

@ **The Pitch:** "The #1 Premium Channel"

@ **They Say:** "Each month, HBO offers more than ninety theatrical motion pictures—ranging from top box office hits to a broad spectrum of popular films—as well as exclusive programming, including original movies, series, comedy, documentaries, family shows, and world-class sporting events."

@ **Wallet Impact:** None

@ **The Skinny:** Not unexpectedly, HBO.com is a highly professional and well-designed site, effectively promoting the cable network. It also has a slick and user-friendly HBO Careers section. Do a search for "Internship" in this section, and you'll get information about HBO's extensive internship program.

@ **Rating:**

@ **Most Useful For:** Finding a job or internship at HBO.

Hollywood Reporter.com

www.hollywoodreporter.com

@ ***The Pitch:*** "Hollywood's #1 news source"

@ ***They Say:*** "We learned early on that the Internet is a medium that demands change and evolution. . . . We update daily. Classifieds hit the Web almost a day before they hit the street. . . . We've slashed the price of accessing full-text stories, production listings, and archived items. . . . Unlimited use of the classifieds, domestic, and international boxoffice charts, and TV pilot charts are all covered under the monthly fee."

@ ***Wallet Impact:*** $14.95/month (plus possible per-view charges) to access full text of articles and data

@ ***The Skinny:*** You can't read the full text of this popular entertainment-industry journal's articles without paying $14.95 a month, and there's not much that you'll get for your money that you couldn't get by subscribing to the print version. However, the site does have one useful free feature, the message board, which has a Hollywood 101 section devoted to discussing how to break into "the biz."

@ ***Rating:***

@ ***Most Useful For:*** Hollywood-related discussion boards.

IATSE—International Alliance of Theatrical Stage Employees

www.iatse.lm.com

@ **The Pitch:** "The International Alliance of Theatrical Stage Employees, Moving Picture Technicians, Artists, and Allied Crafts of the United States, Its Territories and Canada, AFL-CIO, CLC"

@ **They Say:** "The IATSE is the labor union representing technicians, artisans, and craftspersons in the entertainment industry, including live theatre, film and television production, and trade shows."

@ **Wallet Impact:** None

@ **The Skinny:** This union site is ugly but nonetheless useful if you're involved in the technical side of theater or film. It features news, good general information about the union, and a useful Crafts section, which provides a good introduction to the different career fields covered by the union.

@ **Rating:**

@ **Most Useful For:** Learning about the IATSE union; learning about technical film and stage career fields.

IMPALA—International Motion Picture and Lecturers Association

@ **The Pitch:** "The Home of Travel Adventure Filmmakers"

@ **They Say:** "IMPALA, the organization of filmmakers who perform Travel Adventure Film Lecture presentations (also known as Travelogues), is looking for new filmmakers to join the field (see our New Producers Guide). Do you enjoy moviemaking, film production, or video production? Yearn to travel to far off distant places? Are you a natural performer? Love sharing travel slides, movies, or videos with friends? This could be your new career!"

@ **Wallet Impact:** None

@ **The Skinny:** This site covers its unique filmmaking niche with admirable clarity and brevity. Despite the salesman-like tone of its self-description, the site is refreshingly clear of the money-grubbing, starstruck, or self-important tones of many of the other sites covered in this section. This conveys an image that the site is created by people who are in the industry for the love of it, not for the money or the glory.

@ **Rating:**

@ **Most Useful For:** Learning about the career of Travel Adventure Film Lecturer.

Internet Movie Database

www.imdb.com

@ **The Pitch:** "Visited by 8 million movie lovers each month!"

@ **They Say:** "The core of our site is our search capabilities. We catalog all sorts of information on over 250,000 movies made since the dawn of cinema plus even more on over 900,000 people who helped make them. That 900,000 includes over 500,000 actors and actresses, nearly 50,000 directors, over 70,000 writers, and a wide variety of other folks from producers to gaffers and everything in between. Then we take all that information, organize it into a cool structure, and make it possible for you to easily search and browse through it . . . FOR FREE."

@ **Wallet Impact:** None

@ **The Skinny:** This site is nirvana for movie fans. Its central feature is an almost unbelievably comprehensive and ever-growing database of feature films (and television shows, made-for-TV movies, and direct-to-video movies). The database is searchable by multiple criteria and is cross-referenced six ways to Sunday. If you want to research the career of anyone who's ever worked in film, this is the place to go. If you want to find out all about a particular movie, this is the place to go. Just don't get so wrapped up in this addictive site that you neglect your job search! Although this is a great general research tool, it's (obviously) not specifically career-oriented.

@ **Rating:**

@ **Most Useful For:** Researching film releases, past and present.

JobsInSports.com

@ **The Pitch:** "Your Fantasy Sport Job Awaits Inside www.jobsinsports.com."

@ **They Say:** "Welcome to JobsInSports.com, an Internet-based employment service dedicated to helping you find a sports job in the highly competitive sports marketplace."

@ **Wallet Impact:** $29.95/month to access job listings

@ **The Skinny:** This sports-business and broadcasting job board has no extras other than a résumé-posting feature and is a bit expensive to boot. Although its professionalism is encouraging, it gives no indication of the current size of its job board.

@ **Rating:**

@ **Most Useful For:** Finding a job in the sports industry.

JobsintheBiz

@ ***The Pitch:*** "JobsintheBiz delivers up-to-the-minute job postings from nine concise sectors of the entertainment industry. Get top-notch career advice and expert opinions from industry guru Brad Marks."

@ ***They Say:*** "JobsintheBiz was developed by the staff of Brad Marks International, a world-renowned entertainment recruitment company based in Los Angeles. Our candidates inspired the creation of our Web business. During the past year, we have received daily inquiries requesting advice on 'where to find the best entertainment jobs and related information on the Internet.' We realized there was no ideal place and consequently set up our own site."

@ ***Wallet Impact:*** None

@ ***The Skinny:*** This well-designed site has a fair number of job listings (about a dozen or so per week), but its real strength is in its extra informational features, including some outstanding links sections and useful articles. If you're just beginning your job search, looking through these features would be a great place to start.

@ ***Rating:***

@ ***Most Useful For:*** Learning about and finding a job in the entertainment industry.

JournalismJobs.com

@ **The Pitch:** "The Job Board for Media Professionals"

@ **They Say:** "JournalismJobs.com is the largest and most-visited resource for media jobs, and receives more than one million page views a month. It has the best variety of jobs and the largest database of résumés for journalists."

@ **Wallet Impact:** None

@ **The Skinny:** This is the very model for what an industry-specific job site should be: It's professionally designed and maintained, is easy to navigate, has a large number of current job postings, and is entirely free. One might wish for more extensive career advice and industry news, but you can find that by exploring the many sites in the Media Links section.

@ **Rating:**

@ **Most Useful For:** Finding a job in journalism.

Live Sound! International

@ **The Pitch:** "The #1 Pro Audio content site in the world"

@ **They Say:** "Join the thousands of Live Sound regulars. . . .
Sign up for a FREE Web Membership to get all the cool
features on this site."

@ **Wallet Impact:** None

@ **The Skinny:** A companion to the print magazine of the same
name, this site offers an extraordinary amount of information
about the pro audio industry—though you will have to
struggle with the ungainly site design in order to sift through it
all.

@ **Rating:**

@ **Most Useful For:** Plumbing the depths of the technical side of
pro audio.

Los Angeles International Short Film Festival

www.lashortsfest.com

@ **The Pitch:** "The premiere festival of short films in the U.S."

@ **They Say:** "The Los Angeles International Short Film Festival (L.A. Shorts Fest) is the premiere festival of short films in the U.S. . . . [It presents] an array of extraordinary programs and the spectacular talents of filmmakers and industry professionals from around the world."

@ **Wallet Impact:** None

@ **The Skinny:** This top-tier short-film festival has a professionally designed site and some useful links (in the News section, for example) to other similar festivals. The site is in need of some more content, though—there's no information about how to apply for next year's competition, nor is there any good general introduction to the festival.

@ **Rating:**

@ **Most Useful For:** Learning about this prestigious film fest.

Louisiana Film Commission

www.lafilm.org

@ ***The Pitch:*** "Louisiana: always camera ready"

@ ***They Say:*** "The Louisiana Film Commission is the public agency that is responsible for promoting film and video production in the state. Our office represents the state of Louisiana in all matters dealing with film and video."

@ ***Wallet Impact:*** None

@ ***The Skinny:*** This nice-looking film commission site has some basic information about filming in Louisiana—more details would be nice, though. The strongest feature here is a detailed locations database.

@ ***Rating:***

@ ***Most Useful For:*** Learning about what's involved in planning a shoot in Louisiana.

Lucasfilm Ltd.

@ **The Pitch:** "Lucasfilm Ltd. is proud to offer exciting internship opportunities in the business aspect of the entertainment industry, as well as in various operating departments within the Skywalker Ranch facility."

@ **They Say:** "Assignments may be available in the following departments: THX (Pro THX Theatres, Consumer THX, the Theatre Alignment Program, and the Digital Mastering Program), Marketing, Finance/Accounting, Human Resources, Information Technology and Services, Ranch Operations (Facilities, Fire/Safety/Security, Organic Garden), Internet, Archives, Library/Research, Business Affairs (Legal), Guest Services, Food Services, and Corporate Fitness.... [Y]ou may also apply to Lucas Licensing Ltd., which may have opportunities in their Domestic Licensing, International Licensing, Merchandising, and/or Publishing departments."

@ **Wallet Impact:** None

@ **The Skinny:** George Lucas's media empire offers a number of internships to students. These well-designed pages tell you everything you would want to know about these internships, including how to apply.

@ **Rating:**

@ **Most Useful For:** Finding out how to apply for a student internship at Lucasfilm.

Make-Up Artist Magazine

@ **The Pitch:** "The premiere magazine for make-up artists and movie enthusiasts"

@ **They Say:** "[The magazine] began as a two-sided newsletter and has developed into an internationally read magazine, featuring cover stories and articles on the entertainment industry's top make-up artists, the most innovative make-up techniques, current product news, and invaluable information available nowhere else but *Make-Up Artist Magazine*."

@ **Wallet Impact:** None

@ **The Skinny:** The rather ugly online version of the industry journal *Make-Up Artist Magazine* includes only a fraction of the content found in the print version. The most useful feature is an FAQ section that gives a brief introduction to breaking into the career field. The job board, sadly, is completely empty.

@ **Rating:**

@ **Most Useful For:** Learning how to become a professional makeup artist; keeping up with entertainment-industry makeup news.

Makeup Artist Network

www.makeupartistnetwork.com

@ **The Pitch:** "This site is designed especially for all areas of the Makeup Industry."

@ **They Say:** "This site is designed to help new and advanced Makeup Artists advance their careers. We invite newcomer's questions and appreciate advanced Makeup Artists sharing their knowledge."

@ **Wallet Impact:** None

@ **The Skinny:** This alarmingly garish site fails to cover the promised "all areas of the Makeup Industry." Instead, it offers a collection of makeup-related links that you may or may not find useful. There's also a message board, which is marginally useful.

@ **Rating:**

@ **Most Useful For:** Finding out a bit about the makeup-artist industry.

Mediabistro.com

@ **The Pitch:** "Connecting all media professionals to new opportunities—and to each other."

@ **They Say:** "The mediabistro.com website is dedicated to anyone who creates or works with content, or who is a non-creative professional working in a content/creative industry: editors, writers, television producers, graphic designers, production, circulation people in book publishing, magazines, television, radio, newspapers, online media, advertising, PR and graphic design."

@ **Wallet Impact:** None

@ **The Skinny:** This slick, highly professional "media community" site offers media-related news clippings, original articles, a lively bulletin board, a résumé-posting service, and an excellent job board. There's even information on obtaining reasonably priced freelancer's health insurance. The site is so friendly and useful, you might be tempted to make it your browser's homepage, especially if you live in New York, toward which the job postings and other content are severely slanted.

@ **Rating:**

if you live in New York,

if you live elsewhere

@ **Most Useful For:** Finding a job in media-related industries in New York; keeping up with media-related news.

Mediaweek.com

@ **The Pitch:** "The online news magazine of the media"

@ **They Say:** "The resources of Mediaweek's editorial staff are combined with the knowledge of our online editors and the multi-media capabilities of the World Wide Web to create a total experience for media professionals."

@ **Wallet Impact:** $39.95 for three months' worth of the "Job Seeker's Special," which gives you, among other things, access to job ads "at least 1 week" before they appear in the free Classifieds section. Details are at www.mediaweek.com/adweek/career_network/index.jsp.

@ **The Skinny:** For a site that's produced by a company that covers advertising (*Adweek*), you would think that Mediaweek.com would know how to sell itself. But in fact, the site is unnecessarily ugly and cumbersome to navigate. Furthermore, the job listings for Mediaweek are mixed in with listings from Adweek's other publications, making it tedious to sort out the entertainment-industry listings—which are in any case alarmingly sparse. This leaves the site's main feature, entertainment-industry news, as its only truly useful function.

@ **Rating:**

@ **Most Useful For:** Keeping up with entertainment-industry news.

Miami Film Commission

www.filmiami.org

@ **The Pitch:** "The most thorough source of information for filming and conducting entertainment-related business in Miami-Dade County"

@ **They Say:** "[This is] the official website of the Miami-Dade Mayor's Office of Film & Entertainment."

@ **Wallet Impact:** None

@ **The Skinny:** This site provides good, basic information for those considering filming in the Miami area, including a few location photos, permit info, and a short list of projects currently in production. More detailed information about available local talent and services can be found in the sites listed in the Production Guide section.

@ **Rating:**

@ **Most Useful For:** Learning about what's involved in planning a shoot in the Miami area.

Monster.com

@ **The Pitch:** "Work. Life. Possibilities."

@ **They Say:** "We are the leading global online network for careers, connecting the most progressive companies with the most qualified career-minded individuals. Monster.com is committed to leading the market by offering innovative technology and superior services that give consumers and businesses more control over the recruiting process."

@ **Wallet Impact:** None

@ **The Skinny:** This industry-leading job site is not focused on entertainment and media, but it has such an overwhelming number of job listings that it's one of the best job-searching sites for these industries. It has an ever-growing list of extras, including résumé-posting and career advice. Not too long ago, this would not have been the site to go to for any kind of detailed advice or information about media and entertainment, but now there are dozens of pertinent articles; go to content.monster.com and explore.

@ **Rating:**

@ **Most Useful For:** Finding a job in the media or entertainment industries; learning about employment in these industries.

MovieBytes

@ **The Pitch:** "Screenwriting Contests & Markets Online"

@ **They Say:** "Register . . . to receive MovieBytes' FREE e-mail newsletter featuring contest deadline reminders, contest news, screenplay marketing opportunities, and much more. You'll also receive a password to access the MovieBytes bulletin board and contest evaluations."

@ **Wallet Impact:** $20 for six months or $30 for a year's worth of access to the Who's Buying What section

@ **The Skinny:** There are a lot of screenwriting contests out there, but this is the only site that compiles them all. These contests offer everything from cash awards, which are nice, to production deals for chosen scripts, which are even nicer. The contest list on the site is free; equally interesting is the nonfree (but cheap) Who's Buying What section, which is sort of a writer's market for screenwriters. MovieBytes also has a small job board, which unfortunately is merely a list of production companies looking for script submissions. The site's amateurish design is a minor annoyance.

@ **Rating:**

@ **Most Useful For:** Finding out about screenwriting contests; finding a market for your screenplay(s).

Music Business Journal

www.musicjournal.org

@ **The Pitch:** "The Internet Publication for the Global Music Business"

@ **They Say:** "This independent resource website has been conceptualized and developed in order to increase the global understanding of all issues pertaining to the music industry."

@ **Wallet Impact:** None

@ **The Skinny:** This small U.K.-based site has an academic style and focuses on the study of the international music industry. It's interesting for its international perspective but may not be of particular use to job seekers.

@ **Rating:**

@ **Most Useful For:** Learning about international aspects of the music industry.

Musical America.com

@ **The Pitch:** "The business source for the performing arts"

@ **They Say:** "Thank you for your interest in MusicalAmerica.com, the business source for the performing arts, [and] the most comprehensive business resource on the web for performing arts professionals."

@ **Wallet Impact:** $11.95/month or $115/year to access the listings features

@ **The Skinny:** This elegantly designed site is a good source for information on the performing arts (classical music, ballet, opera, etc.) industry. It includes industry news, links, and performance schedules. It also includes a listings feature that allows artists, managers, and employers to find one another; this feature is difficult to evaluate because no samples or other information are provided.

@ **Rating:**

@ **Most Useful For:** Keeping up with news from the performing arts industry.

Musician's Guide

@ **_The Pitch:_** "The Musician's Guide to Touring and Promotion"

@ **_They Say:_** "With over 4,000 completely updated contacts, the Musician's Guide to Touring and Promotion is the essential tool for booking gigs, contacting record labels, finding a manager, and more."

@ **_Wallet Impact:_** None

@ **_The Skinny:_** The self-description above refers to the print version of this musician's resource, but now you can search its listings online, for free. Because you can search by various criteria, it's actually more convenient than the print version. Use it now before the publishers figure out that people would pay to access it.

@ **_Rating:_**

@ **_Most Useful For:_** Obtaining invaluable musical touring- and promotion-related contact information.

Musicians Network

@ **The Pitch:** "Where Musicians & the Music Industry Meet!"

@ **They Say:** "Networking is the key to success . . . for musicians and people in the music industry—Musicians Network ® is here to help you make it happen."

@ **Wallet Impact:** $14.95/year to post contact information; $100/year to post a portfolio

@ **The Skinny:** This site allows musicians and music-industry types to offer their services to one another by posting contact information and brief pitches. Your $14.95 also gets you some "Members Only" features that are inadequately described. The site's creators also offer Web-design services for your band. This site has managed to attract several hundred subscribers, which shows that it must be doing something right.

@ **Rating:**

@ **Most Useful For:** Advertising your musical services.

National Diversity Newspaper Job Bank

@ *The Pitch:* "Diversity Makes The Difference"

@ *They Say:* "Welcome to one of the nation's most comprehensive newspaper & media job banks. The National Diversity Newspaper Job Bank (NDNJB) is devoted to diversifying these industries and is primarily aimed toward women and minorities. Here you will find job openings in all aspects of the newspaper & media industries, from advertising and public relations to management and editorial. The goal of the NDNJB is to create a link between employers who believe in diversity and those who are searching for a job where they will be able to perform to their full potential."

@ *Wallet Impact:* None

@ *The Skinny:* This site appears to be a valuable resource, but a lack of information about the volume of job postings, some nonworking links, and outdated pages raise concerns.

@ *Rating:*

@ *Most Useful For:* Helping women and minorities find newspaper jobs.

New York Assistant Directors Training Program

www.dgatrainingprogram.org

@ *The Pitch:* "A Career In Film Production"

@ *They Say:* "The New York Assistant Director Training Program is designed to provide opportunities for a limited number of individuals to become Assistant Directors of Motion Pictures. This is a two-year program consisting of up to 350 days of on-the-job training combined with seminars and special assignments. A rotation system places Trainees on the sets of various features, television series, and commercials shooting primarily in the New York City vicinity."

@ *Wallet Impact:* None

@ *The Skinny:* This program, sponsored by the Director's Guild of America, is a wonderful opportunity for anyone who would like a chance to work (for pay!) on a set. Note, however, that the application process is rigorous and the competition stiff. This site explains it all with admirable clarity.

@ *Rating:*

@ *Most Useful For:* Finding out how to apply for a chance to gain valuable on-set film-industry experience.

New York City Mayor's Office of Film, Theatre, and Broadcasting

www.ci.nyc.ny.us/html/filmcom

@ **The Pitch:** "Welcome to Production in New York!"

@ **They Say:** "For nearly three decades, the Mayor's Office of Film, Theatre & Broadcasting (MOFTB) has been the central clearinghouse for the international production center here which provides 78,000 New York entertainment professionals with employment and generates just over $5 billion annually. This office is an advocate for all kinds of productions, from major feature films and television series to commercials, music videos, documentaries, and student films. We provide a free permit and services to assist your project, and we look forward to working with you. We have a reputation for finding a way to say yes."

@ **Wallet Impact:** None

@ **The Skinny:** New York City may well be, as former mayor Rudolph Giuliani claims, the Entertainment Capital of the World; should you want to shoot some film or video there, this is the site to visit. It provides news and information about production resources in New York, and basic information about permits and other regulations. As far as employment goes, the site provides a phone number to call about interning at the Film Office.

@ **Rating:**

@ **Most Useful For:** Learning about the red tape that's involved (and help that's available) when filming in New York.

New York Exposition of Short Film and Video

www.nyexpo.org

@ **The Pitch:** "The Nation's longest-running festival of independent shorts"

@ **They Say:** "The New York Exposition of Short Film and Video, now celebrating its 35th year, is the nation's longest-running annual festival of independent short film and video. Over the years, the Expo has sought out and presented challenging, unconventional, and technically innovative films and videos that have often had a difficult time finding a venue."

@ **Wallet Impact:** None

@ **The Skinny:** This site promotes one of the country's most prestigious short-film festivals and provides clear information on both the program's history and how to submit your work for consideration.

@ **Rating:**

@ **Most Useful For:** Learning how to submit your work to this festival.

NewsJobs.net

@ **The Pitch:** "Because you need to eat"

@ **They Say:** "NewsJobs.Net is an exhaustive resource for editors, writers, PR staff, and other editorial workers in the English-speaking world who want to find the top sites that offer jobs. We offer links to every conceivable site we can find that advertises jobs—weeding out the junk so you don't have to—and provide advice to job seekers."

@ **Wallet Impact:** None

@ **The Skinny:** Despite the fact that it's really just a links site, NewsJobs.net is one of the best sites for freelance writers. It provides a list of virtually every website of interest to writers, along with a few site reviews and some useful career advice articles. A good starting place for job surfing writers.

@ **Rating:**

@ **Most Useful For:** Locating writing- and editing-related websites.

OpenCasting.com

@ **The Pitch:** "Put Yourself in the Action!!!"

@ **They Say:** "Welcome to OpenCasting.com, a full-service Web resource for the entertainment community. We provide a free bulletin board for posting casting notices, crew calls, and other entertainment-related information. Feel free to browse our database or to post your own notices."

@ **Wallet Impact:** None

@ **The Skinny:** Though this site shows up in many search engines and link lists, it should have long ago been given a decent cyber-burial: It is dead, dead, dead. One line near the bottom of the page says it all: "Last Updated: 11/12/00."

@ **Rating:** 0

@ **Most Useful For:** Learning the sad truth that just because a website is available doesn't mean that it's still a going concern.

Paramount Pictures Career Opportunities

www.paramount.com/studio/homecareer_frame.html

@ **The Pitch:** "Film professionals click here."

@ **They Say:** "Leadership in the competitive universal field of entertainment takes the dedicated talents of a diverse, highly motivated team. It also takes a deep respect for each team member, without whom success is unattainable. With this at the heart of Paramount's corporate philosophy, the resulting career environment is interactive and supportive."

@ **Wallet Impact:** None

@ **The Skinny:** Although the design of this page is strikingly terrible, the content will likely make any would-be Hollywood player salivate, with lots of available jobs at this major studio. The internship opportunities are particularly interesting.

@ **Rating:**

@ **Most Useful For:** Finding a job or internship at Paramount Pictures.

Planetmedia

@ ***The Pitch:*** "Media Jobs From Around The Planet!"

@ ***They Say:*** "Over 300 Television Jobs."

@ ***Wallet Impact:*** $10 per month or $20 for six months to access job listings

@ ***The Skinny:*** This site features an extremely crude design and uses Java (an advanced Web-browsing feature that is problematic on many computers) for its navigational features, which undermines the ability of many potential users to navigate the site without difficulty. Despite the low price tag, you should proceed with caution. The site does have some good links pages, however.

@ ***Rating:***

@ ***Most Useful For:*** Finding a job in a media industry; exploring industry-related links.

Playbill On-Line

@ **The Pitch:** "THE Theatre Source on the Web for Broadway Theater Information"

@ **They Say:** "Since launching the Playbill On-Line Club in early 1996, Playbill has offered its club members discounts and advance purchase opportunities on some of the hottest Broadway shows and theatre merchandise. In addition, Playbill has secured discount opportunities in more than a dozen states in the US and Canada."

@ **Wallet Impact:** None

@ **The Skinny:** This comprehensive online guide to the upper echelons of the theater world may not have the slickest design, but it has just about everything else you could ask for, including discussion boards, comprehensive coverage of Broadway and beyond, and a good job board. An essential site for theater professionals.

@ **Rating:**

@ **Most Useful For:** Finding a job in theater; keeping up with theater news.

Redwood Curtain

www.redwoodcurtain.com

@ ***The Pitch:*** "Because Life Shouldn't Be All Work And No Plays"

@ ***They Say:*** "We choose our plays with you in mind. Plays to delight and entertain you. Plays that celebrate the human spirit or illuminate the human condition beyond our own experience. Plays by authors who are recognized on the world stage and plays that will leave a lasting impression."

@ ***Wallet Impact:*** None

@ ***The Skinny:*** This Northern California–based site is a good example of a small theater company's website. It includes information about current productions, press releases, and explains how to help support the organization. Though small theater companies like this one may lack the resources, a more modern and attractive design would probably improve its Web presence.

@ ***Rating:***

@ ***Most Useful For:*** As an example of a small arts organization's website.

Reelmind.com

@ **The Pitch:** "They need your creative genius, show it to them!"

@ **They Say:** "Consider the power of placing examples of your work in a location where millions of people can see it. REELMIND offers filmmakers, animators, and musicians the most powerful tool conceivable for promoting themselves using their own work and their own words. We are not simply a large database of short content posted to entertain the masses; rather, we are striving to provide individual artists with an online presence to assist them in gaining the exposure needed to advance their careers. Producers, ad agency directors, studio heads, film directors, festival coordinators, and a slew of other industry decision makers look to REELMIND for the next generation of production talent. They need your creative genius, show it to them!"

@ **Wallet Impact:** None

@ **The Skinny:** This site for aspiring filmmakers allows members to post up to thirty-five minutes of film, animation, or music and up to 5MB of textual work, photos, drawings, or storyboards on a personalized "micro" Web page. Members can post contact information; projects can also be plugged in the monthly newsletter. Reelmind has some good original content, such as "Electronic Media Law and Regulation" and "My First Film Festival." Other features include a large and lively discussion board.

@ **Rating:**

@ **Most Useful For:** Posting an online filmmaker's portfolio.

Review.com

@ **The Pitch:** "One of the most popular sites on the Internet for students seeking information about college, graduate school, and careers"

@ **They Say:** "More than half a million students, parents, and counselors visit www.review.com each month to take advantage of the free interactive tools designed to help them find schools, submit applications, and research career and financial aid options."

@ **Wallet Impact:** None

@ **The Skinny:** We may be biased, but we think that this is the best website of any kind on the entire planet. Although not specifically geared towards media and entertainment, this subsection of the larger Review.com site has some useful features, the most helpful of which may be its Career Quiz. Answering a group of questions yields a set of results that define your professional interests and the likely style in which you would enjoy pursuing them.

@ **Rating:**

@ **Most Useful For:** Assessing your professional interests and educational options; finding an internship; getting general career advice.

Screen Actors Guild

@ **The Pitch:** "Information is the key to success in any career"

@ **They Say:** "Welcome to the Screen Actors Guild online.... We hope you will find this website providing more and more useful facts to assist you as the days progress. I have asked our staff and board members to make certain that this website continues to improve both in content and style as it already has over the last several months. There are any number of misconceptions about our union and its services to all of us, and much of the future growth of this website will be to help provide the correct answers to our members."

@ **Wallet Impact:** None

@ **The Skinny:** It's hard to believe that this actor's union, one of the most powerful organizations in Hollywood, can't afford to buy better Web design than this. Nevertheless, this site has some good basic information about the union and what it does. The best intro is on this hard-to-find page: www.sag.com/filmmakers.html. There's a useful links page, and a small job board listing positions available at SAG. One of the job listings is for Web producer; if you're a good Web designer, you should apply—SAG obviously needs your help.

@ **Rating:**

@ **Most Useful For:** Learning about the Screen Actors Guild.

Sebastian LaCause

www.sebastianlacause.com

@ **The Pitch:** "The astounding Sebastian LaCause"

@ **They Say:** "If on some rainy night a your car breaks down outside Broadway's Circle In the Square Theater, you are in luck. Inside, you'll be welcomed by familiar characters from The Rocky Horror Show—among them the astounding Sebastian LaCause as Rocky."

@ **Wallet Impact:** None

@ **The Skinny:** This is an excellent example of an artist's personal website; it serves to promote Mr. LaCause's acting career. He apparently had it professionally designed, which is a good option if you can afford it—slick design like this will always make a good impression. One oversight that you should not emulate is that the main page lacks any explanation of who Mr. LaCause is and what he wants visitors to learn from his site.

@ **Rating:**  **+**

@ **Most Useful For:** An example of a personal website.

Showbizjobs.com

www.showbizjobs.com

@ **The Pitch:** "The Entertainment Professional's Network"

@ **They Say:** "Showbizjobs.com is an entertainment industry job center—a destination portal for both job seekers and employers. Founded in 1995 by Human Resources professionals, Showbizjobs.com specializes in Administrative Jobs within entertainment-related companies. From niche boutiques to entertainment giants—companies use our services and get results. Our site has assisted hundreds of people in finding their job in the Industry. We hope that you find our services useful."

@ **Wallet Impact:** $70/year in order to access "Premium Services," including résumé-posting and discussion boards, as described at www.showbizjobs.com/dsp_user.cfm

@ **The Skinny:** The pay features are a bit overpriced, and the free job board should be much less sparse, but this straightforward and well-designed site is nevertheless a decent entertainment-industry job board.

@ **Rating:**

@ **Most Useful For:** Finding a job in the entertainment industry.

South by Southwest Conferences & Festivals

@ **The Pitch:** "A unique global event focused on the creative side of the entertainment business"

@ **They Say:** "South by Southwest (SXSW, Inc.) is a private company based in Austin, Texas, with a year-round staff of professionals dedicated to building and delivering conference and festival events for entertainment and related media industry professionals. Since 1987, SXSW has produced the internationally recognized Music and Media Conference & Festival. As the entertainment business adjusted to issues of future growth and development, seven years ago, SXSW added conferences and festivals for the film industry as well as for the blossoming interactive media. Now three industry events converge in Austin during a Texas-size week, mirroring the ever-increasing cross-pollination of entertainment/media outlets."

@ **Wallet Impact:** The site's free, but the festival itself can cost as much as $775 to attend, depending on how many events you want to get into and when you register. If you want to perform at the music festival, it'll cost you $10 to apply for a spot; submitting a film for consideration for the film festival will cost you up to $50.

@ **The Skinny:** South by Southwest is the premiere music festival in the United States, bringing hordes of established and aspiring artists and music-industry professionals to Austin for a once-a-year, five-day orgy of performing, showcasing, seminaring, and conferencing. The festival has expanded in recent years to include film and Internet media. This well-designed, easy-to-navigate site promotes the festival and gives you a chance to register to attend, either as a conference attendee or an artist.

@ **Rating:**

@ **Most Useful For:** Finding out how to (possibly) get your big break or do some productive networking, or just get inspired by other artists at this festival.

SteadiCam Operators Association

@ **The Pitch:** "Represents Steadicam Operators around the world"

@ **They Say:** "The Steadicam Operators Association (SOA) was formed by Garrett Brown, the inventor of the Steadicam, and Nicola Pecorini in 1988 to connect skilled Steadicam Operators with motion picture directors and producers."

@ **Wallet Impact:** $150 one-time fee to post your résumé

@ **The Skinny:** It's difficult to imagine a more narrowly career-specific site than this comprehensive and useful, though awkwardly designed, site for Steadicam operators. The site offers general information about Steadicams (including how to become a Steadicam operator), an extensive bulletin board, information about workshops and training opportunities, and a résumé-posting service.

@ **Rating:**

@ **Most Useful For:** Learning all about the profession of Steadicam operator; attracting employers via your online résumé.

Sundance Institute

@ **The Pitch:** "Community Creativity Courage"

@ **They Say:** "The Sundance Institute is a nonprofit organization dedicated to the support and development of independent filmmakers, screenwriters, playwrights, composers, and other film and theatre artists."

@ **Wallet Impact:** None

@ **The Skinny:** Perhaps you have what it takes to compete at the country's most prestigious independent film festival. Or perhaps you'd just like to attend, do some networking, visit some panel discussions, and get some inspiration. Either way, this site will tell you what you need to do. Intriguingly, there are also a number of job opportunities for those who would like to work *for* the Sundance Institute—click on the Employment Opportunities link at the bottom of the page.

@ **Rating:**  **+**

@ **Most Useful For:** Finding out how to attend Sundance; finding out how to apply to compete; exploring the institute's job opportunities.

Talkin' Broadway

www.talkingbroadway.com

@ **The Pitch:** "Your home on the Internet for theatre news, talk, and information"

@ **They Say:** "Talkin' Broadway is in its fifth successful year providing readers worldwide with up-to-the-minute news, interactive discussion, and information about Broadway and the current theatre scene in San Francisco, Las Vegas, Toronto, and other cities across the United States. The entire staff of Talkin' Broadway volunteers their time and efforts in either writing columns or maintaining the site."

@ **Wallet Impact:** None

@ **The Skinny:** Probably the best site on the Web for theater fans, Talkin' Broadway features an attractive, easy-to-use design, a lively message board, reviews, and extensive information on pretty much everything you'd want to know about what's happening on Broadway. The site has also recently incorporated the ITDb, an Internet Movie Database–style site devoted to theater.

@ **Rating:**

@ **Most Useful For:** Keeping up with Broadway-related news; researching past theatrical productions using the ITDb feature.

Themeparkjobs.com

www.themeparkjobs.com

@ **The Pitch:** "Jobs in and around the world's theme parks"

@ **They Say:** "A targeted recruiting tool toward theme-park job searchers!"

@ **Wallet Impact:** None

@ **The Skinny:** This is a unique concept for a job site, but having only twenty-eight listings in its database, almost all of them more than six months old, does not make for a very useful resource.

@ **Rating:**

@ **Most Useful For:** Getting an opportunity to compete with thousands of other people for a handful of currently available theme-park jobs.

TVandRadioJobs.com

@ **The Pitch:** "Click & listen to our library of air talent free! Click & post your aircheck [radio skills demo] in our library."

@ **They Say:** "If you're a job seeker, you may send out a dozen tapes and résumés a week hoping to get a bite. This costs you cash in postage, duplicating tapes, and other supplies. In the final analysis, your tape may sit on the program director's desk with hundreds of envelopes . . . unopened, despite the 'attention getting' package you sent it in. TVandRadioJobs.com has 13,000+ Unique Visits a day. Almost half our visitors are radio management types looking for fresh talent. That's what makes this the most efficient and economical way to find a job."

@ **Wallet Impact:** None

@ **The Skinny:** This clunky-looking site has a decent-size job board (with many more jobs in radio than in television), along with a service that allows you to post your "aircheck," or demo of your radio skills, but that's about it.

@ **Rating:**

@ **Most Useful For:** Finding a job in radio or television.

TVinsite

@ **The Pitch:** "TVinsite is a vertical [i.e., comprehensive] news and information portal targeting professionals in the global broadcasting, cable television, satellite, interactive television, and new media industries."

@ **They Say:** "TVinsite is the only online destination that targets a global television professional audience and provides aggregated branded content from the leading news sources in the industry: Broadcasting & Cable, Multichannel News, Cablevision, Multichannel News International, Television Europe, and Television Latin America. TVinsite is the single point of entry online to the global television industry, with news, research tools, directories, and links to other industry information sources."

@ **Wallet Impact:** None

@ **The Skinny:** TVinsite is notable for the breadth of its coverage of the television industry, its clean, professional design, and for its outstanding job board. If you're seeking work in this industry, the only other thing you could possibly want might be some career advice—which, because this is not primarily a jobs site, is not to be found here.

@ **Rating:**

@ **Most Useful For:** Finding a job in the television industry; keeping up with industry news.

TVJobs.com

@ **The Pitch:** "Broadcast Employment Services"

@ **They Say:** "[We are] an Internet-based employment service dedicated to helping you find employment in the highly competitive broadcast marketplace."

@ **Wallet Impact:** $20/year to access job listings

@ **The Skinny:** Though this is not the most professional-looking site in cyberspace, it is exactly what it claims to be: an excellent resource for those looking for employment in television. You have to pay a modest fee to access the remarkably extensive job listings, but the site has a number of great free features as well, including a large discussion board, contact information, and career advice.

@ **Rating:**

@ **Most Useful For:** Finding a job in television.

TVSpy.com

@ **The Pitch:** "The leading website for broadcast professionals"

@ **They Say:** "TVSpy's mission is to be the leading website for broadcast professionals by providing job seekers, professionals, and employers with 'insider' content, community and business services. With its daily ShopTalk newsletter and its Watercooler, it unites network presidents, station executives, broadcasters, technicians, journalism professors, and students in a forum unlike any other."

@ **Wallet Impact:** None

@ **The Skinny:** TVSpy.com is fairly well designed and has some strong features—especially the Agent and Audition Guide advice section—but falls short of its goal of being "the leading website for broadcast professionals." The Situations Wanted feature is of doubtful usefulness, and the job board is woefully tiny.

@ **Rating:**

@ **Most Useful For:** Getting advice on the role of agents and audition tapes in securing a broadcasting job.

U.S. Directory of Entertainment Employers

@ **The Pitch:** "The Industry Resource: for job searching in the entertainment industry; as a reference tool to locate top entertainment companies."

@ **They Say:** "About The 9th Edition: Over 3,500 Entries; 49 Major Industry Categories; 2,500+ Web & E-Mail Addresses; Job Hotlines, Affiliations, Project Highlights; Stock Symbols; Available in soft cover book or online!"

@ **Wallet Impact:** $79/year to access directory listings

@ **The Skinny:** This no-frills site tells you simply how to order the print version of this resource and how to pay for access to the online version—after which you will have access to a searchable, categorized database of over 3,500 entertainment-industry employers. This resource might be useful if you're having trouble locating potential employers, but you should probably check out the Internet's numerous free resources before turning to it.

@ **Rating:**

@ **Most Useful For:** Obtaining very comprehensive lists of entertainment-industry employers in many categories.

Variety.com

@ **The Pitch:** "The premier source of entertainment news"

@ **They Say:** "Recognized and respected through out the world of show business, *Variety* is the premier source of entertainment news. Since 1905, the most influential leaders in the industry have turned to *Variety* for timely, credible, and straightforward news and analysis—information vital to their professions."

@ **Wallet Impact:** $59/year to access most of the content; free for subscribers to the print version.

@ **The Skinny:** If you want to keep up with entertainment-industry news, then there's no more comprehensive and efficient way to do so than to subscribe to Variety.com. If you're just looking for a job, the free classifieds section could provide some leads.

@ **Rating:**

@ **Most Useful For:** Keeping up with entertainment-industry news.

Viacom

@ **The Pitch:** "The No. I platform in the world for advertisers with preeminent positions in broadcast and cable television, radio, outdoor advertising, and online"

@ **They Say:** "With programming that appeals to audiences in every demographic category across virtually all media, the company is a leader in the creation, promotion, and distribution of entertainment, news, sports, and music. Viacom's well-known brands include CBS, MTV, Nickelodeon, VH1, BET, Paramount Pictures, Infinity, UPN, TNN: The National Network, CMT: Country Music Television, Showtime, Blockbuster, and Simon & Schuster."

@ **Wallet Impact:** None

@ **The Skinny:** This homepage for the gargantuan media company Viacom offers a few corporate-headquarters jobs—but click on the Visit Our Sites link, and you'll have access to all of Viacom's subsidiary companies, which, as you will note from all the extremely familiar names, account for a large percentage of the U.S. entertainment industry. Some of these sites have job listings.

@ **Rating:**

@ **Most Useful For:** Learning about a media conglomerate; finding a job at Viacom.

View Askewniverse

www.viewaskew.com

@ **The Pitch:** "Home of View Askew Productions"

@ **They Say:** "Your official news source for Kevin Smith and View Askew."

@ **Wallet Impact:** None

@ **The Skinny:** This slick yet endearing site is the Web home of View Askew Productions, slacker/wiseacre/indie-hero filmmaker Kevin Smith's production company. The site promotes Smith's films and various other projects, sells merchandise, and contains many articles and commentaries by Smith and his associates.

@ **Rating:**

@ **Most Useful For:** Via commentaries and production diaries, getting an education on the filmmaking process; getting ideas on how to structure a production company website; getting inspired (it looks as if everyone at View Askew is having a great time).

Visual Elixir

@ **The Pitch:** "Stupid Cat"

@ **They Say:** "Animation by Sandy Wu. Directed by Dennis Tamayo and Sandy Wu."

@ **Wallet Impact:** None

@ **The Skinny:** This is very well-designed example of an aspiring animator's site. You could follow this format to display your own work. Unlike this site's creator, however, you should add some basic biographical and background information, so that prospective employers can get a good picture of who you are and what you want, and have multiple options for contacting you.

@ **Rating:**

@ **Most Useful For:** An example of an animator's online portfolio.

Webnoize

@ **The Pitch:** "Digital Entertainment Intelligence"

@ **They Say:** "Comprehensive, end-to-end informational services for the new entertainment economy. The only vertical intelligence network serving the entertainment space."

@ **Wallet Impact:** None

@ **The Skinny:** Although you won't find a job on this site, you will learn all about the ever-growing intersection between the entertainment industry and the Internet.

@ **Rating:**

@ **Most Useful For:** Learning about Internet-related aspects of the entertainment industry.

Women in Film

@ **The Pitch:** "Moving Forward Together"

@ **They Say:** "Women In Film's purpose is to empower, promote, nurture, and mentor women in the entertainment, communication, and media industries to achieve their highest potential through a network of valuable contacts, educational programs, and events. Women In Film also increases the visibility of women and recognizes their achievements in these industries."

@ **Wallet Impact:** None

@ **The Skinny:** This organization offers a variety of opportunities for aspiring and working female film-industry professionals, including workshops, grants, and networking opportunities. The site itself is a bit shaky, with some poorly designed graphics and broken links, making it at times difficult to navigate. The Announcements section, in addition to containing news, also occasionally lists internships, job openings, and similar opportunities.

@ **Rating:**

@ **Most Useful For:** Learning about opportunities for women to get ahead in the film industry.

Workinpr.com

@ **The Pitch:** "Premier recruitment for the PR industry"

@ **They Say:** "Workinpr.com is dedicated to providing global PR professionals with strategic career resources and industry information. As the only jobsite endorsed by the Public Relations Society of America and the Council of PR Firms, workinpr.com is working to advance the PR profession by giving employers all over the world access to the most qualified PR talent."

@ **Wallet Impact:** $75 for résumé-review service

@ **The Skinny:** This is an extremely professional and well-designed site. Job listings are a bit meager, but it is, at the very least, an excellent resource for learning about the public relations industry.

@ **Rating:**

@ **Most Useful For:** Helping to find a job in the public relations industry.

WritersMarket.com

@ **The Pitch:** "Instant Access to Thousands of Editors and Agents"

@ **They Say:** "Writer's Market has been the freelance writer's 'bible' since 1921, providing complete market contact information, query letter clinics, pay rates, submission guidelines, and more. And now it's available online."

@ **Wallet Impact:** $29.99/year to access the heart of the site: the listings

@ **The Skinny:** If you're a freelance writer, you would be foolish not to subscribe to WritersMarket.com. At $29.99 per year, it's a bargain and even more useful than its venerable print version because the listings can be electronically searched. There are also some excellent free features on the site, providing general information about freelance writing. The only drawback is that the listings search procedure is strangely nonintuitive.

@ **Rating:**

@ **Most Useful For:** Researching the writing market and finding out how to sell your work.

dir.yahoo.com/Business_and_Economy/Business_to_Business/
Corporate_Services/Human_Resources/
Recruiting_and_Placement/Career_Fields/News_and_Media/

dir.yahoo.com/Business_and_Economy/Business_to_Business/
Entertainment_and_Media_Production/Film_and_Video/
Studios_and_Production_Companies/

dir.yahoo.com/Business_and_Economy/Business_to_Business/
Entertainment_and_Media_Production/Film_and_Video/
Talent_and_Crew/Talent_Agencies/

dir.yahoo.com/Business_and_Economy/Business_to_Business/
News_and_Media/Magazines/Publishers/Organizations/

dir.yahoo.com/Entertainment/Actors_and_Actresses/
Organizations/

dir.yahoo.com/Entertainment/Employment/Jobs/

dir.yahoo.com/Entertainment/Movies_and_Film/Downloads/

dir.yahoo.com/Entertainment/Movies_and_Film/Film_Festivals/
Short_Films/

dir.yahoo.com/Entertainment/Movies_and_Film/Organizations/
Regional_Film_Commissions_and_Boards/

dir.yahoo.com/News_and_Media/Industry_Information/
Journalism/Organizations/

dir.yahoo.com/News_and_Media/Television/Networks/

dir.yahoo.com/Regional/U_S__States/New_York/Cities/
New_York/Entertainment_and_Arts/Organizations/

@ *The Pitch:* "An online guide to the World Wide Web"

@ *They Say:* "Created by a staff of editors who visit and evaluate websites, and then organize them into subject-based categories and sub-categories."

@ **The Skinny:** There are other sites that provide Internet directory services, but none of them do it as well as good old Yahoo!, the most comprehensive and well-organized site of its kind. Yahoo!'s strength in the directory area makes it a good place to go to look for various kinds of website lists (or directories, as Yahoo! calls them). Listed above are a number of Yahoo! directories that should be particularly useful to you in your job search. Some of the sites listed in these directories will have job listings; others will help you learn about the industry in which you're seeking work.

@ *Rating:*

@ **Most Useful For:** Finding comprehensive website directories covering thousands of different subject areas, including many of great interest to job surfers.

Index

Electronic media 105, 243, 256, 301

Emmys 221

Employment statistics 20

Engineers 96

Eno, Brian 74

Entertainment Employment Journal 258

Entertainment law 104

Entertainment marketing 35, 107

Entertainment Professional's Network 305

Entertainment Weekly 85

EntertainmentCareers.net 75, 103-105, 107-108, 112, 119, 257

EntertainmentJobsNow.com 259

Entrepreneurs 54, 65, 131, 222, 262

Entry-level jobs 33-34, 55-57, 66

ESPN 28-29, 46

Ethernet 136, 144, 150-151

Ethics 89, 99

European touring 39

Evening newscast 18, 85, 93-94, 98

Executive job postings 108

Executive producer 36

Expansion cards 146

Faculty positions 75

Family shows 268

Fan sites 71

FCC 80, 105

Feature film 18, 43-45, 48, 61, 236, 249, 252, 272, 293

Federal Communications Commission Audio Services Division 80

Festivals 31, 43-45, 62, 65, 222, 225, 253, 277, 294, 301, 306, 308

Fiction writers 90

File size 72, 163, 195, 197-198

File Transfer Protocol 131, 159, 168, 185

File-sharing business 71, 75, 109

Film crews 93

Film design 53

Film development 46

Film directors 7, 42, 51, 53, 301

Film music 69, 102, 245, 260-261

Film production 47, 68, 271, 292, 324

Film publicity 105

Film school 28, 263

Film writing 61

Filmmaker.com 263

Final Fantasy 10

Finance/Accounting 279

Financial analyst 103

FireWire 146, 194

Font sizes 175, 180

Food services 279

Formatting features 172

Fosse, Bob 68, 109

Fox 18, 29, 44

Frank, Jonathan 70, 72-73, 91, 110

Freelancing 16, 33, 43, 88, 98, 101, 127, 208, 267, 282, 295, 323

Freeware 164, 167, 169

FTP 131, 159, 168, 185

G3 processor 136

Gaffers 16, 55, 272

GAG 100

Game shows 30, 54

Garage bands 31

GarageBand.com 74, 114

Gates, Bill 123, 144

Gay Journalists Association 90

GB 136, 143

General manager of a television station 108

General office worker 55

General-assignment reporter 87

General-interest job-board sites 207

Geocities 38, 185

GIF format 90, 194, 197

Gofer 55

Goldberg, Whoopi 68

Goldblum, Jeff 57

Golden Globes 50

Google 126, 204, 209, 216

Grace of My Heart 84

Grammatical errors 165, 173

Grammer, Kelsey 9

Graphic design 85, 97-101, 116-117, 146, 173-174, 184, 187, 197, 282

Graphics cards 136, 146-147

Great American Song Contest 78

About the Authors

Jeff Adams is a Web producer for The Princeton Review's Review.com website, where he supervises product development and content creation as well as the synergy with the division's books (such as the one you're reading right now). Prior to that, he was a Web producer at a public relations firm where he worked on sites and Web-based press kits for TDK, Toshiba, and Fujitsu. Before shifting his focus to the Net, he spent ten years in journalism running the gamut from construction-equipment maintenance for *Equipment World* magazine, where he is still a contributor, to writing about satellite television in both a trade journal and a TV listings guide. Along with David LaBounty, who authored *Job Surfing: Sciences*, he cofounded and coedits *The First Line*, a literary magazine that is online at www.thefirstline.com. He lives in New York City and you'll find him attending live theater whenever possible.

Jim Blau is a freelance writer, copyeditor, Mac tech support guy, database designer, and all-'round technogeeky wordsmith. He is 32 years old and lives in New York City with Greta, Partial, and Shovel, two of whom are cats.